ACCIDENTALLY

ON

PURPOSE

ACCIDENTALLY ON PURPOSE

A MEMOIR

KRISTEN KISH

WITH STEF FERRARI

LITTLE, BROWN AND COMPANY
New York Boston London

Little, Brown and Company
Hachette Book Group
1290 Avenue of the Americas, New York, NY 10104
littlebrown.com

First Edition: April 2025

Little, Brown and Company is a division of Hachette Book Group, Inc.
The Little, Brown name and logo are trademarks of
Hachette Book Group, Inc.

The publisher is not responsible for websites (or their content)
that are not owned by the publisher.

The Hachette Speakers Bureau provides a wide range of authors
for speaking events. To find out more, go to hachettespeakersbureau.com
or email hachettespeakers@hbgusa.com.

Little, Brown and Company books may be purchased in bulk for business, educational, or promotional use. For information, please contact your local bookseller or the Hachette Book Group Special Markets Department at special.markets@hbgusa.com.

Print book interior design by Jeff Stiefel

ISBN 9780316580915
Library of Congress Control Number: 2024950423

1 2025

MRQ-T

Printed in Canada

For the two people whose story I do not yet know,
but who set my own in motion.

For my mom, dad, and Jonathan,
who gave me every opportunity to live a memorable,
character-building life.

And for Bianca,
who makes every day feel like a fresh page,
full of possibility.

ACCIDENTALLY

ON

PURPOSE

1

For most people, the first photos that exist of them are probably from a hospital room. They're in pink or blue blankets, surrounded by doctors and nurses, and in the arms of their parents, who look haggard and maybe a little bit terrified but are beaming with pride and joy. It's a captured moment that everyone is fully aware will be cherished, treasured, and revisited often for decades to come, so the people are usually giving their best. These photos are visual touchstones, evidence of the initial life-altering moments for a family.

Mine were no different in that sense—except that instead of a hospital room, it was a tarmac with an airplane in the background. And instead of a doctor, it was a judge holding me, conferring my US citizenship. But my parents are there, smiling and beaming with pride just the same. My brother, Jonathan, is featured, too. I've been informed repeatedly over the years, whenever the story is retold at birthdays or upon request, that he was insistent on being the first to feed me a bottle, and there are photos of him doing just that at the airport and in the RV they drove back from Detroit, where they had picked me up.

I know these images so well that even though I couldn't possibly recollect how I felt at four months old, I feel like I have memories of those moments. They are the first impressions of my life as I know it. My mom has always shown me these photos, so what was depicted in them never seemed unusual to me. I've always known I was adopted. These photos weren't hidden in a drawer or an attic somewhere while my family tried to conceal my true origin story in some way. I didn't stumble upon evidence and have to muster the courage to ask questions. In fact, I don't remember asking any questions at all, nor do I recall any intervention-style moment in which I was told to sit down for some major reality-shifting announcement.

It wasn't until many years later that I understood the implications of the airplane in those photos—it indicated that I had come not by way of the stork but on a commercial jetliner. That I was delivered into this world by a woman on the other side of the globe, and the only real information I have about that day are records that I was born in a clinic, in room number 2, along with a small image of me, the size of a passport photo, on my birth certificate.

What I do know is that at some point in the months prior to my arrival, that unknown woman was contending with the decision to part with her child, for reasons I do not and may not ever know. Simultaneously, the family who collected me that day at the airport had been going through their own grueling process—the bureaucratic obstacle course of the American adoption system. Under any circumstance, bringing a child home for the first time requires extensive planning, preparation, and emotional heavy lifting. Mine also included a lot of paperwork, jet fuel, and patience. But as the infant at the center of all this—the one who connected those strangers on opposite sides of the planet—I was spared the knowledge of the extraordinary investment on the part of all involved as well as any pain my birth parents might have experienced.

To people looking at these photos, more than four decades old at this point, it may seem like a remarkable entry onto this earth, and as an adult who understands what the images imply off camera and behind the scenes, I now know that to be true. But to me, my birth—much like the childhood that followed—was never anything but totally normal.

By today's standards, a childhood in the 1980s seems serene compared to the way kids live today. I was without the distractions of social media and pocket-size screens, and there were almost no limits to what I could imagine for the future. Those were simpler times, and in the Michigan suburb where I was raised, we were just like every other family. In fact, we could have been candidates for our own sitcom on TGIF—the Friday night TV lineup that was so big on screens across the country during that era, featuring shows like *Family Matters, Full House,* and *Step by Step.* Despite the fact that I came from Korea, the Kish family would've fit right in; we could not have been more born-and-bred all-American. Two working-class parents in a heterosexual marriage, two children—one boy, one girl—two dependable jobs that kept them busy from nine to five Monday through Friday.

Weeknights meant the end of the workday for my parents and a family dinner, no matter what. No one had cell phones or emails to follow them home, and if the corded house phone rang from its mount on the wall, it went unanswered. My parents were dedicated, hardworking people, but family time was sacred. On the weekends, there were activities we liked to do as a family. My dad took us ice skating. My brother was a swimmer, so we'd go to his meets. I had softball and Little League in the spring and summer.

Of course, like any civilized American family, we valued order and responsibility, and we had chores to keep up. Like most kids, I couldn't say I was in love with that part of the family dynamic, but I participated because it was expected and because I wanted to make my parents happy. Fortunately, they made our routine fun. My favorite by far was Saturday—laundry day—when my dad would let me help. He'd make a game of it, pulling the warm sheets from the dryer, wrapping me up in them, and tossing me on the bed. I felt safe and seen and cozy in our family bubble.

If this all sounds like a dream, that's because it was. But it was a purposeful one that my parents conceived of together, and with a lot of love, foresight, and perseverance, they made it come true for us.

Being adopted, I've often considered the circumstances—the millions of factors and decisions on the part of so many people—that have to come together in order for humans to find one another in such a vast world and become a family. You can call it fate or divine intervention or an aligning of stars, but in my parents' case, it was a little more down-to-earth: a shared Midwestern geography and a grounded pursuit of education.

My mother, Judy Adams, was born in 1949 in Niles, Michigan. Her father, a World War II navy veteran who was raised in Texas—and whom I remember as having a bit of a twang to his speech—married and raised his family in Buchanan, Michigan, after his time in the war. They settled on a few acres of land, and my mom's was a very rural Midwestern upbringing. My father, Michael Kish, was born in Hawaii in 1948. His own father was in the military as well—the army—so they moved around a lot and lived in San Francisco and Germany for a time before moving to Michigan. Ultimately, he was raised in Lansing, and though he wasn't a city boy, his suburban life definitely contrasted with my mom's experience. In the end, though, their paths converged in pursuit of higher learning. They met at Michigan State University, where my dad was studying engineering and my mom was building the foundation for her future as an educator. They fell in love and were college sweethearts; then they married and never faltered. To date, they've been married for fifty-three years and counting.

That kind of resolve and conviction served two people who decided to take on the complicated, tumultuous terrain of international adoption. I've asked my mom why they chose to adopt, to open themselves up to such a challenging and potentially heartbreaking endeavor, when they had a biological son at home. She explained very clearly that she always knew she wanted to be a mother, and my parents were also certain from the start that they wanted to have a child biologically but also adopt.

The motivations for couples or individuals to adopt can range widely, from difficulty in becoming pregnant to medical conditions to concerns about population growth. For my parents, it was a simple equation of need and fulfillment. There were children in the world who required a loving, stable home, and they had the means to provide it. Simple as that.

So five years after Judy and Michael married, they had their biological child, Jonathan. Eight years later, I arrived on that airplane, dropped from the sky and into their loving home.

———

I can't remember ever wanting for anything in my life. I had all my needs met, whether they were for food, clothing, and shelter or for love, attention, and support. But my parents knew long before I did that although I didn't feel it, I *was* different just by virtue of being adopted and being Korean. I was destined to have a life experience different not only from my peers' but also from their own. They would never be able to directly relate to the identities I would inhabit in America.

They did everything they could to provide me with what I needed to grow into myself as I became older and aware of my identity as an adoptee as well as an Asian American. My mom used her resources as a teacher to introduce me to exchange students. I remember one girl—a high school student—who came over with Korean dolls. These were not just dolls *from* Korea but also dolls that *looked* Korean. Dolls that looked like me. This was long before toy companies became progressive enough to start manufacturing multicultural toys in all sizes, shapes, and colors, and representation was virtually nonexistent, so for me, this was beyond special.

Fortunately, I was also raised in a very diverse place. My school had plenty of kids who were not white, and I was far from the only Asian kid in town. In fact, not only were there other Korean kids in my classes and neighborhood, there were also other *adopted* Korean kids. I'm asked so frequently these days what it was like growing up as an Asian adopted kid in the American Midwest. The truth is that I honestly never really felt "othered" in those days—an experience that can seem miraculous when compared to stories I hear from other Asian Americans and adoptees about their upbringings. That is never lost on me; I always think about this and try to drive the point home when people discuss the importance of diversity. I'm certain I'd have had a very different outlook on the world had I been the only one like me.

That's not to say I wasn't on the receiving end of some bullying and teasing—from dopey kids who contorted their faces, pushing their eyes in a way that made them look Asian. But I've always chalked that up to the fact that kids are just jerks sometimes, and they're products of their culture. At the time, in the 1980s and 1990s, that kind of thing was common on TV shows and in movies. It was "comedy." The culture at large was unaccommodating and downright cruel at times to any human experience outside the straight white one, but the truth is, I was teased more painfully for wearing boys' clothes than I was for being Asian, and overall, I had great friends from all walks of life at school.

The relative comfort in my environment, coupled with my lack of need in general, is probably why I don't recall being adopted as feeling like a very big deal. I'm not sure when I even really came to understand the word, especially given that the context in which I heard it wasn't always positive. To this day, it gets under my skin when people use it as a sort of threat for their kids ("If you don't behave, we're going to put you up for adoption") or a cheap joke ("You don't have your father's [insert negative trait here], so you must be adopted"). But I felt eased into my understanding. I knew that my parents didn't make me, but I can't say it was something I considered part of my identity, certainly not as a child preoccupied with playing with friends being among classmates.

I was also empowered by my parents. When I was old enough, they offered me the opportunity to pursue a search for my birth parents if I wanted to. I know there are some people who want and need that. They can't feel whole until they have that information, that experience, until they've at least tried to reach out and make that connection, but it honestly just seemed unnecessary to me. Later, when I was eighteen and the adoption paperwork was made available to me, my overwhelming feeling was that I *should* want to seek my biological parents out—not that I actually wanted to or needed to—because society makes you feel as if this is part of the adoptee "journey" no matter your personal experience.

This created a lot of guilt for a time. I wondered if I was scared, if I was avoidant, if there was something wrong with me. Only in recent years have I come to understand the difference between circumventing something out of fear and simply not needing it. My parents gave me the offer. They empowered me to express my feelings and to say the word if I wanted to do this ancestral excavation. I had every opportunity to say so if I wanted to. But I had a full, loving, complete family and a happy, joyful home, and I didn't need anything more.

The problem with creating a happy, joyful, safe, and complete home for your children? They may never want to leave it.

I was a good student. My mother was an early childhood development teacher, and the teachers within her professional network would keep her informed of my progress. She's told me that they almost always had positive reports; they let her know I was kind and pleasant. That's probably because I enjoyed school enough and did pretty well. I was confident in music, art, and certain forms of creative writing. I absolutely *crushed* in typing class when the time came. Math, on the other hand, was a struggle and remains so to this day— although cooking has helped by contextualizing scales and measurements, and running my own business has given me very good reason to get familiar with economics. Overall, I had a good reputation. In fact, I still hear from teachers now and then who will reach out because they've seen me on TV or found me on social media. While they often send sweet reminders about what a good student and a happy, positive kid I was, I'm also occasionally reminded of one of my tendencies that stuck with them—my intense separation anxiety.

I was a clingy kid, always hanging on to my mom's leg and following my parents around. And anytime I was away from home for something like a field trip, I cried. Like, inconsolable, uncontrollable, bawling, heaving sobs. It got to the point where my dad would have to come on field trips because I was *not* having it without at least one of my parents.

Judy and Michael Kish wanted to give their kids all the best. They wanted us to have opportunities, and I think they took some pride in being able to provide something they considered really special, something maybe they hadn't been able to have themselves as kids. They wanted to condition me to being away from them, which may have been part of the reason why, despite my track record of hysterics, summer camp seemed like a good idea. I'm sure the other kids found the whole sleepaway situation to be a dream, but not me. Total freaking nightmare. I could not stop crying. And crying. And crying. And then on day three—the second to last—smack in the middle of the cafeteria crowded with other happy kids, I cried so hard that I threw up my blueberry cobbler. Later, I called my dad and asked him to come pick me up, but he gently insisted I finish. Maybe somehow he knew that with reassurance that camp was almost over, and that I'd be back home with the family in just a day and a half, I'd be able to relax and have a little fun. If that was the case, he was right. I finally enjoyed myself.

Today I look back and wonder if some of my anxiety had to do with being adopted. I know it's common for kids who have come from unstable family situations and gone into foster care to develop that kind of attachment and insecurity, always subconsciously fearing they might be forgotten about or left behind. But honestly? I think I just really, really loved my parents. Despite my obvious devotion to them, my family didn't have a history of deep heart-to-hearts the way some TV families did. They didn't say "I love you" every five minutes. No one was overly effusive. Not until much later, when I went to college and we didn't see one another on a regular basis, did my father become vocal in this way.

Instead, my parents made my brother and me feel cared for and protected through acts of service. It was the little things. The way my dad took me to work with him to the plant where he was an engineer. The way I could feel his pride as he paraded me through the halls where the secretaries would give me candy and his coworkers—big, burly men who seemed like giants to me (and were probably swearing like sailors above my delicate ears)—operated huge machinery. He would take me out on the forklift and drive me around, and I absolutely loved the ride and the attention. The way my mom, whose job as a teacher was never really finished, would let me "help" her with grading on the weekends. Which meant I got to put the A at the top of a paper or even just sit next to her while she worked.

My parents were extremely hardworking, but they always found ways to include me, and my brother followed their example. Because he's eight years older than me, he was parental in many ways. Maybe at times I was just an annoying kid sister, but I also remember that, when he was old enough to have his own job at Pizza Hut, he'd take me with him to help him fold boxes. He always looked out for me, even later in life, when he helped me find apartments, celebrate my twenty-first birthday, purchase a car, and plan my finances.

I think my parents also demonstrated for both of us a model of love and marriage to which I still look for guidance. They showed love to each other in the same ways as they showed it to us. My dad, always the engineer even off the clock, built my mom a little lap desk for the La-Z-Boy in the basement so she could be comfortable while she did her paperwork. They had an impressive system of sharing responsibilities that I think strengthened their relationship and gave my brother and me confidence that we had a sturdy family foundation.

And fortunately, when they needed time to themselves, I had three living grandparents on whom they were able to lean occasionally for childcare. In the fall, one of their favorite ways to get away for a break together was to catch a football game at their alma mater—and one of my grandmothers happened to live near the MSU stadium. I loved going to her house, because although for the most part she sat in her recliner and crocheted (not exactly the most riveting activity for a child), she did have the most spectacular glass jar filled with foil-wrapped Werther's Originals and sugarcoated Sunkist Fruit Gems. I loved the Werther's until one of those slippery suckers got stuck in my throat and I almost choked (I'm still scarred from this experience).

But the Sunkist Fruit Gems were my absolute favorite and remain so to this day. I'm not discerning with them the way I am with Starbursts and Skittles, for which I have certain favorite flavors. Those chewy Sunkist candies were *all* the best, and I loved every flavor—equal opportunity. I would suck the sugar coating off and then bite them lengthwise with my teeth, splitting them open like a hamburger bun, and I still consider this one of the most satisfying textural experiences. Later, when I became a chef and worked pastry at a fancy French restaurant, I made pâte de fruit and did my damnedest to channel those fruit gems of my youth.

But truly, nothing can ever compare to those Sunkist Fruit Gems, and at my grandmother's house in those days, I went hard.

I stashed all the empty wrappers in her couch cushions, thinking I was pretty slick. Of course, she knew what I was up to, but she let me do it anyway.

If my childhood sounds perfect, that's because for the most part it was. So perfect, in fact, that it started to give me anxiety when I became aware of the possibility that I could lose some of the most important elements of my perfect life. That all the joy and happiness could be taken from me. That people I loved could be taken from me.

I've never been especially religious, but my father was raised in a Catholic household and went to an all-boys school. His mother was devout, so we grew up with at least some of the trickle-down. I remember praying the Our Father and going to catechism class so I could receive my first Holy Communion, and at some point around that time, I began to pray every night at home. I would lie face up in my bed with my eyes closed and recite those famous words at first, but then I developed my own personal addendum:

> Please watch over my dad, my mom, and my brother.
> Please make sure they're happy and safe. Please don't
> give anyone heart attacks. Please don't let our house
> catch on fire.

My fear that something bad could happen to the people I loved—that something could puncture my perfectly happy bubble—developed as I naturally became more aware of the world around me and the dangers outside our walls. It was paralyzing. I was just a powerless kid, so I reached out to a higher power to prevent my greatest fears from coming true, and once I started, I couldn't stop. That fear bloomed into anxiety and an obsessive, urgent need to pray. It went from preventive to proactive—I was convinced that if

I missed even one day, one of those terrible things would happen to someone I loved, and so I was fanatical about these daily recitations. My spirituality was less rooted in a belief that I could leverage a relationship with God than in a faithfulness to and belief in the power of habit and ritual to protect my people.

Later, when my grandmother passed, during my middle-school years, we lapsed, and I never went back to organized religion, but my fears only deepened when my family was touched by this loss. And even without the structure of church, I would still plead, repeatedly, every day, that same personal prayer. This went on for a long time, and to be honest, I'm not even sure when I finally let it go, but I can trace the foundations of some compulsive behaviors that persist today to that feeling.

As far as rituals went, to me, true proof of the divine was my mother's meat loaf. This was a weekly meal: meat loaf and baked potato with sour cream, dried chives, and a can of French-style green beans.

My dad cooked, too. He would make homemade chicken tenders with Dijonnaise sauce (Miracle Whip and Dijon mustard). On the side, we'd have an iceberg salad with grated carrots, tomato, cucumber, bagged croutons, and ranch dressing.

This was not fussy food, but God, I loved it all, and we got a little creative with it. On holidays, there were always a lot of casseroles and pot roast, and my mom would take the leftover pot roast, chop it up, put it in a food processor with Miracle Whip, pickles, and onion, then slather this pâté-like creation between two pieces of generic white, wheat, or rye bread. To this day, I crave those sandwiches.

The meal I often requested for my birthday started with lightly floured chicken breasts cut into strips. My mom used an electric skillet to brown them on the outside in some oil; then she combined them with a little more flour, canned chicken stock, and green beans. She simmered all that down until it became gravylike, then added potatoes until it became a chicken–green bean stew situation. I remember digging around for the crispiest bits of the breaded chicken, and oh, my God, it was prayer-worthy. In the summertime in Michigan there were more green beans—the fresh kind—and tomatoes and sweet corn, which I shucked on the back deck. We picked strawberries by the basket, which we'd smother with sugar and just let them hang out and macerate until they were juicy and syrupy enough to spoon over store-bought angel food cake along with a mountain of Cool Whip.

I helped out here and there and definitely picked up an interest in cooking, especially from the early days of food television. When I was as young as five years old, I would watch *Great Chefs of the World*, totally mesmerized. I tried to mimic what I saw, and even though I had no context for the flavors or dishes they were creating, I was drawn to the process. Sometimes I pretended my tennis racket was a frying pan and tried to re-create the simmering I'd heard on TV with crunchy leaves in the front yard.

Today, I'm often asked about cooking from my heritage, which I now recognize as a question about Korean food. But the truth is, the Midwestern creations my parents fed us are the foods of my culture. The most "ethnic" dish I remember was stuffed cabbage with sausage, rice, and sauerkraut, made by my Grandma Kish, who was German, and my Grandpa Kish, who was Hungarian. Hardly the kimchi jjigae people expect me to bust out.

It's a kind of study in nature versus nurture—a recurring question in my life, as it is for most adoptees. So often I hear people say to others, "You have your father's eyes" or "You look just like your grandmother." That will never be my experience, but I have definitely inherited so much from my mom and dad. My dad's inability to remember to close a cabinet or clean up his crumbs after he eats, for example (you can always tell when one of us has been in the kitchen), and my mom's tendency to worry. But one thing I've always wondered about is what I may have inherited from my biological parents. What did they look like? Were they creative? Did they struggle with math, too? Did they cook?

Today my interest in exploring the Korean parts of me is rooted in my sense of curiosity. When I hosted travel shows, my tendency to question everything was the driving force. I'm interested in seeing how other people live, in knowing what another life could be like. I'm interested in diving deeply into the culture, the food. I want to know the places to visit that aren't in the guidebooks. Maybe because there's part of me somewhere deep down that senses a parallel universe, one in which I was raised in Seoul, South Korea, instead of western Michigan. But that curiosity and compulsion aren't as much about wanting to connect with the people whose lives once came together forty years ago to create me. I know now that it's not about avoidance or fear or even anger at them for giving me up. It's just an absence of need, a sense of fulfillment cultivated in me at a very young age. A lack of want that has always given me peace.

My mom, after retiring, made it clear that one of her needs is for us—my immediate nuclear family—to spend time together. This family that she created with my dad. We're all so scattered, and my lifestyle and career regularly send me in so many directions, but I make a point to prioritize that family time now. Because when I think of family time and how my parents made that a priority—how they made my brother and me a priority—I want to fulfill that need as much as possible. Another thing I inherited from my mom is a desire to provide care. It's a distinct role reversal, the minute I had the means to do that for my parents in return. I want to make them as happy now, in the later years of their lives, as they made me when I was starting my own.

In some ways, though, this happy childhood created channels for anxiety and guilt as I got older and became more aware of the world beyond our family table. First because I was worried I would lose it, and later because I wondered if I deserved all that happiness. As I matured and entered my teenage years, and as I began to have questions about the person I was becoming, I realized that—nature and nurture aside—I might not be what the world at the time wanted from a girl.

2

n the mid-1990s, when I was coming of age, the women's voices I heard coming out of boom boxes and car radios were the Spice Girls, Mariah Carey, Celine Dion, and LeAnn Rimes—and that's when there were women on the radio at all. When actresses walked the red carpet, they were asked about their gowns and their boyfriends long before they were asked about their creative process. It was evident that the world wanted women—and girls—to fit in a very specific, clearly defined, and mostly homogenous box.

Luckily, all the elements one needed for that box could usually be found at any suburban shopping mall, especially if you were an all-American teenage girl, which—as I came out of my Midwestern grade-school bubble—very much described me. It also summed up my friends at the peak of middle school (a historically terrible time for tween girls), who were swept up in mainstream culture. And the pinnacle of female mainstream culture at the time? Makeovers.

Makeovers were absolutely everywhere. Magazine covers blasted every starlet's latest decision about her looks, from her lipstick color to the shape of her shoes to her (holy shit, *unthinkable*) decision to change her hairstyle. TV segments and episodes were dedicated to this phenomenon. Later, it was the basis for entire series of television shows: even the gays got in on it with *Queer Eye*. The process of transformation usually started with a sob story and ended in a tearjerker finale that brought families closer, healed relationships and hearts, and changed lives—not to mention made damn good television. The message was clear: change your look, improve your life.

This message also reached and galvanized a whole lot of young girls who just wanted in on the grown-up glamour of it all, and my friends were no exception. All they needed to have their makeover dreams come true was a target, and toward the end of middle school, they found one: me.

In elementary school, my style could be summed up as suburban '90s kid chic. When my mom took me shopping, it was to the little girls' sections of Kohl's and Hudson's. Then, in middle school, I transitioned toward baggy clothes, like windbreaker pants and especially the sporty pullover Starter jackets that came in team colors. These things sold out everywhere, and to be "in" in any way meant having at least one. It was a boyish style, but my aesthetic was "the baggier the better," because comfort was my top priority. I preferred to keep my long hair pulled back in a zero-fuss ponytail and stick to clothes that wouldn't cling to me or my changing body. I was teased at times for dressing like a boy, but most of the time I didn't care, because even if it stung, being comfortable was worth it, and it was so much better than the alternative.

I had always been a skinny kid, but it never really occurred to me to consider my body type. At the time, everyone's bodies were kind of the same. But as puberty descended upon my peers like a tidal wave, washing us all in hormones and leaving in its wake a totally transformed group of awkward adolescents, our differences became very apparent.

While I was growing vertically, I remained super thin, and I wasn't the only one taking note of my body type. My girlfriends recognized that my frame had a lot in common with the ones they saw on billboards in those days. They also saw that I wasn't using it quite the same way—or the way that they might have—buried as it was beneath my sporty boys' clothes. Like a lot of kids at that age, I was unsure of myself, malleable and unformed and extremely impressionable. I wanted to be liked, and honestly, I didn't even know yet what I *didn't* like for myself, so when my friends realized I was an easy mark for their makeover ambitions, I agreed pretty willingly.

It was summertime, and the style of the era and the season was "less is more." This was a time when your look was most on point if it appeared that your mom shrank your shirt with an over-enthusiastic spin in the dryer. One of my friends raided her closet to find something that would fit me, and the outfit she produced is seared into my memory to this day: a white baby-doll top, cropped enough to expose my midriff above my short jean shorts. *She's All That* was still a few years from hitting theaters, but I can assure you, I was no Rachael Leigh Cook, suddenly flush with confidence in my newfound hotness. In fact, this little glow-up had the complete opposite effect.

We went as a group (tween girl gang?) to KBL—the Kentwood Baseball League fields, as they were known at the time—to watch the boys play. It was an oppressively hot day; I can still remember the steam coming up from the asphalt and knowing that there'd be no possible way to cover myself with a jacket without coming off as super weird—or risking heatstroke. The fields were behind Saint Mary Magdalen, the church where I'd received my first Holy Communion. The fact that it was a place I knew so well made the disconnection from my own body and appearance all the more stark.

It hadn't even been that long since I'd played on those fields myself, wearing a uniform that matched everyone else's—an outfit indicating that I was part of something, that I belonged. Now I was watching from the sidelines, where we'd circled up as a group, sitting on the grass. I felt like a sore thumb that had been slammed in a car door.

It's not even that I was dressed so differently from the other girls. In fact, we were all wearing the same style. But even though I was in step with the '90s trends, I *felt* different. For one thing, I was so much taller and lankier than my friends that my short shorts and cutoff shirt were even more revealing than theirs, and I was so aware of it, so aware of everything. I can still feel the itchiness of the freshly cut grass, which I focused on while some of the popular boys milled around us. I'm sure it's safe to say that the attention of my friends was more occupied by the presence of the opposite sex than by the way I looked, but I couldn't help feeling like they must have been staring at me.

What made it worse was that thanks to a recent growth spurt, I had stretch marks around my knees. I had gotten a bit of a color on my legs from running around in the sun in my regular, pre-makeover life, and because stretch marks are technically scars, and scars don't tan, the snaking marks just shimmered conspicuously in contrast. In my own clothes, these lines were mercifully concealed, but in those short shorts—which I never in a million summers would have chosen for myself—they were exposed and eye-catching in all the wrong ways, much like the rest of me in that getup. I wanted to melt into the grass, just totally disappear. All I could do was desperately try to cover the lines up with my hands, which only drew more attention and questions from my friends, who didn't have stretch marks of their own and hadn't ever seen anything like them.

I wonder at times whether those girls ever remember that afternoon. I can't imagine why they would. It was just another day for which they found a way to pass the time, an activity with friends on one of the dog days of their many Michigan summers. Who knows? Maybe they have that moment in their memory for their own reasons. Kids are myopic, and I can't say I know whether one of them might've been having a private nightmare of her own for some reason, because I was too busy living my own. That said, I'm pretty sure none of them has given much more thought to the whole experiment that was Operation Makeover Kristen or to how they made me their plaything for a day, mimicking what they'd seen on tabloid covers and four-minute segments of their mothers' favorite morning shows. That's the thing about that age. Everything is about *right now,* with very little foresight or notion of how it might affect the future of anyone involved. I don't think my friends gave me a makeover to hurt me, and they could have had no way of knowing that those few hours would still come to mind for me three decades later. But that single afternoon was pivotal for me. It informed me of what the world was going to want from me as a girl, and as a woman, and what it would take out of me to give it.

Although my amateur makeover experience was not a home run at the baseball field, around the same time, a full-grown professional took an interest in my appearance as well—this time in a setting that felt much more appropriate for fashion conversations.

One day while shopping at 5-7-9—a store named for the sizes it sold for tween and teenage girls—my mom and I were approached by a man who explained that he was a talent scout for models. He was a roundish Black gentleman, probably in his thirties (although at my age at the time, it was hard for me to accurately guess anyone else's), who introduced himself as Edward. I stood by watching as he gave my mom a quick spiel, explaining who he was, what he did, and why he thought I was a good candidate for modeling. I don't recall the details of the conversation, but when he presented her with a business card for his agency, Prestige, the name made my ears perk up. It sounded so fancy. The whole scout thing I was a little fuzzy about, but prestige and *talent*—now, those were concepts I knew. And I understood that this man thought I was special, that I had value. Something I had told myself otherwise.

The whole thing happened quickly—my mom, unprepared for the conversation, wasn't exactly asking a million questions, and we moved on with our shopping trip. My mother was absolutely not a stage mom. She did not look in my direction that day in the cargo-jeans section and see dollar signs floating around my head as if I were some child-star solution to whatever financial problems she and my father might have had. In fact I had to plead with her, persuade her to let me do this thing. To be clear, I didn't know what the hell this *thing* was. Not exactly, anyway. Modeling wasn't some great dream of mine, and frankly, even as I begged my mother to call this man and seal my fate as a future runway star, I didn't really grasp what that meant or would require of me. I just knew there was that sense of approval I so desperately craved when he picked *me* out of a crowd at the mall.

My mom relented eventually, but my first shot at doing the job was a serious reality check. It was a runway show for Paul Mitchell hair-care products. Again, I knew there was an element of prestige, because Paul Mitchell was a brand I'd heard of before. We were called to a hotel nearby for casting, and even though I didn't *really* understand what was going on, it still felt so cool to be there, in this exclusive place, and I knew enough to know that it was a rare experience.

We gathered in a vast ballroom, where chairs had been set up for auditioners. I can't tell you how many girls were there in reality, but it seemed to my anxious brain back then that it had to be in the hundreds. They were all there with their parents, and I was no exception. My mom was by my side, and we listened as the agents described what they were seeking for the show with respect to hair. Mine at the time was long, black, silky, and thick, and apparently it was exactly what they wanted, because within a few days, we got the call that I'd been cast. That feeling—*getting* the thing—was so validating, even as ambiguous as it was to me.

Doing the thing, on the other hand, sent me into hysterics.

When we returned to prepare for the show, those of us who were selected were given a demonstration of what the client wanted to see: elaborate, wavelike arm motions, side-to-side shimmying, and strutting down the runway with a type of confidence and ferocity that was totally foreign to me.

Seeing in action what they were going to expect of me, I wasn't just uncomfortable with the assignment, I was also horrified. I turned and buried my face in my mom's shoulder and let the floodgates open. It was almost the blueberry cobbler all over again, except this time, I had my mom right there beside me, and she had no trouble turning us around and heading for the door. In fact, I don't remember her having much of a reaction at all, which I believe is a testament to how comfortable I was being honest with her. She never made me feel any cause for shame.

I was mortified, but somewhere deep down I was grateful to my parents for empowering me not only to speak up when I wanted something but also to feel okay saying I'd changed my mind.

Though it would come back into my life later on, my first brief foray into modeling reinforced what I had learned from my friends' makeover experiment—that the world wanted women and girls to be a very specific thing that fit into very narrow parameters (and tight clothes), whether on the sidelines of a ball field or on a billboard. And I was certain that no matter the setting, I wasn't going to be able to fit.

———

After that, I did my best to adjust to the brand-new world of High School Girl (which to this day is no easy feat), with its entirely new slate of rules and expectations. I didn't understand what had changed or why so much had to, but I knew I had to adapt if I wanted to fit in. And damn, did I want to fit in.

The problem was, I knew I was different. Not just in my body type and choice of clothes. I knew it went deeper than skin-level stretch marks or any kind of visible scars. As I listened to and watched my peers reshape their interests and rearrange their priorities—from playing with American Girl dolls to gossiping about which boys were cutest, both on TV and in our classes—I felt like the ground beneath me was shifting and a chasm was widening between me and the people to whom I once felt so close. I just...*did not care* what they seemed to care so much about.

And I didn't understand *why* I didn't care. It's not like I knew I was into girls at that point. Not exactly. But I knew I was definitely *not* preoccupied with the male dating pool or with dating at all. I would have been happiest if we could have all gone back to the way it was before, when no one talked about any of it. Whatever it was that prevented me from having a boiling-over interest in these suddenly urgent, all-consuming topics, I couldn't let on. Instead I realized quickly how critical it was to camouflage. To try to at least *look* like the rest of them, even though in my mind, I was clearly some kind of alien who couldn't relate.

The idea that I might become an outcast was terrifying, and I was doing everything in my power to stay in the pack. I observed other girls my age and tried to adopt their interests. When my mom took me to the mall, I lingered in the racks at Abercrombie & Fitch, picking out clothes I could be certain the *Dawson's Creek* kids would have complimented. I started keeping a journal of what I wore every day so I would never repeat an outfit within a week and a half. It was like something straight out of the *Mean Girls* script. I look back now at a tendency like this and see the seeds of my chef-brain, where being organized and prepared is a way to circumvent disaster—a fashion emergency being the high-stakes threat in question at the time.

By the time I was sixteen, I was fully swept up in it all. I may not have had any real interest in parties and drinking, but when you're that age, you commit to the hive mind wholeheartedly—individuality earns you no bonuses. I went to the ragers the kids threw when their parents were away. I drank a few sips of Zima when it was handed to me and did my best to hide the fact that I hated it. I pretended to be wasted because that was what was going to get me the most cool points. I was doing exactly what I'd seen teenagers do on TV, what my friends were doing or seemed to be doing around me, and switched over to autopilot like a sort of teenage robot.

Obviously, dating boys is a requisite component of the teenage-girl character sketch, so I would occasionally ask a friend to ask a boy to go out with me. I went to the dances and talked a good game when the situation called for it, which, in Teenage Girl World, was often. I think part of me believed that if I went through the motions,

I might eventually start to feel it all, and I'd be transformed into the malt beverage–loving, boy-crazy, pink-crop-top-wearing, just-like-everyone-else teenage girl I was supposed to be.

Still, teenagers want to have *some* kind of personal identity—little quirks to separate them from the pack. Not enough to be *too* different, but just enough to be memorable and give the clique a good reason to keep them around. I remember trying on personalities. I wanted to be someone different because I felt so boring. I started trying to change anything I thought I could control. I faked an eye exam to get glasses. Later, I got colored contacts, eventually landing on purple and light brown—which I alternated depending on my mood and outfits. I even made retainers out of paper clips just to have something unique about me, even if it wasn't the "coolest" quality. Looking back, I know I just didn't feel like me yet—that when I looked in the mirror at the girl in the trendy clothes trying desperately to be someone I wasn't, I didn't connect with the reflection at all.

It was during this time—searching for a thing that could be mine, and in need of relief from mounting anxiety—that I discovered smoking. I loved cigarettes instantly, after I got over the first few coughing fits. Not only did smoking fit my perception of what was cool, it also had an added bonus I hadn't expected just from watching people on TV do it: it was *relaxing*. It satisfied the ravenous little anxiety animal inside me. I fed that creature a cigarette, and it quieted right down. Smoking gave me a sense of calm I hadn't known I needed. It also gave me a direction for my restless energy and something to do with my hands. I didn't realize at the time that by picking up the habit, I wasn't just mimicking what other kids were doing. I was also, for the first time, self-medicating. And it was the beginning of a more than two-decades-long relationship with nicotine.

Smoking wasn't the only toe I put out of line in high school. Even though I didn't love drinking and partying per se, I still wanted to fit in and was no longer the perpetual "good kid" I was in elementary school, the one about whom my mom received glowing reports from fellow teachers. Once, I went on a camping trip with my friends, and we were caught drinking Busch Lights. (Because if you're going to go, go hard, right?) Let me tell you, nothing sobers up a bunch of rowdy, beer-buzzed teenagers like the stern questioning of uniformed officers—and I should clarify these were camp rangers, not actual police. They didn't even have to do much. In this case, the simple threat of calling our parents ("Either you do it, or I will") was enough to make us all break down in tears and confess, with varying levels of distress and drama. We spent the next few months volunteering at a home for senior citizens as penance.

But despite my few indiscretions, my parents maintained their trust in me. They supported me when I needed them to and gave me a wide berth. They were always giving me privileges and tools to help me develop a sense of independence, including the keys to their car on a regular basis (which I had no business using, because I smoked in it often and furiously tried to cover it up with air freshener). They weren't fools, and I know now that sometimes when I thought I was getting away with something, my parents were just looking the other way, giving me the space to sort things out on my own. I know they would have intervened had they believed I was in any real danger of fucking up my life or being truly destructive.

I couldn't be more grateful to my parents for this liberty, this almost-invisible-safety-net style of parenting, because I am certain it made me who I am today. But at the time, that freedom, and their love, actually began to fuel bad behavior on my part. I knew something in me was making me depressed and irritable, and what made it so much worse was just how great my life was. I had loving parents who encouraged and supported me in all the ways they knew how to. It was that awareness of my privilege and my inability to *feel* as happy and grateful as I knew I *should* be that started to make me into a little monster.

The thing is, certain kinds of pain, especially the emotional kind, can be ignored. My parents and my brother loved me and even *saw* me, inasmuch as I allowed them to, and they made that evident. I had friends and attentive, engaged teachers for the most part. When I look back, I see that there were people who would have likely made themselves available to me had I tried to talk to them. But I didn't. Part of my problem was that I didn't even know what was wrong with me. I couldn't put my finger on it or identify it, and I *definitely* didn't have the language for it.

Even if I did, would I have said anything? This was not an era during which my parents would have been handed a PFLAG brochure and given a pat on the back. I just knew I was different, and that was terrifying to me, so I pushed all those feelings way down, into some deep, dark, unknowable place. Keeping secrets like that— even as an adult—is corrosive. As a teenager, it can feel claustrophobic, oppressive. Actually life-threatening. Eventually, though, it will catch up to you.

With the growing knot of shame, guilt, and irritation at my inability to be myself or fix the thing that was wrong with me or even talk about it, just being around my mother was hard. I became irrationally furious with her. I was so angry that she had given me this wonderful life. When you're a teenager, your feelings are big and uncontrollable, and you don't know what you're feeling or why. It's like a fire hose of feelings spraying full-force in all directions, and no one is able to get a grip on how to aim the thing. I think you often unleash those feelings where and when you know you'll be the safest. For me, that was with my family, especially my mom. She got the brunt of my pain—the misdirected anger-depression-guilt-shame I was mixing up and shaking like a warm soda—in little explosions.

One evening at a local coffee shop, a group of my friends and our mothers met to have a meeting about senior spring break—where we'd be allowed to go, who would chaperone, baseline rules, that kind of thing. I was terrified that my mom was going to embarrass me, so before we walked in, I'd given her my code of conduct for this gathering: We were going to go, sit quietly, drink water, and get the hell home. Apparently, I assumed this was a very reasonable set of ground rules for a seventeen-year-old to provide to her parent. To my mother's credit, she took this speech in stride, but when it came time to put it into practice, Judy Kish went rogue on me.

It was wintertime, and we were all seated at a long table. My friends and their moms looked like they were having a great time together, picking out drinks and snacks when the server took orders. But my mom did not request water, as we had discussed. She asked for something that might as well have been an atomic bomb as far as I was concerned.

"I'll have a hot chocolate with whipped cream," she said.

For some reason, the fact that she ordered this particular beverage was utterly humiliating to me. And what was so much worse was that after the offending drink arrived and she took a sip, she got whipped cream on her nose.

Of course, if this happened today, I would lean over and wipe it off for her. But not when I was seventeen. At the time, my insecurities were completely out of control, and I projected them onto my mom in public. I tried to keep it in check because I couldn't totally lash out in front of everyone, but I was incubating a massive tantrum during the rest of the discussion. By the time the bill was paid and we were all parting ways, I wasn't just clipped with my mom; I was also mean and on a rampage. As discreetly as I could, I stood and said to my mom, "Let's *go*."

Everyone else was lingering and exchanging their goodbyes, and I played along, but once we were out the door, I stormed to the car. Mind you, this was my *mom's* car. But I still commandeered the thing, and when we got in, I peeled out of the parking lot, pedal to the floor, and started speeding through the neighborhood. I just wanted to piss her off, to make her feel some of what I was feeling.

At first, my poor mother was confused. But then she reacted.

"Kristen, *what* are you doing?" she shouted, trying to get me to slow down.

Eventually, we made it home, and I was grounded—rightfully so. To this day, I can't fully explain why this scene sent me into such a spiral. I could say that it was average teenage shit, being over-dramatically and inexplicably embarrassed by your parents. But I know it was compounded by my secrets, my guilt, my shame, which became a vicious cycle. And because I couldn't articulate it, I also couldn't ask for help.

Naturally, my parents did try to get to the root of the problem after this. Because I remained so thin, one theory was that I might have an eating disorder. I still liked baggy clothes, and without another possibility to explore, since I wasn't any help in understanding what was going on with me, they clung to this explanation.

I did not have an eating disorder, but without knowing what else to do, my parents came up with the idea to arrange for therapy.

Looking back, I can see that this was actually a pretty evolved decision on their part. It wasn't like it is today, with psychologists in schools and plenty of kids at all ages and with all different lifestyles seeking support for mental health—openly, in networks that encourage them to do so. In those days, parents were more inclined toward punishment if a kid's behavior was out of step with their (or society's or school's) expectations.

I didn't want to go, in part because I didn't have an eating disorder and in part because I found the idea of therapy embarrassing—something to be ashamed of. At the end of the day, though, it was a lot *less* embarrassing than trying to articulate my queerness, especially since I wouldn't have known how to at the time.

The woman my parents found specialized in eating disorders, so when we made our way inside the institutional brick building for my first appointment, my mom and I took up two of the six brown chairs in a waiting room surrounded by pamphlets about how to talk to your kids about anorexia, bulimia, and similar conditions. I slumped in my seat, anxiously waiting for my turn, and I remember watching as other patients entered or emerged from doors behind which they'd just completed their sessions and feeling increasingly out of place.

We are not the same, I thought on a loop, watching all these girls who had very clearly been battling something serious but entirely different from what was going on with me. Even there, in a place that was supposed to be healing, helpful, welcoming, and nonjudgmental, I felt like I didn't belong.

More than anything, I remember that almost-always-there feeling of discomfort in that brown chair, intensified by anticipating what I knew would be a difficult and fraught conversation with a stranger whose sole purpose was to analyze me. I never wanted to be looked at. I always tried to disappear, blend in, be *normal*. And there I was going into an hour-long session in which the entire time would be spent focusing on me and my differences. Even now, I remember that I clung to the sole source of comfort I had on that first day—my favorite pants. They were dark denim jeans so worn-out that the stitching on the back pocket had come off. I'd patched it up with a red bandanna iron-on detail, and that day I noted the feeling of those jeans, taking some solace in something I knew well, something that felt like part of me when everything else was so foreign.

Once I was called into the office, I took a seat on the big, overstuffed leather couch. Christine—who went by Chris—was kind, and her desk was on the opposite wall. There were big windows in the room that looked out onto the street, and I remember looking out those windows so many times during that session and the ones that followed. I was conflicted at times between wanting to be outside and on the other side of those glass panes and knowing that out there, I always felt out of place.

At first, I disputed the eating-disorder diagnosis. Partly because it was not true but partly in the hope that I could quickly put an end to the sessions. But then, after a while, I didn't argue or try to correct the narrative. It was just easier to let everyone believe a lie than to try to explain a truth I didn't understand myself.

Whatever the reason for leaning in to it, over time, I became comfortable with Chris, and I started to see the benefit of those hours together. It was frustrating to feel misunderstood and misdiagnosed, but I came to value the conversations, because even though I couldn't talk about the thing that was *actually* bothering me, I *could* just talk. And while I was always dancing around anything related to being gay, I did find some comfort on that couch.

Although I went to therapy somewhat reluctantly, I went willingly and enthusiastically to work. In high school, a job isn't always just drudgery and obligation. It can be an expression of—and, in my case, an escape from—the self. Tasks have always alleviated my anxiety. At a job, I knew exactly what was expected of me. When I was on the clock, I had a sense of purpose, and I knew what to wear and how to act, because I had instructions. At work, I also made the confidence-boosting discovery of skills and talents I'd never have imagined were in me and frankly wouldn't have thought to seek out otherwise.

At Twist & Shout, the shopping-mall pretzel franchise, I would clock in for my shift wearing an orange visor and an oversize company-issued T-shirt with a Comic Sans logo, ready to roll. The place smelled like a combination of cleaning supplies, pungent Asiago cheese—which we had in abundance because it was one of our best-selling varieties—and raw, yeasty dough. But it was the buttery, cheesy aromas that drew passersby as they came through the mall. People, especially little kids, would come up to the window to order and marvel at the process of making the doughy twists.

It was the suburban fast-food version of the fine-dining open kitchen. There were always a few people on the shift, and we operated a little assembly line. The pretzels were rolled and twisted, then set off to the side before they went for a bath in a solution of baking soda and water. From there they were arranged four to a tray and passed through the baking machine, emerging to be brushed with melted butter on the other side. Someone handled the dipping and topping, and a cashier helped customers.

We rotated through the positions, but I realized I had a knack for whipping the ropes of dough into their iconic shape and twisting them up with ease. It was a meditative act, and when I got into a groove, it was a confidence boost, too, especially during a massive rush. That deftness didn't come super easily to everyone else, and knowing that I was not only capable but also exceptional gave me a sense of pride. I got to feel like I was good at something. Like I excelled.

I also had some of my first really satisfying creative experiences. In the back room, there was a huge mixer, and one of the parts of my job was to make the dough. The only instructions were to combine the prepackaged mix with a specified amount of hot water. But I noticed that sometimes, depending on the temperature and humidity of the room, the dough would feel too hard and didn't roll well. It required a lot of extra effort to work it into a long rope, and I realized that when I added more water at those times, the dough turned out soft and supple. I started messing with it, trying to find a new formulation that felt better in my hands and that made it easier to speed through the twisting process. That was always the goal for me. When I was on a roll whipping pretzels, when that dough was perfect—oh, my God, I could have been there all day. I loved it so much. I had never understood math and science the way I did when I was thinking through time and measurements like that.

My nonsanctioned experiments extended to my own snacks, too. On breaks, we were allowed to eat just about anything we wanted. I would make myself an Asiago pretzel with mountains of cheese— so much that when it baked, the holes in the pretzel would fill with gooey, salty pools of the stuff. I topped it with Italian seasoning and marinara dipping sauce, essentially making a pizza. And because that wasn't enough, I then doused the whole thing in nacho cheese sauce and sprinkled Parmesan on top. When I was in the mood for something sweet, I hit the soft-serve machine for a vanilla-and-chocolate twist loaded with Reese's peanut butter cups. (If my parents and therapist could have witnessed this "snack," the idea that I had an eating disorder would have gone out the window.) And on the days when I was less inclined to prepare a culinary masterpiece for myself, I hit McDonald's for a number 2 combo: two cheeseburgers with fries and a Sprite. Call it opposition research.

Later, I got a job at Surf City Squeeze, which was our local version of Jamba Juice. I was practically a bartender at that place. I got a rush from the morning hustle and spent downtime concocting new smoothie flavors. It was an early glimpse at what my life would look like in just a few years.

More than anything, the work removed me from the academic pressures and social land mines that were my day-to-day reality. When I was shaping dough into hot, butter-soaked twists of perfection or mixing up creamy drinks for customers, I could forget about the fact that I felt lost everywhere else.

There were times when I wished I could hide out in those roles for the rest of my life, wearing the aprons of those quick-serve food concepts instead of having to decide on jeans or a sundress. I preferred answering questions about whether the peanut butter smoothie came in a larger size rather than the ones about what I was going to do with the rest of my life. I was far from being able to answer that latter question, but at work, I'd found an environment where I felt comfortable and confident. I had no idea how long I'd struggle to maintain those two feelings throughout the course of my life, but this was the first time I saw them as being possible and where and how I might find them.

3

Julia Roberts has appeared in at least fifty-four movies. She has received four Academy Award nominations plus God only knows how many other awards. She remains a fixture in American cinema to this day. She has reached an untold number of people through her work as an actress and has a list of credits to her name that could fill a book all its own. She is, and always will be, America's sweetheart. But what she may never truly receive due credit for is the way she changed *my* life. Because even though Julia is most remembered for being "a girl, standing in front of a boy, asking him to love her," it was her face on the screen in front of *me* that was a revelation.

"Oh, my God," I thought, sitting in the dark, watching her deliver that line. "I'm *gay*."

I was fifteen when *Notting Hill* was released, and even though I've been gay from the minute I was born—halfway around the globe a decade and a half earlier—this was the moment it really hit me. All the awkwardness and fears, the knowledge that I was definitely different—it all crystallized in the image of Julia Roberts's smiling face on-screen when I saw that movie.

If that sounds like the memo arrived late, consider the time I was living in. Around the millennium, there were only a handful of out celebrities. About 2 percent of the population admitted to being gay, and women made up less than half that number. Today, we use the word *identify* as if it comes from a place of power and pride. In those days, it was an *admission*—a word more indicative of guilt than any sort of assertion of self-actualization. If you came out as gay at the time when I realized it, you were setting yourself up for a lifelong struggle to prove your worth to people, to defend yourself and your "lifestyle" from the judgment of society at large and protect yourself not only emotionally but also physically, since your safety and well-being could very well be compromised (something that is, sadly, still true). You were also committing to a very particular undefined future. And though I didn't have any idea what that future was, I knew it wasn't the one I'd envisioned for myself.

I think that's one of the most destabilizing things about realizing you're gay. The view suddenly goes fuzzy, like your eyeglasses have been knocked off your face. You no longer know what is ahead of you. There aren't enough examples of what a happy, joyful queer life could look like to enable you to imagine one for yourself. At least, that's how I was feeling at the time. Today, queer culture accommodates so many ways of living. That's part of the beauty of being part of the LGBTQIA+ community. You can create your own rules and find people who are just like you or who might be able to introduce you to a world you didn't know existed. And if none of the paths on the map looks appealing, you can, and are empowered to, carve out your own.

At that time, I saw only one path—a tunnel, one with no discernible light at the end. It seemed to me that being gay was a one-way ticket to the fringes of society, which was not a place I wanted to be and not a place where I thought my parents would want to see me, either—especially after they'd worked so hard to bring me into their home almost two decades before, when they received me from that airplane.

To be clear, this had nothing to do with anything my parents explicitly said or told me about gay people. They did what open-minded, well-intentioned moms and dads did at that time, which was to raise me with their same core values, expose me to and educate me about different kinds of lives, and emphasize that we are accepting of good humans from all walks of life.

Once, when I was a kid, we traveled to Cape Cod and Provincetown, Massachusetts, on a big East Coast family adventure. P-town is known for being a gay mecca, and we happened to be there during Pride weekend. I remember holding my mom's hand, and there were rainbow flags everywhere. It was chaotic but bright, and I recall a clear sense of lightness and joy. I remember my mom saying to me, "Kristen, these boys like these boys," trying to explain that vast concept to a child. I'm not sure I completely understood the details, but it felt no different from her description of the contrast between cats and dogs. One wasn't better or worse than the other. They just were, and they were different from my mom and my dad.

I'd spent so much of my high school life trying to fit in, to be like everyone else, so with my post-Julia epiphany, to think that I'd have to try fashioning some form of a life in a world I was sure would never in a million years accept me was not just daunting, it was also devastating.

That said, that realization was loaded with so many emotions, because while it was a realization, there was also a little bit of a thrill. There's a reason a crush feels so fucking good. There's all kinds of chemistry going on in your brain—liking someone in that way actually gives you a high, and I hadn't really had a chance to feel that yet in my life. My friends all went on about this phenomenon in high school, and I could finally relate. It's not that I'd never had butterflies before, but prior to that moment, I hadn't made the connection between the flutter and the feeling they'd all been talking about.

When the movie ended and the credits rolled, there was no question in my mind. I just kept thinking on a loop, *Holy shit. I'm gay.*

———

While this information was a sort of answer, in the absence of some guidance or road map as to what to do next with it, and since there was no way I was prepared to process it, I had no choice but to focus on the part of my future about which there was no question whatsoever. I was going to college.

Today, there is a recognition that there is more than one way to live, thrive, and find one's definition of success. Kids now might graduate from high school and launch straight into tech start-ups or careers as influencers or TikTok stars, but when I was growing up, particularly if you had a certain level of means and privilege, like I did, you followed more or less one path: from the locker-lined corridors of your local high school to the hallowed halls of an institution of higher learning.

There were a handful of kids taking gap years or doing a year or two at a community college, but I never entertained any other option than a four-year university. Not because my parents would have objected or because the other kids in my graduating class would have called me a loser, although either or both of those things might have been true. It was because even though I can't say I was especially excited about the idea of another nearly half decade of tests and teachers and increasingly anxiety-inducing forms of math, I did see the value of a degree for my own purposes. If being gay was a one-way ticket to the fringes of society, a degree was a boarding pass to freedom.

To this day, I think it's ludicrous that we ask seventeen- and eighteen-year-olds to try to choose something they'll want to do for the rest of their lives and then sink unholy amounts of money into it at a time when really all they want to do is fuck off and hang out with their friends. But that was the process, so I tried to narrow it down. Travel had been of interest to me as far back as I could remember. Maybe it started with episodes of *Great Chefs of the World*, which opened my eyes to the possibilities and realms that were out there beyond the borders of Michigan. Maybe because I'm Asian, I'd always been aware of the existence of other cultures, or maybe it was just a deep, innate curiosity, but seeing the world had always seemed thrilling.

When I landed on my gay identity, though, travel wasn't a daydream anymore: It was an imperative. It felt less about being drawn to other places than it was about escaping to them. I was pushed by my own hand away from the reality I was in. I thought that if I wanted to have any chance at an authentic life, one in which I could be my true self, I had two options: Wait until my parents and all the people I loved were long gone or get as far away as I possibly could, to a place where I wouldn't bring shame upon them, a place where they'd never have to know a version of me that would disappoint them. For a kid who got homesick just going to summer camp because of how much I loved and missed my parents, this idea was... well, you can imagine.

And while it was never anything my parents said that scared me, it was what they *didn't* say—what they could never have known to say and what the world in general didn't say to people like me because in those days, there was no way of knowing it was true: *It'll be okay; you'll be okay; you will be loved. The world will change.*

What the world—and college brochures—*did* say was that if you got a college education, you could be anything you wanted. And what I wanted was to put a safe distance between my home and myself so I could live a real life. The business school catalog didn't exactly thrill me the way my crush on Julia did, but putting on a power suit and flying around the world, finding places where I might be able to be myself? Sign me up. So in the fall of 2002, I packed my bags and my extra-long bedsheets and became an international business major.

I stepped onto the campus of Grand Valley State University feeling optimistic. The imposing brick buildings and the clean, crisp autumn air uplifted and inspired me. It gave me a sense of forward movement in my life; I had a new setting for my story. High school was finally behind me, and this was my shot at building a future. It was a change and a fresh start, and at least for the moment, I had a solid plan. Like twisting pretzels and making smoothies, this was something to which I could dedicate myself and my focus.

With the gift of time-won wisdom, I know now how often I've had the sense of "Okay, I've arrived only to find out that what I've arrived at is another question, another crossroads—a detour or a roadblock." But I don't think I'm alone in that rush to have your shit figured out, especially in a culture that presses its youth—not its elders—to be leaders and stars. By comparison, those of us (meaning the majority of humans) who do *not* rise to the upper echelons of their fields by their midtwenties, with a heterosexual marriage and a mortgage and 2.5 kids to quickly follow, wind up feeling like total failures. I didn't need the added layer of being a closeted queer kid to feel that. But at least for the moment, I walked into that first semester with my head up, my eyes on the prize. A cap and gown. A power suit. Plane tickets.

Getting into college hadn't been a cakewalk. Literally everyone in my family had gone to Michigan State, and even though my parents never put any pressure on me to do so, I tried to continue the legacy. I'd done well in high school, but apparently not well enough, and my application was rejected. So instead of following in my family's footsteps, I did what many kids my age did and followed the lead of my friends, one of whom had been accepted to Grand Valley State, a college forty minutes from my parents' house. It wasn't exactly the far-off reaches I had in mind for the future, but for the moment, it was accessible.

When I got in, my friend and I decided to be roommates. I didn't love the idea of trying to make new friends—I remained an introvert, totally uncomfortable with social situations, especially when I didn't have familiar faces around me—so at least I could count on having one friend for sure.

Even with at least that one constant in my life, college was different in so many ways. There was the initial thrill of independence, the throngs of new faces, the academic challenges. But there was also plenty that felt the same, and pretty quickly, I got swept up in trying to fit in—again. My roommate was a social butterfly, which had pros and cons for me. I didn't love that she was coming back to our room hours after I'd already gone to sleep when I had crack-of-dawn classes the next morning. But she did manage to get me into the social scene in a way I might not have done on my own.

She loved to party, and even though I hadn't suddenly developed an interest in getting wasted since my high school Zima-sipping days, I joined in anyway, because—college. I tagged along with her and her new friends to frat parties and played wingwoman, much as I had in high school.

So many times in my life, I've done something because I thought it was what was expected of me. This was no different. What *had* changed, though, was I already knew I didn't like those things. In high school, I'd been experimenting. It was all new: I was still testing the waters to see what might be fun. But by this point, I didn't need to dip a toe in. I was already certain I had no interest in, for example, going to a Halloween party on campus dressed as a sexy kitten. Just…no.

And yet one frigid October evening during my freshman year, that's how I found myself, in that exact getup, with the ears and all, standing at a party surrounded by frat bros and girls in similarly weather-unsuitable getups, feeling so uncomfortable I could die. One of the guys we were with was dressed as a slice of pizza, and all night, all I could think about was, first, how badly I wanted to be eating pizza and, second, how badly I wished I could have been wearing *that* instead of my costume.

I also knew that I absolutely didn't want to kiss boys. And yet this was another thing that I began to comply with because that's what was expected. In high school, you can kind of fly under the radar and avoid dealing with some of the dating stuff. At some point, though, it became really hard to hide from it, and I didn't want to draw attention to myself. I couldn't give anyone a reason to think I wasn't interested. And so it came to pass that in my first semester of my freshman year of college, I wound up briefly going out with the punter on the football team. Let me tell you, this was *nothing* like dating Julia Roberts.

I knew college served a bigger purpose beyond an education—as I perceived it, my survival relied on my ability to power through the next four years. But if you've ever been truly depressed, you might know that it stretches and morphs time in disorienting ways, and it started to feel impossible that I'd make it through what then seemed like an eternity. I didn't even have the joy and refuge of a job I liked to buoy me. I'd taken a gig as a receptionist at an assisted living facility for seniors. My friend's mom ran the facility and got me in, and the job had its positive moments—elements that made me smile (the guys who would zip by in their wheelchairs, saying hello to me) and feel purposeful (checking in families who were there to visit loved ones). But compared to my high-intensity smoothie- and pretzel-making days, this was sleepy. The phone rarely rang during my shifts, and I found myself looking at the clock, always wanting more.

There were some parts of college that brought me joy, though. Even though it was hardly an introduction to haute cuisine, I was *obsessed* with the food. College cafeterias are seriously unreal. What an experiment—to drop a kid into a massive room where there is everything from soft-serve ice cream machines to full-blown dessert buffets and say, "Have at it!" And thanks to the magic of the dining plan my parents had chosen for me and the invoices I never saw, it *felt* like it was all totally free. I was in awe. The fact that every day I got to eat a full 3 Musketeers bar with my turkey sandwich at lunch? Unbelievable. Even though I'm not a huge chocolate lover anymore, those bars still stir up a lot of good nostalgic feelings for me.

Still, the magical cafeteria menu wasn't enough to sustain me entirely. I didn't officially move home, because I wasn't ready to admit defeat, but I started going back there more, beginning with just a few trips to see my parents for a meal or to do laundry. I could frame it as just a visit, nothing unusual. But then I started staying for a few overnights, then weekends, and eventually I fully moved home, driving the forty minutes for class for a while.

I did continue to try to participate in the world in some way. I went out with a guy named Gary for a few ill-advised dates. Mostly, I did it to prove to the people in my life—and maybe a little to myself—that I was still trying. When he showed interest in me, I jumped at the chance to go out with him because he was the kind of dude other girls would have gone crazy for, and I thought, *I've got to make something happen with this guy.* He was beautiful. I mean, his hair, his bone structure—he was *pretty*-beautiful. In retrospect, maybe I just saw him and thought, *Well, close enough!*

I remember trying to look alive for the date. I put on a nice pair of jeans and my North Face fleece because, like the Starter jackets and Abercrombie cargo pants of my younger years, this piece of clothing telegraphed coolness and status. I don't remember the movie (let's just say it didn't have the staying power of *Notting Hill*), but maybe that's because I spent the whole time feeling so utterly lifeless. I couldn't understand how I'd arrived at this place. Gary and I cordially parted ways. I hope he found someone who makes him happy.

I finished out the school year living in my parents' place and mostly avoiding social situations. Pretty soon, I gave up on my power-suit globe-trotting dreams and withdrew from school—and that particular four-year plan. It felt like such a massive defeat at the time, but as I look back, although I didn't walk away with a whole lot of knowledge about international business, I did learn what I *didn't* want in life. And that may have been much more valuable.

4

When you get to a certain point in your career as a chef, people start asking about your culinary point of view. What is the message you try to send with your food? What is your food story and how did it start? What is your vision and how has it evolved? Well, I had a very clear vision for my first culinary effort. I was going to make a thick, creamy, deep dark chocolate pudding.

I was maybe six years old at the time, and the idea was inspired by my regular viewings of *Great Chefs of the World* plus a personal love of the wiggly dessert. I worked so hard on that recipe, carefully formulating and tinkering until I had the texture exactly right. Just like I'd seen on TV. Just like the Jell-O pudding I knew and still love. I was very proud of this creation.

Sadly, it was entirely inedible. That's because nothing about my chocolate pudding was chocolate or pudding at all. I didn't know what the fuck I was doing. I was a child who could grasp visual sensory cues like color and texture, and I had a great imagination. I found soy sauce in the cabinet, which had the general hue of what I was going for, and cornstarch, which I knew—thanks to watching my mom make Thanksgiving gravy—would thicken it up. They say with food, it's all been done. But I beg to differ. I'm pretty sure what I came up with that day—that milky, starch-thickened, soy sauce "chocolate" concoction—was an entirely original recipe, a Kristen Kish signature. I might've added other "ingredients" that I can't recall, but the point is this: My journey to *Top Chef* had officially begun.

At least that "dish" probably tasted like something. Later, when I was old enough to use a knife and an oven, I remember trying to make dinner for my parents. What I served them—plain chicken and couscous entirely without seasoning—was the blandest, most boring meal imaginable, but they were gracious and complimentary.

Still, it'd be hard to imagine these examples of my culinary prowess providing the inspiration behind my mom's suggestion for my next step in life after my year at Grand Valley State University. I'd moved back into my parents' house and was nursing my wounds, at a total loss for what to do next. Mostly I was sitting around in my pajamas, eating spaghetti with red sauce and drinking creamsicle floats, both of which are comfort foods for me to this day.

As a teacher, my mom had a good handle on the available options for higher education. And despite how much spaghetti I was putting away on a regular basis, there was still a lingering concern that I had an eating disorder. I think the concept of culinary school was comforting to her in a way, to think I'd be surrounded by and learning about food.

Whatever the motivation, when she presented the idea to visit Le Cordon Bleu College of Culinary Arts in Chicago to check out the program, it piqued my interest. For one thing, even though I was deeply depressed, I hadn't counted myself out. I just didn't have a sense of direction, and this was at least *something*. Also, while it wasn't the other side of the world, or in one of the far-off places I'd envisioned an international business degree might have promised, Chicago *was* a way out of Michigan, one with which I'd already had some experience.

———

The summer before starting college at Grand Valley, I'd taken another swing at modeling. Though the runway show in middle school was a bust, I remained on the Prestige agency's radar and occasionally picked up small jobs throughout high school—photo shoots for back-to-school catalogs, that kind of thing. It wasn't hard; it wasn't easy; it wasn't fun; it wasn't miserable. It was fine, and it was just a thing I did sometimes.

After I graduated, my agents suggested I explore representation with a larger agency. At the time, in my mind, there were really only two major names in modeling: Ford and Elite. The latter had an office in Chicago. My feeling was, Why not? It was at least a good reason to take a train into the city, so I made an appointment.

The office was the kind of thing you see in movies: an open space with lots of desks, beautiful faces everywhere, high-powered people having conversations that sounded very important, receptionists placing people on hold so they could answer more incoming calls. It felt so exclusive, so fucking cool. I loved the whole scene and the idea of being part of this system.

After the meeting, the Elite agency officially signed me, which felt like big news. But now I understand how these things work. Signing guarantees nothing, and I was probably one of hundreds of girls carrying around what they called comp cards—a kind of modeling-specific business card—and feeling like that carried some weight, some clout, the promise of some dream.

What I also came to understand during that time was what was most valued in a model. All my life, I had only ever wanted to fit in. But what bookers really wanted were models who stood out—maybe they had a gap in their teeth or, like Cindy Crawford, a birthmark. The only thing that made me stand out was how clueless I was about that world. I was still super uncomfortable with the idea of a catwalk, but my height and build made me desirable for the category, so I agreed to attend a runway class. I showed up in head-to-toe Abercrombie, right down to the oversize men's flip-flops. The other girls were dressed like, well, aspiring models, in spiky heels and formfitting clothes. Needless to say, even with the additional training, I didn't book a lot of jobs during that time, and though I wasn't quite finished with modeling (it would come back into my life in later years), that experience was fresh in my mind after my brief business school attempt, so it helped me rule it out as a path forward.

Still, there were two important takeaways from that experience. The first had to do with one of the agents. I can still picture Shannon Hill, a young Black woman with short hair, as she welcomed me into the office and gave me the rundown. I listened closely, interested in how she could help me with my future, but I was even more intrigued by her past. Shannon had moved to Chicago from Omaha, Nebraska—which to my mind was a very small town, a place that seemed not unlike where I was coming from, and she was probably not a whole lot older than I was. But she managed to land what appeared to me to be a very impressive job, and I thought she was the coolest fucking thing ever.

I didn't aspire to become an agent—I wasn't even sold on the idea of being a model—but sitting there with Shannon, I couldn't help but think that if she could carve out this spot for herself as a badass professional in her industry, I could make things happen for myself, too.

To this day, I sometimes think about Shannon and wonder if she is still an agent or whether she's ever imagined that her impact reached far beyond booking runway shows. But it was her example, and the fact that she moved to a big city to pursue her ambition, that brought me to the second important takeaway—Chicago was a place you went when you wanted to make things happen.

A couple of years later, I was back in Chicago. It was summertime when my parents and I toured Le Cordon Bleu for an info session. I still remember the tour guide, Toby. He was a short guy wearing a sweater with a button-down shirt underneath and glasses, and he spent the day taking us around and selling "the dream." Every institution has one, and there, it was all about Chef Life. I could feel it instantly, how different it was from my previous college. I was entranced by the sea of people—with their cravats and white skull caps, their checkered pants and black shoes, and the pristine white jackets embroidered with Le Cordon Bleu's logo. I was mesmerized when I caught a glimpse here and there into classrooms where lessons were being conducted not on a chalkboard but at real cooking stations, with working equipment and real tools and ingredients. It wasn't the abstract kind of teaching to which I had been accustomed.

It's a rare thing in life to realize the moment when a dream begins to form. It's so seldom like a lightbulb in a cartoon. For some people, it's a gradual process as they recognize a passion for a thing. For others, it's something they've wanted for so long that they don't even remember when or how it started. But walking those corridors gave me a stirring feeling. In business school, there was a practical element. It wasn't a dream: It was a plan, and there's a big distinction. I have a very logical side of my personality, but I'm also a dreamer. And this guy, Toby, with his sweater and button-down and glasses, pointing out the equipment, highlighting faculty and student accomplishments, and selling the cooking-school dream, tapped into both sides of me. I was sold.

Before we left that day, I turned to my parents. "I want to do this," I said.

The next few months were all about preparation. I was getting out of bed again with energy, dressing to go purchase off-brand slip-resistant shoes from Payless for kitchen work, marveling at the selection of knives and smallwares that was included in the price of tuition. My parents and I also returned to Chicago to scout out an apartment. Living on campus wasn't a thing, so my parents—who always prioritized my safety—researched and asked around for a place that would be close enough to campus and in a part of town that felt secure to them. We settled on a high-rise building in the Gold Coast neighborhood. It was a studio apartment in a doorman building, small but still so much more than a college kid could possibly want.

I was so grateful. It's never been lost on me, especially now, in hindsight, how much my parents invested in me—and what a vote of confidence those investments represented. Not only were they financially supportive in so many ways, they were also generous in their expressions of encouragement. My parents were hardworking people, frugal in their own lives so that they could provide advantages for their children, but they seemed to have a limitless budget for emotional resources. They never made me feel bad about changing my mind or my path. On the contrary: They helped me plot a new course and gave me a compass, tools, shelter, and everything else I could possibly need to move forward and succeed. I knew I had no way to repay them at the time, but as I stepped into my new future, I thought maybe someday, I'd be able to at least make them some edible chocolate pudding.

Except when I was working at my mall jobs, getting dressed had always felt fraught to me. Whether because of my friends' makeover attempts, the expectations of model culture, the customary college-girl Halloween costume, or my continued desire to be comfortable, I could never seem to feel okay about putting on a single outfit without second-guessing everything.

That is, until I suited up for culinary school. In that uniform, there was no guesswork. No questioning whether it would fit the style or be on trend. No agonizing over accessories. No reason to keep track of my outfits in a daily journal. Oh, what High School Kristen would have thought of this aesthetic repetition—not to mention the "style." The uniform was hardly anything fancy. The jackets were comfortable enough, even though they were too big even in the smallest size. The pants, on the other hand, were rough and starchy with a thick elastic waistband that was super tight despite the fact that the pants themselves were absolutely huge. (The pursuit of comfort having always been a major consideration in my life, I still wonder at times if this is part of why I'm so sensitive to scratchy clothes today.) I woke up before the sun every day to perform this readying ritual, which concluded by sliding on the Payless nonslips. These started out fitting well enough in the morning but would come to feel tight later, after ten hours standing caused my feet to swell. I would tie my hair back in a ponytail low enough to avoid interference with the skull cap. And then, rain or shine, Midwestern blizzard conditions or peak city humidity, I would walk down the hallway and step outside with my head high.

It was liberating to have this reliable routine, but most important, when I looked in the mirror, I felt *good*. I felt as if what I had always wanted to feel on the inside—that I was a person with a purpose—was how I looked to the outside world, too. When I walked the fifteen minutes to class, I held my head high, imagining what others might be thinking of me: that I was a chef somewhere; that I possessed specialized knowledge they didn't have; that I was capable, even accomplished.

Of course, I wasn't *quite* embodying those things just yet. A fact of which I was reminded on day one. Given that the first class was Knife Skills 101, we weren't exactly whipping up Michelin-worthy menus. Our first task was to tackle mountains of cabbage, practicing our cuts—dice and chop, julienne, chiffonade, that sort of thing. I'd never been a cook at home, but I had attempted some of this stuff. I'd devoured *Great Chefs of the World* as a kid, but by the time I started school, I'd seen other food television, too. There had been a percolating interest in so-called stand-and-stir shows, the kind in which a chef or cook (like Rachael Ray or Sara Moulton) would make a dish and describe the process step-by-step. For me, learning has always been about visuals like this. If you ask me to sit and read a book or listen to a lecture, I'm not going to retain a thing. But show me a YouTube video on how to build a table, and I'll open you a furniture store in a week. There wasn't much attention paid to diverse learning styles back then, and those of us who didn't fit squarely into traditional academic spaces had to arrive at that recognition on our own. For me, it happened slowly, and in fact it's an ongoing process to this day. But I know now that this is part of why cooking school clicked for me.

The physical space also felt so generative compared to my previous learning experiences. The rooms felt vast—nothing like the claustrophobic lecture halls and seminar rooms at the university—with tall ceilings and exposed ductwork, gray tiled floors and stainless-steel prep tables pushed together to form big rectangles. The classes consisted of around thirty students, and there would be four or five of us on either side facing one another. Each station had big, capable gas stoves and ovens. The school felt new and clean, which was helped by the fact that when lessons were over, we were expected to sweep and mop, clean up after ourselves, and perform the kind of duties that would be required of us in the real world. I remember the hum of exhaust fans while we worked—a calming white noise that allowed me to think, to focus.

It helped to have my skills recognized, too. That first day, despite having no kitchen training whatsoever, I accessed knowledge I didn't even know I had absorbed and had only exercised at home for my own amusement and edification.

Our chef-instructor, Mr. McGinnis, surveyed everyone's work. He was a calm guy—not at all the caricature of a screaming, loose-cannon kind of chef. He smiled a lot and was very approachable. And when he arrived at my station, he stopped.

"You've done this before," he said with a nod.

My chest filled with pride—a kind I can't recall ever experiencing before then. I'd felt proud in my life when my parents praised me, but this was different. This had nothing to do with how this man felt about me. We'd met only hours before. This was entirely about my ability, about something I was capable of doing. The closest I'd come in the past was maybe making pretzels, but that was child's play. This was no part-time job. This was my future.

From that moment, I was on fire. I excelled at cooking school in ways I never once had in any other setting. It appealed to so many parts of me. Classes weren't about sitting around in a lecture hall; we were up, moving our bodies, *making* stuff. And not just for the sake of practice—our food was used to really feed people. There was a sense of structure, order, and preparedness. We were busy in a way that kept both my hands and my mind occupied. There were lectures, but they were short and broken up by practical courses rather than the interminable sitting that always put me to sleep in other academic settings.

And then there was that propulsive pride. I was shining in almost every class, and despite all the times I'd tried to hide and be invisible before then, I never once tried to dim my light in cooking school. I was standing out, but for all the right reasons.

And I couldn't wait to share what I was learning. After baking and pastry classes, I almost always had something to take away with me. We made choux pastry eclairs with a light, vanilla-flecked pastry cream and chocolate mirror glaze, buttery tarts with fresh Midwestern seasonal fruits, and cherry clafoutis that reminded me of the Michigan cherries from back home. But instead of going home and having a personal feast on my latest pear frangipane tart, I would bring treats like that to my doorman—a friendly older guy with a mustache, always looking dapper in his uniform—who was amused and grateful whenever I showed up with an aluminum tin. To this day, this is how I get the most joy out of creating food. It's never about feeding myself—in fact, I really never cook for me. It's always been about connecting with others, sharing a little piece of myself and hoping to make someone else feel happy and cared for and seen.

Of course, I encountered some constructive feedback at times— a few early brushes with the sensation of being judged, which I would become familiar with later, during my *Top Chef* days. One instance occurred at the hands of a sauce instructor who bore a striking resemblance to the animated food critic Anton Ego in Pixar's *Rata-touille*. This guy scared the shit out of me for no real reason beyond his stern reputation and ability to wield a white plastic tasting spoon like an executioner's ax. I still believe that my performance, which he deemed subpar, had more to do with my fear than my actual sauces and stocks. It was the only class for which I received a C, and while I was briefly crushed, even that couldn't suck the joy out of cooking school for me.

By and large, though, my instructors over the course of two years were encouraging, patient, kind, and approachable. At Le Cordon Bleu, I began with lessons on how to chop and dice and julienne and went on to learn the complex chemistry of cooking, the funda-mentals of sauces and stocks, techniques for braising and brûléeing, and how to break down ingredients into the refined components that could become complete dishes. Even if those creations were not quite culinary masterpieces just yet, I had the beginnings of a career.

Today, I'm sometimes asked whether I believe culinary school is necessary for a career in food or if it's worth the price tag. My feel-ings are complicated, and to be honest I believe there are ways into the industry without accumulating debt.

But for me, maybe more than anything, culinary school was the first place I really felt like myself. I had confidence, a sense of purpose, and from the vantage point of a classroom cooking station, I began to make out the image of a promising future in front of me again.

Still, as self-assured as I was in the classroom, within the armor of my white jacket and skull cap, when I stepped off campus, it was like a spell was broken. My social anxiety was intense, and without my schoolwork, I found myself spinning when left to my own devices. I didn't explore Chicago's food scene or spend time adventuring around the city. My off-hours meals mostly consisted of bags of chips and protein bars from the health food store twenty feet from my building or delivery from a Thai place I loved (massaman curry with fried spring rolls and rice—enough for leftovers a few hours later), all of which felt safe because I barely had to step outside, if at all.

As it had been in the past, though, having a paying job where I punched a clock—an obligation—was a lifeline. It kept me from careening into total isolation. Although my parents were very generously involved with my living expenses, and I had student loans, I still had to work for spending cash. Besides, working was just *in* me. I didn't know how to not work.

I got a job at the Chicago Chop House, an institution in the city. It's still there, occupying a massive Victorian brownstone in the River North neighborhood, serving seafood towers and prime rib and molten chocolate cakes. Despite how much I was learning at school about how to create those classic dishes, I didn't work in the kitchen. As I look back, it was probably for the best—I'm sure I would have been eaten alive.

Instead, I took a job as a hostess because it was something I perceived as "easier," although certain moments provided insight into the challenges of other restaurant roles—insight that proved valuable when I became a manager and leader later in life. Being the primary point of contact with the public was taxing on my anxiety, but I found a groove and committed to the work the same way I always did when given a task. I'm very good at pushing myself through uncomfortable situations—for better or worse.

The job prompted me to be at least a little social outside of work, too. School had many positive elements, and I liked my classmates. The environment was diverse. Agewise, it ranged from students who were my contemporaries, coming straight from high school or transferring from college, all the way to older career changers. There were plenty of women, too, and for the most part I never felt outnumbered or othered. But school was not a place where I went to make friends. I was laser-focused in class, and while I had some cordial relationships, none was lasting or translated into off-hours, off-campus hangs.

But as most industry employees will tell you, working in a restaurant just about guarantees you an instant family. While I would experience that to a far greater degree in the years that followed, my time at the Chop House was an early introduction to that dynamic. My main source of sustenance outside of school and protein bars was family meal, along with group outings to a spot called Bijans. To this day, if I could associate a single meal with my college experience, it would be the salad that was practically my standing order there: creamy mustard dressing, shredded roasted chicken, goat cheese, dates, romaine, and almonds. So fucking good. I also ate enough portobello mushroom burgers in those days that I literally can't even look at one anymore, but they were great at the time, and at least I was getting some real nutrition beyond the mounds of french fries I ate.

I got by going out with that crew because there was always a big enough group to allow me to disappear a little. I can't say I was anywhere near as confident or comfortable as I was at school, but it beat the hell out of frat parties and Halloween kitten costumes, and I was able to make some happy memories. I felt like I really was part of something, and it was one of the first times I got to experience the kind of camaraderie for which the hospitality industry is famous, the kind that calls to people who consider themselves outsiders and brings them together for the purpose of serving guests—the kind that creates bonds and would become such a huge part of my life going forward.

School was a relief in other ways, because being focused on my studies gave me a very good excuse to completely avoid dating. If I had to explain it to others or to myself, there was my discipline to lean on. I was simply unwilling to be distracted.

That said, when an old connection from high school resurfaced, I had my first real brushes with gay culture. In our Michigan days, speculation swirled about Vinny's sexuality. When you're gay and closeted, other gay people, who seem to be lightning rods for the wrong kind of attention—the toxic, frankly traumatic, and cruel kind—are almost scary to be around. Even if you feel for them (and you most likely feel very deeply for them), and even if you're fascinated by the fact that you might actually, personally know other gay people *in the flesh,* and even if you want to know them so much better and even be their friend, they are an example of the kind of notice you want more than anything to avoid. That it can be so achingly lonely is one of the great sadnesses of queer life. And yet seeking out connection—reaching for the cure to that loneliness—feels dangerous, because the association is too great a risk. It's gut-wrenching and illuminating and paralyzing all at once.

In Michigan, Vinny and I were friendly, but we didn't run in the same circles. I didn't avoid him, exactly, but we didn't cross paths much outside of school. Then in Chicago, I learned he was attending school there, too. These were the days before social media, before

you knew your ex-schoolmates' every move. I had no way of knowing Vinny's entire life story since graduation, but what I found when
we reconnected was a young man who was living his life as an out
gay man in a major American city. While I was inspired by Vinny's
openness, I wasn't anywhere near ready to follow suit. Still, I willingly went as his "straight" girlfriend to the gay bars in Boystown—
a historically queer neighborhood in Chicago—and experienced for
the first time since I went to P-town with my parents all those years
before what gay pride could really mean. There were the same rainbow flags I remembered, bright and vibrant, and it was just so utterly
joyful.

In those days, if you believed what popular culture would tell
you, being gay was a miserable experience. A death sentence. A life
defined by struggle and pain. But this? This was pure celebration. It
was a testament to the enduring spirit of the community, and I was
so grateful for the introduction. I felt safe and welcomed. And even
though I wasn't prepared yet to identify as part of their community, I
felt like I belonged and just maybe had something to look forward to.

My time in culinary school in the Windy City blew by. I started at Le
Cordon Bleu with the intention of completing an associate's degree,
which was a two-year program. I'd already earned the necessary
general education credits at Grand Valley, and while a bachelor's
degree was an option, when I enrolled I wanted more than anything
to just be done with school as soon as possible. I hadn't expected to
love it. Now, with the end of the program in sight, I had conflicting
feelings about finishing. I was excited in some ways to begin living
the dream I'd been sold that summer afternoon during our tour with

Toby. But I was also apprehensive about living in a world beyond the school walls, which had come to feel like a place of safety, personal empowerment, and purpose.

I clung to that sense of purpose to get me through the transition. Toward the end of the program, students were required to work in an externship. For me, that was a gig as a banquet cook at the Union League Club of Chicago, where I was hired on in an official capacity when I was through, and when the time came for the graduation ceremony, I opted to work instead of walk. My parents asked if I was sure—they said they didn't want me to miss out on a memory. But I couldn't see the point.

To this day, I struggle to do anything that doesn't feel as if it has an express purpose, a quantifiable outcome that generates or leads to something else. For that reason, it's been impossible to relax and incredibly difficult to celebrate myself even when it might be customary, even when I know on some level that it is deserved. I didn't yet realize then how important, how critical and healthy, that practice is—to pause and look at what you've done with some pride, to invite in those feelings of joy not only for yourself but also for the people around you who helped you get there. I still have a hard time putting that into practice, and though I don't regret my decision, these days I see the value in doing something simply for the sake of recognizing a moment and commemorating a milestone. I'm just usually better at celebrating others than celebrating myself.

While there was no cap and gown involved, I did receive a degree, which I knew I had earned and was hard proof that I had a specialized knowledge, a skill, and that no one could take it from me. But after two very positive, happy years in which I didn't have to wonder about my future and could just focus on what was in front of me, I felt a creeping fear. It was just like the one I had as a child when

I said my prayers: I was afraid that it was all so precarious, that I could lose this precious happiness, attributing all the joy, confidence, comfort, and self-assuredness that I'd found to external elements— coming from without rather than within.

We're sometimes told that anxiety is resistance to what is real. It is clinging to what you can't control. And for me, the sensation was growing with every day closer to graduation. I was a ball of nerves, and with looming uncertainty, I would go into the next stage of my life searching to take the edge off in far less productive ways.

5

Today, wellness culture emphasizes the benefits of being present and living in the moment. It's advice you see in Instagram captions and painted on signs and stitched into pillows you can purchase for your home, but it's also fundamental to philosophies like Buddhism. It seems to be grounded in a lot of good research and intention, regardless of where it's coming from, and yet for some reason, even as our society advocates this practice in think pieces and podcasts and professional coaching, there is an equal or maybe a more powerful and opposite emphasis placed on looking ahead. Sure, today is great, but: *What's next?*

Coming up with an answer to this question is an exercise in futility—or at least in attempts at educated and anxious guessing. It requires that people evaluate so many possibilities, search their souls and their hearts for their desires and dreams, then cross-reference those with what society and the asker of the question want to hear—and finally, adjust for variables as well as what is actually possible and realistic, so that whatever the answer is, the answerer has half a chance at making good on it later and avoids feeling like a failure as their future selves. In short, it can be a straight shot to an existential tailspin.

When culinary school ended, this question kept me up at night. Having a plan and a point of focus for those two years felt so good. It allowed me to relax a little. It calmed me. Now I was facing adulthood, a time when a human is supposed to start doing the things they've been saying they're going to do. And my answer to the question "What's next?" was what many culinary grads say once they have a degree in hand: I will eventually open a restaurant. Never mind that I wasn't even sure if that's what I *actually* wanted. But it sounded good. It seemed logical, and it had the makings of a plan.

After graduation, I opted to stay in Chicago in part because, as far as professional opportunities go, there was no real reason to return to Michigan and because I was well positioned in Chicago to begin pursuing my path. Thanks to my externship at the Union League Club of Chicago, I was able to roll right into the workforce. It was a private members-only club, kind of ritzy, and I liked it enough. It was ideal for the moment because it allowed me to have a sense of purpose, but I also enjoyed the job because of the people. They were patient and lovely, took me under their wings, and made me feel included and welcome.

There was Fernando, an older Mexican gentleman who worked the grill. He made it look so cool, and he graciously entertained my questions in good humor. Then there was Ginny, an older Vietnamese woman who worked the 6:00 a.m. to 2:00 p.m. shift. With her shiny, silky black hair pulled back with a white bow, she showed me how to make and decorate the egg salad with meticulous care. She was so good at her work, but I also remember the way she would punch out and go home, and it was clear that she had no further ambition in that place or any intention of climbing her way up to a chef position. Today, I wonder what her life was like outside the restaurant, what fulfilled her beyond those walls.

At the time, I was young and hungry and had found my greatest moments of affirmation through cooking. Work—and the status and recognition that came along with it—was the primary source of value in my mind. I couldn't fathom a world in which I could be satisfied working a station without reaching for the next rung. I'd later fully appreciate what the mentality of those people meant for me as a coworker in this environment. It wouldn't be long before I'd realize just how competitive commercial kitchens could be, but in those early days at the Union League Club, I was working alongside people who weren't jockeying for a top spot, in part because there wasn't a lot of room for upward mobility since the (all-male) upper-management kitchen team wasn't going anywhere. That's not to say they weren't genuine in their generosity, but they offered help and support without fear that I might be an obstacle to their future opportunities.

On the other hand, I was entirely obsessed with upward mobility. Getting ahead, moving up and on. Proving myself and making my way forward. Which is why I started to become restless in my position. Being a banquet cook was fine when I was getting school credits, but with my degree in hand, making egg salad—no matter how much I enjoyed the company of my coworkers—was something I started to feel was beneath me.

I wish I could have a conversation with that version of myself, the one who believed she should be able to skip ahead, past the due diligence and dues paying, the learning and practice that are required to progress in life regardless of the industry. But I also try to give my younger self a little bit of a break because I know the competitive rigors I was putting myself through. Even in the days before social media, I was stacking my own accomplishments against those of my peers, always wanting to be on a par, worthy of equal praise and respect. To be worthy as a person, period. I would speak to friends from Michigan who were at universities, or in art school and already selling art, or doing some other thing I deemed impressive, even though I couldn't have known a thing about the reality of their situations. I couldn't admit that I was (what I considered to be) a lowly line cook. Of course, now I see the respectability of that position, how critical it is not only in the formation of a career but also in the functioning of a professional kitchen. But fuck, I had graduated from culinary school. I was a *chef* and felt that I needed a job and a title that reflected this level of accomplishment in order to be taken seriously, in order to be part of those conversations. In order to feel whole. I started applying for jobs aggressively, all with titles that required extensive experience, but none of the swinging doors I wanted to walk through was opening for me. I was going to have to find another way in.

For better or worse, some of my postcollegiate "extracurriculars" inspired me to get creative with my job search. My weekend outings during school weren't always as wholesome as salads and mushroom burgers with the Chop House crew. In those days, I dabbled in some of the partying for which the restaurant industry is famous. I still didn't love the drinking and the kind of interminable nights in which my peers seemed to revel, but my lack of interest and my social anxiety were both always at odds with my ongoing desire to fit in.

While I was still in school, I kept it in check, mostly just going out on weekends here and there and never letting it interfere with school or work. I was able to prioritize, because again, for me, it was always about having a purpose and a plan. Chasing the high of accomplishment—and the hit of pride that came with a recognition of excellence—was far more satisfying than any vodka buzz. But when my cooking-school cravat was retired, the lines between days and nights, productivity and partying, became less defined. I let some of that intense focus slip, ever so slightly at first. The banquet job I was doing didn't feel high-stakes in the same way, and I was likely to go to work the next morning hungover, or on a lot less sleep than I would have required of myself on a school night, when I needed to wake up fresh and perform to the best of my ability.

Still, I had one major goal to guide me, and that was to get a better job. Predictably, the group I was hanging out with developed a routine, and there was one restaurant in particular where we'd hang out as our pregame spot. It was a new place, and the owner was always sitting at the bar drinking. Maybe he was working in some way, but all I knew and cared about was that he was available to listen to me, and between this familiarity and the boost of a solid buzz, I clocked an opportunity. I knew he needed an executive chef, so I decided to launch a one-woman campaign for the job. I told this guy he needed a skilled professional, and because of my fancy culinary degree and what I described as my robust experience in the industry, I told him he should look no further.

He resisted a little at first, but whether because he really believed in me or just wanted me to leave him alone about it, he eventually relented and gave me the gig. I had been in the workforce officially for just a few months, but there I was—an executive chef.

If one looks at career websites or culinary school advice on how to become an executive chef, they'd find a list of requirements and expected qualities ranging from culinary knowledge and creative cooking ability to time management, communication, and leadership skills. The job postings also tell those interested in pursuing a degree with the school that they should expect those jobs to become available to them after they have around ten to twenty years of experience. Of course, there are always instances in which this timeline is accelerated or slowed, but this average range is a decent point of reference.

There is simply no possible way to accumulate what you need to be an executive chef without that real-world experience. But most twenty-two-year-olds can't see the value in patiently living through those many years, extracting wisdom from each a little at a time, repeating and processing and reflecting until the takeaways become sturdy parts of their philosophy. We're conditioned to this impatience, in a way. The media highlights exceptionalism in youth—"30 Under 30" lineups of people who have accomplished so much in so little time—and we compare ourselves to those people. We want to skip ahead to the "good parts" and over the elements of the journey that don't make the news.

In school, I was so self-assured. Like I was on track and going somewhere. I was complimented for my skill. I stood out for the right reasons. "Culinary student" was an identity with some cachet. "Cook," on the other hand, did not sound impressive at all. But now, less than one year out of school, I was walking around town as an executive chef.

I couldn't wait to sit down and sketch out menus, think through the types of dishes that would work well in the restaurant's environment. With ideas swirling in my head, I counted the days until I could get started. When the time came, setting foot inside that restaurant and taking what I believed would be the next major step toward my future gave me a massive rush. Even though I'd already been to the space, I was seeing it in the light of day, through this new view from the top. The location was prime, and the dining room was colorful and bright and just the right size—not too big, not too small—and I thought we could create really nice guest experiences there. There was an L-shaped bar that ran the length of the space until it gave way to a semi-open kitchen that was nearly brand-new. And then there was *my* office—okay, technically it was a shared office, but I still considered it mine. Maybe some people consider the idea of such a place a type of cage, but in that moment, I couldn't imagine a greater symbol of success.

The team was solid, too. In particular, I remember a garde-manger—a younger woman—who absolutely *crushed* making the house salad. Despite my eagerness to bypass those positions at the time, I have so much admiration for line cooks, especially now that I look back. I wish at times that I could have humbled myself enough to ask them to teach me, but I know now that an element of fear drove my hubris as well. I was terrified because deep down, although I was eager and willing to work hard, I had an awareness that I didn't actually know *how* to do this job. I wanted the title, but to me, that title also precluded me from asking for help—that would have been an admission, an indication that I didn't know what I was doing, in front of people who needed to trust my leadership. Instead of viewing the ability to ask questions, to listen and grow from the experience of others, as a strength—a form of wisdom—I felt it would be an expression of weakness.

This was one element of my confusing love-hate relationship with the job early on, because on paper, it all looked and sounded good. But the fear part was paralyzing. I think I was able to convince myself that it was normal, that these competing feelings are to be expected when you step outside your comfort zone, a signal of growth. And besides, I was too excited to pay it much attention. I was too focused on making it work, not willing to mess with this prestigious position I'd managed to land, always trying to keep my eye on the long game.

Of course, what I didn't see—and what is evident now—were the red flags. The fact that this guy hired me, essentially an over-eager kid, to run his kitchen should have set off alarm bells. Not to mention that I was clearly inebriated when I was trying to make the case that I was capable of doing the job. But I didn't want to acknowledge those issues at first. I was too proud to have the job and the title, telling anyone who would listen where I worked and what I did for a living. I still couldn't see that my personal value came from within me: I found it only in validation, and when someone looked or sounded impressed with the news, I lit up inside. It was the post-graduation version of how I felt in Knife Skills 101.

But as capable as I proved myself in those classes at Le Cordon Bleu, I was a mess running this fully professional kitchen. I wanted to do well and for the restaurant to succeed, but I had none of the experience to execute. My first special was a perfect example. In my mind, I created a beautiful halibut dish with cabbage slaw and soy sauce broth, which, in theory, was appealing, and I couldn't wait to run it. There was just one small problem: I had no idea how to make a soy sauce broth. I kept tinkering with it, and the result was thin, brown, and salty. I had friends in the dining room that night and walked out to introduce myself as the chef. That part felt great, but though they were cordial enough to say they loved it, I knew that what was on their plates was not good *enough*.

I was determined, though, so I kept taking swings. Later I attempted a Grand Marnier panna cotta special. Panna cotta is an Italian custard-style dessert—lightly sweetened cream that's thick-ened with gelatin and then molded. The orange flavor of the liqueur would be a beautiful complement to the natural sweetness of the cream, but I wasn't interested in following a recipe, opting instead to wing it. In my haste, though, I didn't fully burn off the alcohol, which meant not only that the flavor was intensely boozy but also that it inhibited the gelatin from doing its job. Needless to say, this wasn't what one would call a successful attempt, although I did learn important lessons—about both preparedness and panna cotta.

Beyond the actual cooking, I didn't have the wisdom yet to be in a leadership position, and I was understandably naive about the business. Although I was technically in the top job, I was unofficially under the watch of a seasoned cook. He was so good, and so fast, and he guided me when he could tell I was out of my depth but unwilling to ask for help. I was grateful to him for that support, but eventually I guess he saw an opportunity, too, because pretty soon he was acting as a go-between for me and cocaine dealers.

Today, one might call the situation toxic or, at the very least, unhealthy. At the time, though, I wasn't evaluating it. I was just *in* it. Looking back, I can see that the writing was on the wall. I had noticed purveyor invoices piling up and realized that our suppliers weren't being paid. Also, there seemed to be no accounting service in place. But it wasn't until my checks began to bounce—when I received them at all—that I realized the place had zero business infrastructure and that the owner was a bigger mess than my panna cotta special. Fortunately, I had enough foresight and self-respect to get myself out of that situation before the place took a nosedive and closed.

I was crushed for many reasons, including that this was the first instance when my trust in an employer was really rattled. I became aware that not every job would be reliable. But although the restaurant ultimately didn't survive, I didn't feel responsible for it. There were many other factors that contributed to its demise, which helped mitigate the blow to my self-esteem.

But after that, my laser focus on getting another executive chef job was even more intense and high-stakes. Now I had an inflated title on my résumé, and I could *not* go backward. My confidence was shaken. It's not as if I believed I had all the answers, but I did believe I could pretend—just act *as if*—and figure it out as I went along.

To my great disappointment, none of the hiring managers at the establishments where I was applying—flashy spots at the Four Seasons and the InterContinental, among others—seemed to share my optimism. I had a very impressive line on my CV and not a single promising job prospect.

I struggle to talk about the details of the next part of my life for two reasons. First, although I don't think it's unusual for adults to look back at their early twenties with a little (or a lot) of cringe, I knew I wanted badly to feel seen and whole and worthy—to feel a sense of pride—and the ways I tried to achieve that validation still make me anything *but* proud.

Second, this part is difficult to discuss clearly because it was actually very fuzzy. I was almost always extremely fucked up. I have said that partying and drinking never appealed to me during high school and my days at Grand Valley—and during most of my time at Le Cordon Bleu. Aside from the anxiety and the fact that they could interfere with my school or work, I didn't want to participate because it truly didn't feel good. I'm not sure if it's because of the so-called Asian gene (also known as the Asian glow or Asian flush, which is a genetic condition that results in an unpleasant and dangerous reaction to alcohol) or simply because of me and my own body, but I felt like booze didn't work for me the way it seemed to for others. I figured I'd always feel that way and engaged occasionally without much hope that I'd ever have the euphoric sense people described when drinking. But then, in those Chicago days, another element was introduced into the mix that changed everything.

I knew about cocaine. In the restaurant industry, it was kind of an open secret and later would become something of an assumption about restaurant workers, thanks to the behind-the-scenes chef stories that were just becoming popular at the time. You can understand why such a high-intensity, pressurized environment would be ideal for the drug. It helps keep you alert and "on," and when work is over, it keeps you awake enough to party long after the rest of the world has hung up their wineglasses and called it a night.

For me, though, it was the key to the alcohol conundrum. When I combined coke with booze, I suddenly *got* it. I could drink and keep up with my friends, enjoy the buzz, and finally grasp what everyone liked about drinking. It also gave me a major boost of confidence. When I was high, I felt like I could do anything. It's what gave me the guts to go after that first executive chef job. I absolutely *loved* how it made me feel.

I didn't seek it out initially, but I started to become aware of how much cocaine surrounded me. I realized that one of my colleagues at the Union League had been doing it, and that intrigued me. Here was someone I knew and trusted, a superior who was obviously a functioning human who showed up to work every day. This was very different from what all those D.A.R.E. commercials had depicted when I was growing up.

Then eventually, I started getting offers from friends. These were the people I was spending my time with, the ones I wanted to be like and whom I wanted to like me. I was curious and, as always, desperate to *not* be different. So one night when we were at a nightclub, a friend handed me a little baggie and pointed me in the direction of the bathroom, where I could help myself to a bump. She assumed I knew what I was doing, and I didn't correct her. I'd seen enough movies to have a gist of the mechanics. In the stall, I shakily used my fingernail—which I always kept trimmed for kitchen work and was hardly long enough for this purpose—to bring the bitter powder to my nose. I tried to be careful despite my nerves, knowing the price tag of this stuff, and thinking my friend was generous for sharing. But I faltered and, with a breath, blew basically the whole bump all over the bathroom floor.

Still, I played it off when I went back to the bar, answering in the affirmative when she asked if I'd done it and carrying on with no one the wiser. But then the next weekend, when we got together at a friend's apartment for a pre-party session and lines were laid on the table in front of a group of people, there was no hiding. I committed this time, and after my first line, I let the rush rise through me. I could not believe how good I felt, the way everything sharpened, how all that anxiety I was so used to carrying around simply evaporated. How I could go hard on the Ketel One with my friends and actually keep up. I was struggling to get that high of validation in my "real life," but this one? This felt pretty damn good.

After that, armed with this new false confidence, I started putting on a show. I realized that even though I didn't have an impressive job title, I could pretend to be successful and manage to get a version of that acceptance. I went around telling everyone who asked that I was a chef, and because in my mind, money signified success, I started throwing it around like I was printing it. Forget that what I did have wasn't even mine most of the time—it was my parents'. I took care of bar tabs for friends, spent grocery money on drinking and drugs. I wanted to seem fun and successful, like I didn't just show up to the party but also *made* the party happen.

One night, coked up and drunk out of my mind, I tried to foot the bill for a crowd, and my card was declined. Rather than appear embarrassed, I doubled down and called my dad. We shared the same bank, and I knew he could make a transfer to me, and apparently, in the state that I was in, it seemed totally reasonable at 2:00 a.m. to give him a quick ring and ask him to do so. He went along with it, probably to keep me out of trouble and understanding that I was probably in no state of mind to see reason. To this day, it kills me to even tell this story. I absolutely hate to believe I was ever that person, capable of behaving that way—the same person who grew up so deeply attached to my parents, who today would do absolutely anything to make their lives easier, happier, to alleviate their worries rather than cause them.

But I also have a much clearer vantage point now. I try to extend my younger self some grace, recognizing that I was in an immense amount of pain. One of the things that drugs and alcohol did for me, beyond taming my anxiety, was help me avoid the mounting frustration, shame, and confusion about being gay and closeted. I had witnessed just a little of the other side with Vinny—a glimpse at what queer life could be. But I still couldn't square that vision with the future I had decided I wanted for myself—the one I tried to conjure up in my mind whenever I was asked the "What comes next?" question. Dating women might have been my heart's desire, but it did not pass the test when cross-referenced with societal expectations. And the idea that I could lose the people I loved most in the world—the very ones who were sitting at home in Michigan, wondering what was going on with me—was just too terrifying. I couldn't even consider it.

Instead, I continued to do anything I could to avoid being the authentic version of myself. In fact, in an effort to distract the people

around me and "prove" my straightness—that I was just like them—
I started making out with just about any guy, anywhere. Anyone
who has ever been through this performance can likely attest that
the word *hollow* doesn't even come close to describing the feeling
of those moments. For years, I'd listened to friends describe kissing
some guy—the excitement, the flutter, the adrenaline, the joy. For
me, it was practice of a new and unsettling skill—dissociating from
myself in order to tolerate the feeling—which would only become
more necessary as my attempts at relationships with men became
substantial in the years that followed.

In those cases, I leaned heavily on substances to mitigate the pain
and trauma. I did it for a reason—to provide just enough evidence
to keep the people around me from questioning. If I could be the life
of the party, pick up tabs, and parade around as a chef, seemingly
flush with cash and fueled by genuine confidence, I wouldn't have to
contend with the reality of being gay.

For all my dedication to careful planning, it seemed like the only path
I was on at that time was the one leading toward self-destruction. I
was functioning to a degree, because I learned how to measure out
a few bumps during the day, which helped me bypass some of the
anxiety around things like grocery shopping and running errands.
But you can only keep up that pace and punish your body and mind
for so long before both begin to revolt.

I was fucked up so much of the time, self-medicating and dull-
ing the ache in my heart, but the way I felt physically was starting to really scare me and threaten my emotional well-being. I
would wake up with my pulse pounding, alone in my apartment at

dawn—sometimes not even sure how I got there—and feel certain I was going to die. For a while in the years that came after, I couldn't even look at a sunrise; it reminded me too much of waking up on the floor of my apartment in a panic—assuming I'd gone to sleep at all—with the people I'd been trying so hard to impress nowhere to be found.

At one point, I even wound up in the hospital with alcohol poisoning, which was terrifying. I could not imagine my parents getting that phone call—or one that could have been worse. I made sure they never found out.

And fortunately, though they had plenty of reasons to leave me out in the cold, my parents were there for me. They'd been patient for a while there, giving me space to sort things out on my own. But at some point, understandably, they began to press. All they asked was that I get a job—just do that most basic adult thing.

But I couldn't wrap my mind around what I perceived to be a step down. I know that may sound petulant and entitled, and I have wondered at times why my parents didn't just cut me off. Now I see that although they couldn't figure out why, and I wasn't forthcoming or helpful in explaining it, they must've sensed my pain. My desperation for validation wasn't just about a fancy title. It was a yearning to be seen. A need to feel like a whole person, one who deserved to be loved.

Of course, I had that love, even if I couldn't clearly see it. My parents never faltered despite my behavior, despite the fact that I was scaring them, that I was hardly living by the values they'd modeled for me. They loved me profoundly and unconditionally, and even when I felt alone and invisible, they had been there waiting in the wings to catch me all along.

I wasn't ready yet to test the boundaries of their unconditional love by telling them that I was gay, but later, I would recall moments like this to remind myself that no matter what questions came from the outside world about my life, the only answers that counted came from the people who'd known and loved me from day one.

For all the pressure I put on myself looking forward and even in the moment, I have tried to learn to be forgiving of myself as I look back. There were so many ways that period of my life could have ended. I could have been successful at my self-destruction; I could have entirely pushed away the people who loved me most. I could have dug my heels in and refused to leave the city. But although I resisted help in many ways, I think there was a small part of me somewhere who—like that kid at sleepaway camp—just wanted to go home, be with my parents, and not have to think so hard. To try so hard. To feel so much pain and pressure. And so with no job and the end of my lease looming, I faced the reality that my Chicago days were officially done.

6

The concept of home is a difficult one to define. For some people, it's a physical structure or building—one in which they've grown up or one that they've created for their own families. For others, it's a feeling. Something they can distill into a sentence and maybe even stitch into a pillow. It's where the heart is. It's a retreat, a refuge. It's a place of comfort and relaxation.

With Chicago behind me, I was technically back "home" in Michigan, even though my parents had moved since I'd graduated from high school, and their new house was still kind of foreign to me. Still, if people are the defining characteristic of home, then my parents certainly made that true. And yet there also comes a point in life when you're not really at home with your family of origin. The world has drilled it into you that you're supposed to be elsewhere, advancing or climbing or *doing* something with your life. My move to Michigan was no longer a stopover between semesters, and although my parents were gentle in encouraging me toward my next step and no one was throwing me out of the house, there was an underlying feeling of impermanence. Of pressure.

It wasn't just about what the world expected of me as a recent graduate in my early twenties. Much of the pressure came from myself. I already had so much shame around being gay, and now I had these added layers—not being able to hack it in Chicago; knowing that I had behaved terribly. The only way to address that shame was to course-correct. Get out of my parents' house and set out on my own. I also had gotten a taste of independence, and I craved that feeling. I wanted to relive the validation of being recognized for my work and recapture that sense of calm I'd experienced in cooking school, where the pressure was about plating what was in front of me and not about planning the next forty years of my life.

Whatever the impetus, I knew I needed to move somewhere that might provide possibilities for a future in which I could be a whole person. I had some of the same ideas about getting away as in my precollege days, thinking that distance would be the only real path toward the possibility of an authentic life. I still wasn't ready to be out as gay, but I had at least seen city life and felt certain that was the only kind of environment in which I'd have a shot. So during those months in Michigan, while my parents patiently waited and provided support and a *lot* of spaghetti, I would sit at my dad's old desktop computer in their new sunroom, trusting that the ancient technology that my parents moved with them as a touchstone from a former life would help me map out my future.

Without the formula of school or a particular goal in mind, though, there were almost too many options. I could have thrown darts at a map and moved to the first major city I hit, and that lack of parameters was overwhelming. Fortunately, I had at least some direction based on what I definitely *didn't* want. Maybe it was instinctual in a way, but on some molecular level, as a Midwestern kid who grew up with four seasons, I've never been called to the West Coast, and California didn't feature in my dreams of the future. Instead, I focused my search to the east but quickly ruled New York City out. Too big. Too scary in some ways, and I was self-aware enough about my social anxiety to know that that was not the move for me.

As I navigated the internet—a very different information super-highway from what it is today—I recalled a school trip from my childhood. We had gone to Boston in eighth grade on a big East Coast educational adventure. There was also the memory of going with my parents to Provincetown, with its rainbow flags and joyful, queer love on full display. Maybe it was nostalgia for that time, and maybe subconsciously I thought it'd be a welcoming place for people like me, or maybe it just seemed far enough away, but as I explored my options in that primitive digital landscape, I could suddenly see Massachusetts in my future.

It was February when my brother, Jonathan, and I boarded a plane due east, carrying nothing but our backpacks and a few snacks.

I had scoured Craigslist and Apartments.com for a couple of months trying to find the perfect apartment where I could start fresh as a full adult, and I'd found a few options, but when I presented them to my parents, they were insistent that I could not make that big a decision based on grainy low-res internet photos alone. I was going to have to make a trip to Boston if I really wanted to live there.

Given that, in a way, I'd been forced to admit defeat in Chicago, I think my parents knew it was important for me to have a sense of independence and agency when it came to my next move. Just as they had my whole life, they maintained a light touch with respect to their intervention in my life. They gave me space to figure things out on my own—or at least they let me believe I was doing that—but they also found ways to stay involved and watchful from a safe distance. I'm sure they knew I wouldn't react super well to their weighing in on what I did next, wounded as my ego was, and while I've never known for sure if there was some behind-the-scenes familial collusion, I'm sure it was part of the reason Jonathan was on that plane with me instead of my parents.

My relationship with Jonathan has always been like this. He's so much older that we didn't spend as much time together as many siblings do and didn't live under the same roof for much of our lives. But he's a caretaker. Though we may have fewer memories than some brothers and sisters, they are significant. He always showed up for the milestones: Years after the early days of bringing me to Pizza Hut to help him fold boxes, he took a friend and me to an eighteen-plus club when I was of age and then, later, out on the town for my twenty-first birthday with his then wife. All these were opportunities to celebrate as well as for him to keep a big-brotherly eye on me. And when that shitty job went south in Chicago, Jonathan found out and called an attorney friend to intervene and try to retrieve the money I was owed. (This was unsuccessful for a number of reasons, but still, the effort was earnest.) Although I didn't see him as someone I'd go to with my coming out—there just wasn't anyone on earth I was prepared to talk to about that—I never wondered whether I could count on Jonathan for major life stuff. He was there when it mattered most. He was a solid role model but not so much of a parental figure that we didn't have fun when we were together.

The Boston trip was the first time we were going to be doing something so big, just the two of us, as adults. In retrospect, Jonathan really deserves a medal for getting on board that plane and flying with his kid sister to New England in the dead of winter. When we

arrived, it was fucking *freezing*. I remember because I hadn't bothered to pack appropriately, and even coming from Michigan and
surviving winters in Chicago, I wasn't prepared for this level of
cold. I hated bulky coats, so I went around in a lightweight shell of
a jacket that had no business being in Massachusetts after October,
and I shivered for three straight days. We were on a budget, but my
brother rented a car so we could make the rounds more easily and
with mercifully abundant heat.

I had been excited for the trip, or at least cautiously optimistic,
but pretty quickly I started to feel disheartened. In Chicago, I'd been
living the high life in all the ways. My previous apartment was in a
literal high-rise, a doorman building with granite countertops and
a spectacular view. The places we were seeing in Boston were nothing like that. They were low, deteriorating row houses and ancient
brownstones that felt like a massive step down rather than a leap forward. We started with a few spots that seemed promising online and
that *maybe* I could see myself in, but my brother quickly squashed
even those.

"Kristen," he'd say in one place after the next. "This is way out
of budget. You can't afford this."

If it had been my parents' idea to send Jonathan with me, it was
a wise one, because I wouldn't have taken the word *no* very well coming from them, even if the logic was inarguable. With Jonathan, I
had to accept it and—never wanting my big brother to find me petulant or bratty—was less likely to be angsty and combative about
it. I slowly adjusted my expectations as the weekend progressed and
in the process went from hopeful and excited to totally dejected and
lost—again.

The trip was a valuable sibling bonding opportunity. My brother
has always been steady and stable, reliable in the person he is. In

many ways, he is the same person to me now that we're in our forties as he was when I was a kid, and that trip was no different. For example, he is obsessed with Mountain Dew, which he still drinks like water to this day, a habit he is also continually trying to break. In Boston, we made frequent rest stops so he could collect cans of this sugary fuel, crucial for getting him through those apartment visits.

Jonathan has also always been super pragmatic, so we ate a lot of pizza—I think it was his way of conditioning me to what was afford-able and practical—rather than going out for expensive dinners. And while I was happy to have the time together, the trip was a total bust on the apartment front. After expanding our search to areas that were no longer walkable or so far on the outskirts of the city that I might as well have been back in Michigan, we returned to my par-ents' home without having secured a place.

Still, it was worth it in at least one respect: It solidified my desire to be in Boston, despite its differences from Chicago and my disen-chantment with the available housing. It was still far enough from home to feel like a fresh start, and I didn't have another or a bet-ter option. Knowing for certain that this was the destination, I just needed to figure out how to make my way there and where I would lay my head at night when I did.

At major transition points in life, there are so many factors and forces that can play into how things ultimately end up. Maybe it's fate or the stars aligning, or maybe it's a higher power or some supreme being. In the case of my Boston move, it was Jeanne, my mom's work friend.

I sometimes think about the ways my mother was connected to her network—the fellow teachers who checked in with her about me when I was a kid, for example. I feel like it's a testament to her and the kindnesses she must've extended, the people she must've touched, and the way she interacted with her community that others wanted to offer her their help. I'm not sure about the circumstances under which my mom found out—whether she went asking around or a solution simply presented itself in conversation—but it came to her attention that a friend of Jeanne's son lived in Charlestown, a Boston neighborhood. And right around the time I was scouring the internet and the frigid city streets for a place, he was preparing to spend three months in New Zealand, leaving his room vacant and up for grabs.

On the surface, it seemed like kismet. Here was a low-risk, low-commitment way of getting my foot in the door in Boston, giving me a few months to figure things out with boots on the ground and a place to sleep at night.

But there was a caveat: Rather than the amenities of a doorman and a killer view, this apartment came with roommates. I'd never lived with anyone aside from Heather at Grand Valley, and she was a friend—someone I knew well. I was not at all happy about the idea of sharing space, knowing as I did how I felt in social situations. In this one, there'd be no escape, no going home at the end of the night, no place to hide or retreat.

Still, there are times in life when your resolve is really tested, and what you're willing to sacrifice or tolerate or overcome in service of a larger goal comes into question. I'd let my social anxiety dictate a lot of my decisions up to that point, but I could not stay in Michigan. Looking back, I see how high the stakes felt. Getting away wasn't just a matter of self-actualization or some kind of fun adventure. It was a matter of survival. This was my only option as far as I could tell.

And so that spring, with two bags packed and no real plan other than a gut feeling and a primal motivation to persevere, I headed for

Boston. The fact that this was a short-term setup—three months, tops—had built-in pros and cons. The ticking clock meant that not only would I have to find a job and get my life in motion immediately but also that I would need to be on the lookout for another living situation. On the plus side, that meant I only had to make it through those ninety days, which was what I kept telling myself, because the second I moved in, I began counting the minutes—every one of which might as well have been an eternity.

I'd managed to silence my anxiety alarm bells long enough to get myself from Michigan to Boston, but once I arrived at the house, with my suitcases and zero plans for work, they started shrieking uncontrollably. It's not that I felt like I was in any kind of danger. There were three roommates—two guys and a girl—all nonthreatening, young East Coast professionals with nine-to-fives. I honestly couldn't tell you much more about them to this day, not because my memories have faded but because I never made a single memory with any of them. They were totally fine, but they were strangers in close proximity to me, and that was enough to send me spinning.

The living room and kitchen areas were shared, and I did *not* want to interact at all, ever. To feed myself, I managed to carve out a quick path to the Papa Gino's around the corner so I could pick up enough slices of pizza and breadsticks, calzones, and cans of Dr Pepper to sustain me—hardly a wholesome diet. I consumed these meals alone in my bedroom, which was uncomfortable because everything in it belonged to this dude. I never cooked a single thing and even tried to limit going to the bathroom. I remember having my period and was so horrified by the idea of interacting with the world that I waited two full days before going down to CVS for tampons, instead using toilet paper as a makeshift pad so I wouldn't have to risk running into anyone.

In some ways, what ended up saving me was a competing anxiety. I couldn't dwell on those feelings because—survival. No matter how bad it became in my head, there was nothing that scared me more than admitting defeat yet again. Going back to Michigan was out of the question.

I knew I had at least two bankable skills, and in my early Boston days, despite the fact that modeling was nowhere near my top choice for a career move, I had developed enough of a sense of comfort doing it—a self-assuredness rooted in experience—to believe I could get myself some kind of work in the field. And far more than any daydreams about becoming a cover girl, which other aspiring models might've been chasing, it was determination that probably gave me an edge when I marched myself down to Newbury Street, where Dynasty Models had an office.

I walked into the office hopeful that I could walk out with a contract. The office was different from Elite's, which had been sleek and modern. This was in an old brownstone, in an area where row houses had been converted into commercial spaces and several businesses were located on each level. It was run by a husband-and-wife team, Gin and Joe, and it was small—much quieter than Elite, without the movie-ready receptionists answering phones that were ringing off the hook. As I had with the apartments, I was learning that things in Boston were less shiny and chic, even in the modeling world, than they were in Chicago. Still, I tried to look the part: I put on some super low-rise jeans, which were in style at the time, and a semifitted white T-shirt. Then I made my way in and introduced myself to Joe. And maybe I manifested it, or maybe it was the

I-fucking-got-this energy I brought into the room, but lo and behold, shortly after becoming a Boston resident, I was up on a runway.

Surprisingly, I did more frequent and more lucrative modeling in my Boston days than at any other time in my life. I worked a weekly event at the Liberty hotel called Fashionably LATE Thursdays, a show that featured local designers but was mostly a see-and-be-seen kind of event with a nighttime-hotspot vibe, and I participated in Boston Fashion Week, a much more modest affair than the ones in New York and Paris but still significant to those on the Boston fashion scene. In fact, I later went on to win Model Boston, a contest in which one male and one female winner receive photo shoots and styling with five different photographers and their teams, followed by participation in a showcase before industry professionals.

It was a transitional time for me in so many ways, and that applied to my sense of style, too. I was still very much sorting out a look, trying new things the way I had back in middle school with my colored contacts, searching for something that made me feel *me*. I had cut my hair short back in Michigan after I left Chicago and was still adjusting to such a drastic change. Initially, I absolutely hated it. I had asked the stylist—a woman around my mom's age—to give me a short, spiky cut like the one I'd seen on Sharon Stone, which absolutely did *not* translate to my face, my hair type, or my age. I was miserable over it, crying and wishing I could undo it so many times. But in Boston, I think the short hair helped me stand out in a positive way, and I eventually found a funky salon in the South End filled with people who had tattoos and punk-rock hair where the stylists managed to reshape it into something I could feel good about.

It was obviously massively helpful to have the financial benefits of reentering this world. It also felt good that after nearly ten years of on-and-off stints in modeling, I had come to feel somewhat at ease in this world and in the role and to be acknowledged for my work as a professional. It had been a long time since I got that kind of reassurance in a kitchen, because I hadn't worked in one for a while. But that pride in modeling wasn't about vanity or feeling like I'd finally lived up to a certain beauty standard. When you're a gay person, the world rejects a massive part of you, and any moment in which you are seen and valued—regardless of the reason. Those moments were a little bit of a charge in a battery that always felt perilously low.

Still, no matter how many poses I struck, catwalks I strutted, or jobs I booked, nothing could compare to the way I felt when I was recognized for my cooking. Fortunately, the search for a place that would pay me to cook, to create and learn and execute in the kitchen, had also yielded a result.

After a few weeks of searching for cooking gigs from my rented room, I applied for a job at Top of the Hub, the legendary restaurant on the highest floor of the Prudential Center, which had been in operation since the 1960s. The opening was for a sous chef, not an executive chef, but I knew I had to check my ego at the door upon arriving on the East Coast. My hierarchy of needs had changed, and the one at the top of the pyramid was to stay in Boston at all costs. This was a major shift from the way I'd approached my employment search back in Chicago, but having to go back to Michigan for that period in between was humbling and clarifying. I knew I had to do whatever was necessary to avoid repeating that scenario.

To be honest, I really didn't have any business selling myself as a sous chef, either, but that didn't stop me from handing over a résumé that had nothing more on it than a bogus executive chef position in Chicago and a banquet-cook gig at the Union League Club. I didn't know enough to be worried. When I walked into the interview with the executive chef and one of his sous chefs, I wasn't relying on anything you could put on paper anyway. I was confident in my actual, demonstrable skills and what was—as I look back on it now—a comical sense of self-assuredness. This was always the dichotomy for me, part of why I believe I continued to pursue a career in food. As cripplingly self-conscious as I was almost everywhere else, a restaurant kitchen was *the* place where I felt good at something.

Of course, confidence can only get you so far, and despite my feeling ready for the role, the interviewing chefs felt differently. Still, I guess they saw something in me, because two days later I got a call with an offer. It wasn't for the sous chef position but rather for a spot on the line. Initially I was frustrated, still believing I could pull off the sous position. There was a time not long before when I would have scoffed at the idea of taking the job they were offering, but now, with the clock ticking on sink-or-swim in Boston, an offer to be a line cook was a lifeline.

If my title wasn't exactly impressive, at least to me, the view from the top of the Prudential Center made up for it with its grandeur.

Once I accepted the fact that I wasn't going to be in charge of the kitchen, I was able to feel some excitement, in a way. Every big city has a restaurant like Top of the Hub. The kind you find in a beautiful downtown building where they turn up the charm and serve all the hits—the seafood towers, the beet-and-goat-cheese salads, the cold martinis with a twist. It attracted a ton of tourists based on the view alone, fifty-two floors above the street, and it was always packed. On a Saturday night, tearing through five or six hundred covers wasn't uncommon. That kind of volume might've scared some cooks away, especially ones who didn't have the experience to fall back on. But I didn't care. I remembered the admiration I had for the line cooks at my jobs in Chicago, and when I shifted my perspective, I embraced the fact that this was going to be a period of conditioning for me. New place, new position, new skills.

Beyond the learning opportunity, the Top of the Hub job provided me with a proven way to soothe my emotional stress. I'd already learned at school that cooking was meditative for me. But more than anything, I finally had purpose again. Although I took on those modeling gigs occasionally, the money was not substantial, and it was never something I really considered a job, nor did it give me a centering effect or a sense of meaning the way cooking did. It had been so long since I'd worked in a kitchen, and for me, the sense of contributing to something, of forward motion—more than any sort of passion or fire within—was always the antidote to my anxiety.

I hit the ground running and learned that, after many decades in business, the kitchen was an organized and well-oiled machine. Two people handled the grill station; one cook took on the lounge menu; three or four stood in garde-manger, handling cold appetizers and desserts. They started me on the fish station, where I worked with the chef de partie, a kind of line-cook station manager, handling proteins plus the plating and garnish. I got into a groove fast and realized that not only did I love the crush of line-cook work— the rush and ritual, the (partly) controlled chaos of it all—but I was also *good* at it.

What I didn't love, though, and what surprised me in a way, was that I was surrounded by coworkers (mostly dudes—no surprise there) who had no problem fucking off. The same went for the servers who were making substantially more than my minimum-wage cook pay. Of course, I now understand how challenging and demanding the role of a server can be, but at the time all I could see was that they were coming back from the floor into the kitchen to eat piles of french fries while I was sweating and busting my ass for eight bucks an hour.

I have always taken work seriously—whether twisting pretzels or plating tuna—and at times in my life this has probably been both a strength and weakness. But my motivations for performing at a high level always had to do with something much bigger than making sure I had a paycheck to fund a night on the town.

And maybe because I was raised by hardworking parents who valued their jobs, I not only developed a defining personal work ethic but also a respect for that same quality in others. I realized that in comparison to a lot of the senior crew, I was more dedicated and diligent—qualities that are hard to find and maybe impossible to teach—which was frustrating given my role and pay grade as a line cook.

I have also found it oddly counterintuitive at times that this quality does not always win you friends at work. On some level, you'd think it is a good thing to have someone willing to go to battle when the situation calls for it and even pick up the slack if necessary. But I've seen time and again over the years that coworkers, and sometimes even superiors, can feel upstaged and become salty about it. On the flip side, it has frustrated me that so few lived up to my expectations, putting forth what I considered to be a baseline effort. It has been not only disappointing but also isolating at times, especially since that same expectation has narrowed the pool of people with whom I could see myself being friends.

But after a few weeks on the line at Top of the Hub, a new hire emerged from that very small pool of diligent people. Someone who not only lived up to my expectations but also exceeded them and pushed me forward, both professionally and personally. Someone who would go on to become a permanent fixture in my life.

Being a line cook is a dangerous job. Anyone who has ever done it will tell you that. Cuts, bruises, and burns aren't just par for the course; they're also sometimes considered a badge of honor. That said, too many of those injuries can be considered evidence of sloppy work—something for which I had zero patience in those days. I still don't, to be honest, but I'm at least more understanding now.

One day when I came in for my usual shift, I was informed that I was going to be on training duty at my station. Maybe I could have considered it a vote of confidence—my supervisors must have seen me as capable—or maybe it was just that no one else was interested in the extra work and disruption. But it's probably more likely that they stuck her with me because we were both girls. Whatever the rationale, I was less than enthusiastic to have another job to do, especially since we already had such a huge set of responsibilities preparing for service. But I had no choice, so my goal was to get the new girl up to speed as soon as humanly possible and get back to business.

When Stephanie Cmar arrived and introduced herself, I was polite but direct. I wasn't about to get into her life story because I wasn't there to make friends, and honestly, in restaurants, you never know how long someone is going to last, so the investment of time feels frivolous. Instead, I got right down to giving her the lay of the land, explaining our expectations both for the job and for our shift and the immediate needs of the restaurant every night. She listened and observed, and I didn't have any significant feelings about her one way or the other for the first week or so. But shortly after she started, something happened that changed my opinion of Stephanie entirely.

Most of us knew that the restaurant's walk-in freezer could be a death trap if you weren't careful, especially because the door was *heavy*. But because Top of the Hub was such a busy restaurant, we relied on the freezer for a lot of purposes, including storing various preportioned elements of certain dishes. One day, Stephanie stepped away to take preportioned servings of foie gras to the freezer to set. When she disappeared from our station, I thought nothing of it, turning back to my business while I waited for her to return. To this day, I still couldn't tell you exactly what went down in that freezer, but I can tell you that I wound up setting up the station myself and running service without her that night, because Stephanie spent the next few hours in the emergency room after slamming her finger in the door.

My initial reaction when I found out was a head-shaking *Fucking amateur* muttered under my breath, but of course I felt for her. I'd had my share of mishaps. We all had. Beyond that, though, I didn't give it much thought. Restaurant work can be brutal, and I'd seen plenty of another-one-bites-the-dust situations. I assumed it was the last time I'd ever see this girl. Which is why, when Stephanie reappeared in the prep kitchen next to me a few hours later, looking no worse for wear beyond the splint around her finger, ready to get back to business and help clean, I wasn't just surprised, I was also fucking impressed. This girl was the real deal.

After that first day, Stephanie got her sea legs at Top of the Hub fast, and she and I jammed the fuck out. Every day, we ran that kitchen together like a culinary supergroup. Our alliance was founded on a shared work ethic and a rapidly developed under-standing of each other, which didn't need a whole lot of explanation. Today, there are a lot of conversations about women in commercial kitchens—what that experience is like, how to improve it, and how to make those spaces safe and welcoming for people of all kinds. In those days, though, there was no such discussion. If you got into the business, you knew that was what you were stepping into, and for me and Stephanie, this shared experience was an unspoken bond that brought us closer together. We worked circles around the guys, partly because that's who we innately were but also because, as any woman in just about any field can tell you, you have to work twice as hard and fuck up less than never in order to be seen as worthy of a spot or as more than just an object for the male gaze—or to be seen at all.

And while we were at it, we also drew great pleasure in provok-ing the guys into competitions. Though we didn't outwardly chal-lenge them, we were always internally facing off with the grill boys to see if we could get food up faster. There was an expo (restaurant shorthand for "expeditor," a go-between for the kitchen and the ser-vice team) whom we especially did not respect. When it was busy and he was on, he was solid and reliable, but there were many times when it seemed like he spent more time talking to his event-manager girlfriend than doing anything to facilitate the transfer of dishes from the pass to the dining room—all while the two of us were bust-ing our asses to deliver. Mostly I was annoyed because I felt like expo was a job I could and should have had—and would have done bet-ter at—and because Stephanie and I both felt like we were working twice as hard for less pay.

So we fucked with him a little, too. It was a standard step in the service process to make sure plates were warm when they hit the pass, and if our warmers weren't getting the job done fast enough, we'd quickly stash the plates up in the salamander—a commercial-style broiler that sits above a range—to speed things up. When he was working, we threw on a little extra heat once in a while. Not enough to cause any real damage—just enough to startle him when he grabbed the dish—but it was our small retribution, since we couldn't actually say anything.

But even as we were fucking around and finding small ways to either entertain ourselves or get a little payback for being overlooked or ignored altogether, we always got the job done. We executed consistently, at an insanely high volume, night after night. And while it wasn't necessarily the most creative culinary experience I've ever had, I can honestly say that I learned valuable skills that only come from the turn-and-burn pace of a super-busy restaurant, and I hadn't felt the rush of that environment since my days at Twist & Shout.

At Top of the Hub, I was getting a crash course not only in cooking for guests but also in being part of a team. There might have been people in that kitchen I wasn't particularly fond of, but there were enough people to whom I felt accountable to make me care. I also came to understand that without any one of us on the line, the job just wouldn't get done, something that stood in stark relief when there was a weak link. Knowing I was a critical cog in this big machine gave me a deep sense of personal value and opened my eyes to every single one of those humans in the kitchen—maybe especially to the ones to whom others didn't give the time of day.

So many people don't realize the critical role in a restaurant played by stewards, an industry term for what is commonly called a dishwasher. If these people were to strike, believe me, we'd all be fucked—there'd be no restaurants at all. At Top of the Hub, I was especially fond of one of our stewards, Charles. He was a kind gentleman, and I'm not sure what part of town he was coming from, but I always remember that he rode his bike, rain or shine—or he took the bus if the bike couldn't get the job done. It was often a frigid or sweltering commute, depending on the season, after which he punched in and worked grueling hours at a job that was basically thankless. Even if you didn't have a shred of decency or empathy, I would have thought it was clear that his presence was imperative to keeping our kitchen running smoothly. And yet Stephanie and I were baffled by the way so many of our coworkers treated him. They would toss dishes in the pit, barely acknowledging Charles and almost never saying "please" or "thank you." He was recognized only when his station was considered a bottleneck. I remember a time when one of the servers needed cutlery and started barking orders at Charles to get it done on the fly.

I'm sure it has something to do with being closeted, but I've always hated to see anyone treated as invisible. When Stephanie and I spoke to Charles, we inquired about his day, said "hello" and "how are you" and "please" and "thank you" and asked if he needed anything. And while it wasn't our motivation for interacting politely with Charles, we knew that when we needed something done quickly, he made it happen with a smile. He was so kind and positive and truly too good for that kitchen. I think about him often and hope he's doing well.

Kitchen jobs teach you all kinds of skills, far beyond how to cook and create food. Later, when I opened my own restaurant, I remembered all those details I picked up in jobs along my journey, not just about how to julienne herbs or arrange equipment for optimal efficiency. I understood that it was necessary to hire people who were not only talented but also kind and empathetic. Back in those days, I noticed that when workers cook at a high level and treat one another with respect and kindness, this ensures a positive work environment and helps keep the gears turning. Talent may be the hardware, but consideration is the oil critical to smooth operation. My team today is a prime example of this.

And while the kind of food we were cooking at Top of the Hub wasn't exactly stretching the limits of my culinary skill, I learned so much about how to interact with other people. Socially, this job made a huge difference in my life, most of all as a result of meeting Stephanie. During our long days and short smoke breaks, we developed a friendship that endures to this day. We worked hard, but we also laughed together. We slowly started sharing details of our lives and feelings outside the realm of our professional experience. We saw the world in many of the same ways, and we learned from each other. Our work styles are almost totally opposite in technical ways, but they're in total harmony when we're together, and our shared goal is what kept us in step. In Stephanie, I made my first true friend as an adult—something I wasn't sure I knew how to do or would have been capable of with the intensity of my anxiety. It was proof I hadn't had previously—that with the right people, it is possible to feel safe and seen and motivated to be part of a relationship in which you can return the favor.

In those early Boston days, despite being hundreds of miles from the place where I grew up, I began to understand what it means to call a place home—not because of its location but because of what can be built there in terms of human relationships. That alone would have been enough to view my time at Top of the Hub as a success, but to my great surprise, I was destined to meet another major figure in my life on that top floor.

7

There are times when someone enters your life, and you are not entirely sure how or in what capacity, but you are certain that person belongs there. In 2007, when I met Scott, that sentiment could just about sum up the situation.

When I was still living in Chicago, as part of my ongoing attempts to appear as "normal" as possible, I very loosely dated guys. I still wasn't ready to imagine a future in which I might have to explain my perpetual singlehood, and maybe somewhere deep down I thought I could condition myself into living a heteronormative, societally acceptable life. In lieu of actual physical attraction, I went for guys who looked good on paper, who seemed to promise the trappings of an exemplary adult relationship.

Of course, none of them stuck, and in my very early Boston days, I was too busy with work to worry about putting on a performance— for others or myself. But then, as they say, these things happen when you aren't looking for them, and that was definitely true in my case when the most fulfilling and significant relationship of my life to that point simply presented itself in the service elevator with a smile. The whole thing was a shock, and entirely unexpected, but what surprised me more than anything was that it was in the form of a man.

In restaurants, it's pretty common for romances to spark up among the team, in part because of the high-intensity, ultra-emotional, and adrenaline- and sometimes alcohol-fueled environment. Also, because of the long and unusual hours, you rarely interact with anyone beyond the walls of your restaurant, and if you do manage to meet someone in the "real" world, it can be tough to maintain a consistent relationship for very long. So it made sense that Scott was a coworker.

At the time, he was an assistant manager at Top of the Hub. I knew him, but we didn't interact a ton. I mainly went in for my scheduled hours, did my job, and took off. But we crossed paths enough, especially when my shift was over and I actually set foot outside the kitchen. I was always in a rare state in those moments—simultaneously exhausted and fully amped from the adrenaline of service. It was around six or seven months in when I ran into Scott at the employee elevator bank. I always felt so nasty after a shift, covered in the residue of hundreds of meals and hours of accumulated sweat, and I couldn't wait to get home for a shower. Apparently, though, I didn't look as bad as I thought, because this dude—dapper in his full and very professional suit—asked for my number.

It didn't throw me too much; this wasn't the first time in my life some guy had made this request, and my reaction always fell somewhere on the spectrum from mildly horrified to ambivalent to totally avoidant. Plus, when Scott asked, I wasn't sure what his intentions were. We were friendly. It could have been that he was looking for a date, but it also might've been that he just wanted to hang out for a few beers.

Either way, I gave it to him—scribbled it in Sharpie on a piece of paper from the kitchen ticket printer, not giving it too much thought. But as I watched the doors slide shut between us a few minutes later, I had no way of knowing that I'd just opened an entirely new chapter of my life.

First dates have the potential to be painfully awkward, and most of mine to that point had been borderline torture, so I had very little in the way of expectations when I arrived at Tia's Waterfront in Boston on a sunny September day. Whatever Scott's intentions, I figured we'd have a drink and a meal, maybe some decent conversation, and then I'd move on with my life. I certainly did not expect that I would be out long after the sun went down, chatting and laughing and listening and—in the biggest surprise of all—actually enjoying myself.

Much like the guys I'd dated in Chicago, Scott looked good on paper. He was handsome, with a full head of soft brown hair and blue eyes. He had big dimples that charmed everyone when he smiled, which was so often that he developed crow's-feet, even at his young age—something I always found attractive—as evidence of his good nature and affability. He had a solid job and was well liked and respected around the restaurant. But I learned that day that Scott was so much more than a suit with a great smile. He wasn't super macho—maybe because he was raised by a single mother—but he was super smart. He was intelligent in a way that reminded me of my dad and brother, inquisitive and thoughtful and curious. He knew wines like the back of his hand. He was sensitive and a charming conversationalist. He asked questions and listened to the answers. He shared and was honest and humble. He was—like Stephanie— a *good* person. I knew it that day, when the heat of the sun on my face dissipated and the only indicator that time was passing was that the late summer dusk turned the air chilly. We drank vodka sodas through plastic straws and joked about the fact that we'd barely caught a buzz, wondering whether the bartenders bothered to put alcohol in our drinks at all.

Afterward, we took a walk. It was the most relaxed I'd felt in ages, being with Scott—a person I didn't really know. It surprised me and surprised me more that I wasn't questioning it, just going with it instead. I honestly can't remember the circumstances of our first kiss. Maybe some part of me doesn't like to associate this person about whom I still care deeply with something so historically traumatic for me. But it never felt that way with Scott. It was much less threatening, less menacing. It didn't feel like a performance; I genuinely liked sharing my life with him. Being close to Scott in that way was a lesson in what it could be like to be close to someone in any way and actually feel safe. And that was something I'd never felt before.

It's hard to know the mysterious forces that make two people compatible, but whatever it is, Scott and I had it. For the following five years, we were together, always. After my three months in the Charlestown house were up, back in my early Top of the Hub days, my parents helped me find a studio in the North End, an area they'd heard was safe. It was nothing fancy—a walk-up studio where I mostly just dropped in to sleep between shifts—and I never really felt at home there. It was more like a boardinghouse than a place of refuge. Eventually, after around six or seven months of dating, Scott and I decided to move in together. I didn't move into his place or vice versa; we chose and leased a place jointly. And from there, we built a home—together.

I remember how grown-up the whole thing felt. Not just because the apartment we chose had a washer and dryer in the unit (previously, I'd had to venture into the terrifying basement in my building) but also because this—a relationship with a boyfriend, both of us with jobs that had a clear upward trajectory, taking the major step of merging our lives—felt like a recognizable and societally approved life. It was easy for other people to see and understand where we were headed, why and how.

But unlike the people I casually dated in Chicago, this wasn't just about what it looked like from the outside. Prior to this period with Scott, I'm not sure I had a lot of fun in my life, not since I was a kid. I didn't prioritize fun or see a place for it. It didn't seem to be a thing that would help me move forward or advance my life plan. But with Scott, fun came easily.

We did such normal, couple-y things together. We had many of the same interests. On days off, we loved scouring the city for interesting foods, stopping for cupcakes at our favorite bakery. He met my parents and came home to Michigan with me. I got to know his family, too. We hung out with other couples and talked about "someday" the way straight people I knew so often did. I could finally breathe a little and feel *normal*—at least outwardly. If this was my future, I was going to be okay.

Having fun with Scott was possible because he was my best friend. The universe delivered him to me in that elevator and made it clear that this guy was going to be part of my life—for profound conversations, for laughter, for a sort of love that comes with finding a soul connection. But what it didn't make clear was that this man— no matter how wonderful—couldn't change the person I was inside.

In some ways, I was role-playing based on what I thought I was supposed to do in a partnership. That's not to say I didn't love Scott or that I was acting. To this day, I can say with my full heart that my love for that man was genuine, and in all the platonic ways we inter-acted, I felt confident in expressing that love.

But no matter how true that was, or whether I felt life might be better, easier, more stable, more "normal," and more certain if we were together, it didn't—and couldn't—make me straight. And although I tried to see our relationship as a way to be close to a person I cared about, with whom I had a clear sense of safety and trust, when it came to physical intimacy, I struggled. It's difficult to describe the out-of-body experience. Mentally removing yourself from the scenario as a form of self-preservation, the sort of power-lessness, even in a situation that you participate in creating, contrib-utes to shame and despair.

Scott never pushed me; he was patient and accepting. And yet I couldn't shake the feeling of pressure, one that might have stemmed from my own perceptions of what was expected of me. I knew how to be friends with a guy, but beyond that, I didn't have a frame of reference from any past relationship of my own with men, no idea of what was average. For the most part, I crossed my fingers and focused on the many positive parts of being with Scott, hoping that we could keep going and leave things exactly as they were—and I could just be happy to sleep peacefully beside my best friend.

While I was steadily dating Scott, life continued evolving on the pro-fessional front. After a few years at Top of the Hub, I started to get restless, feeling like I was at the end of the road in terms of growth and learning opportunities. I got very good on the line but never really moved around. Beyond that, summers in the restaurant were brutally hot and uncomfortable (thanks to floor-to-ceiling windows, the location on the fifty-second floor, and a criminally insufficient air-conditioning system), and with another summer on the horizon, I couldn't imagine staying put any longer.

I always had feelers out, and when I heard about an executive chef position at a new restaurant, Ivy, I pounced. At age twenty-five, I felt like I'd paid my dues and was ready for the role in a way I hadn't been back in Chicago. Plus, I had a clear head this time around and a stable life surrounded by people I loved. And although I wanted to make a move, I also wanted to keep it that way—which is why when I applied for and landed the gig at Ivy, I knew I had a much more important job: to bring my best friend, Stephanie, along for the ride.

I'm not sure what gave me the impression that we were living in an action movie—maybe because of the always high stakes in my anxious brain—but the speech I gave to Stephanie when I was preparing to leave Top of the Hub belonged in a screenplay.

From the minute I found out I was officially leaving, I played out the conversation with her in my head. Sharing the news that I was leaving felt like breaking up, and I wanted her to know I had no intention of abandoning her. So one day after I officially tendered my resignation, I pulled her aside on our smoke break. We'd taken the elevator down to the first floor and were standing outside the Prudential Center, ripping cigarettes one after another, as we'd done during so many shifts before. But this time, I was nervous.

"I have to tell you something," I said, taking a drag and holding my breath.

I exhaled and all at once explained about the new job, that I had put in my notice. And then, before she could react, I added, "Don't worry; I'll be back for you," as if we were a couple in some wartime film and I was preparing to go off to battle. We still laugh about that moment, but the absurdity of it didn't stop me from making good on the promise. In short time, I was able to hire her on as my sous chef at Ivy, and we were fully back in action—heroes in a sequel with a brand-new set.

Ivy felt like a major move. I once again had the title I'd wanted so badly, and this time I had some of the experience to back it up. I'd also gone from hourly to salary, which felt like a very grown-up step, and I got to hire my own sous, who just so happened to be my best friend. It was yet another time when I felt I was taking a giant step forward. But this one would wind up being more like a precarious skip, albeit in the right direction—not quite a stumble, but not the major stride I'd hoped for.

Initially, Ivy was fun at times, primarily because Stephanie and I had each other. Together, we made the best food we could based on what we knew at the time, because we really cared. We even had brushes with stardom, like when we served Ben Affleck an order of beef carpaccio (the most truly Boston story of my life—and the very first time I'd ever made the dish). But it wasn't all star power and daydreams. Once again, maybe I should have been suspicious of how quickly the owners hired a still relatively inexperienced line cook to lead their restaurant, because Ivy gave me a fast case of déjà vu. Checks bouncing. Unprofessional behavior. Rumors about a general mishandling of funds—not to mention mistreatment of people.

At least this time I wasn't totally alone in trying to negotiate a way out of the situation; Stephanie was there beside me. She and I both fought for our money, and also for our team. There were times when I told the owners to just take the cash out of my own check to pay my cooks, some of whom had family to care for. I knew I had a safety net and support system.

It didn't take long to realize that this position wasn't going to be setting me up for any kind of future—other than maybe personal bankruptcy. I had already learned it's a better idea to jump ship before it's swallowed up entirely, so when I heard whispers about a Michelin-starred French chef coming to open a restaurant at the Fairmont hotel on Battery Wharf, I packed my knives again.

To that point, my culinary journey had been a little all over the map. The restaurants in which I'd cut my teeth were what was called Continental in those days—American classics with influences from all over. They were designed to be crowd-pleasers. Sensing, though, was going to be distinctly French. That excited me, both as a new challenge and a focused culinary point of view. It reminded me of those childhood days glued to the screen watching *Great Chefs of the World,* and it seemed like the closest thing I could get to cooking abroad.

Scott and Stephanie were both super supportive and encouraging, and it was winter when I went in for the meeting in the brand-new hotel. I wore little black booties and jeans, a black jacket and a scarf, and really tried to look nice—in a way I thought might earn the respect of my corporate interviewers. The process was a multistep situation, and when I got a callback to return to the hotel a few days later and cook for the powers that be, I was feeling really good.

Of course, I had no way of knowing how this kind of cooking evaluation would factor into my life in just a few years—that this was essentially a *Top Chef* training session—but I remember a sense of confidence as I cooked for the chefs, carefully constructing a creamy fennel risotto with seared scallops and an orange glaze. That might sound surprising, given how deeply anxious I was in so many ways.

Maybe it's because I knew if it didn't work out, I'd be okay. I had Scott at home. I had a best friend in town who had also left her toxic job at Ivy and struck out on her own. I was also, perhaps for the first time, applying for a job that was not a major reach in terms of my experience. I wasn't gunning for executive or sous chef—this was simply a cook position. If I could work in a restaurant with that level of prestige, it wasn't as important that I have a fancy title. And maybe my food reflected that confidence, because when the chef tasted my dish that day, his response was entirely positive. It was a time-machine moment back to that Knife Skills 101 class, a reminder of the power of a pat on the back, of being able to serve something I'd made with my own hands and have someone appreciate it. Except this time, it came not with a grade but with a job offer.

After my three years of marathon shifts, Sensing was a totally different way of working and a new trajectory. The restaurant itself was gorgeous and, as most fine dining establishments are, designed for a quiet, calm, memorable experience. I remember seeing it for the first time and being blown away by how *fancy* it was. After emerging from the employee locker rooms and passing through a small cafeteria, you passed a refrigerated room entirely dedicated to seafood, followed by a window which looked into a beautiful pastry room. Upstairs was a dining room anchored by an open kitchen where guests could see and feel connected to the people creating their meals. It was unlike anywhere I'd ever dined, let alone worked, but I was really ready for it.

And while it had its technical challenges from a culinary perspective—I had to adjust certain practices to match the restaurant's style and adhere more closely to the true French brigade system (a traditional structure of responsibilities in a professional kitchen)—my time at Sensing for the next two years was mostly uneventful, in the best way possible. It was the difference between the chaotic and the truly organized and professional. I'd gone from six hundred covers on a Saturday to sixty. I wasn't worried that my payroll money would come in on time. I had a reliable job that I didn't fear would fall apart. I could focus on my craft, and the relative calm gave me space to truly learn.

I also had my first real mentor in Gérard Barbin, Sensing's chef de cuisine, who was for the most part a very positive influence. Gérard, with his thick-as-Dijon-mustard French accent, was kind but rarely cracked a smile and operated with a strict sense of discipline—for himself maybe even more than for his team. I think he liked me quickly for the same reasons I liked Stephanie. I was reliable, hardworking, and conscientious—maybe because of my own motivation, or maybe because I had empathy for him. The guy was clearly trying to earn respect from his own boss and run a tight ship, while so many of the employees had no problem clocking out and taking off regardless of whether a project was done for the day. I could sense that Gérard was under pressure as well—he'd been appointed to run a restaurant very much expected to be a shining star in Guy Martin's culinary empire on a very tight budget with a lot of opinions from hotel bosses, so he was grateful to have someone who actually gave a shit.

His trust in me was a double-edged sword, though. I was given extra responsibility and overtime. He even handed the badge to his office to me so I could put in orders. As someone who so badly craved validation and visibility, I loved that sense of purpose and could almost feel the professional growth in real time. On the other hand, I can guarantee that because I was the only girl, the rest of the cooks—dudes (no surprise)—were convinced that something was going on between Gérard and me. Not because there was a single ounce of truth to it or even because they saw anything that could be construed as improper but because that's how it is for women in this industry—and in the world, for that matter. These were not days during which you would speak up about something like that, though. At the time, if anything, you doubled down to prove your worth through your work, regardless of how those efforts could wreak havoc on your body and personal life.

Eventually, I got up the nerve to ask for a raise and a promotion but was told there was no budget for that kind of thing. I was disappointed, but I understood that it was business. That is, until they brought in a new sous from Paris. A guy (again, no surprise). After that, with no further discussion of increasing my status, I was hurt and disillusioned, feeling overlooked by my mentor, frustrated and stagnant once again. My contract was for two years, so, much like that first Charlestown apartment, there was an end date. I stuck it out, knowing that I'd be moving on and by then fully prepared to part ways.

On the personal front, things with Scott had been stagnating in a way, too. And I was far less prepared for another inevitable separation.

Codependency can set in quickly, especially when you're young and far from your family and not entirely sure who you are just yet. It's easy to latch on to another person—particularly one who sees you, one whom you love and who you know loves you, too—and pretty soon you lose track of where you start and that person ends.

Although our romantic relationship didn't last very long, Scott and I were a unit for almost five years. I think we needed each other in many ways, and we loved each other so much that the idea of ending the relationship and threatening our friendship was just too scary. At some point, though, Scott started to realize he needed more intimacy. In retrospect, I probably needed that, too, but I hadn't yet come to know how it feels to have that closeness and its benefits, both personally and relationally.

I don't know if Scott ever suspected that I was gay, and if he did, he was kind enough not to put me in the hot seat about it. I think I knew somewhere in the back of my mind that we couldn't go on forever and that I should also let Scott go and live his life and allow him to have a truly fulfilling love. But I couldn't help but cling to the idea of us. Scott was exactly the kind of guy I'd want to be with if I wanted to be with a man, and I spent the relationship trying to convince myself I could just block out the part of me that didn't and be grateful for the love I was given, convinced that it'd be the only love I might ever receive. Of course, you can only convince yourself for so long. And when Scott finally did bring things very gently to an end, I knew in a way that he was releasing us both.

Still, I was devastated. I was sure I'd never feel love again. Being gay was hard work that I wasn't ready to do, and I was angry with myself for not being able to overcome this thing. Suddenly, after several very good years, I felt at sea again, without a job and at the end of my relationship, so I started to think about running away from everything, feeling again that the only way I could survive was to self-isolate. To be alone. The only problem was that this time, I had created a real support system, and I couldn't leave it behind.

Most Boston residents have at least one major life memory at a Dunkin' Donuts location. I am no exception.

One day, after Sensing and Scott were both fully over for me, Stephanie and I were sitting on a brick wall outside one such location, drinking coffee and smoking cigarettes, and I was explaining what I thought I might do next. The company that owned the Fairmont hotel had properties all over the world, including in London and Dubai, and I thought I could leverage my experience with the group to get a gig at one of those other locations. I thought moving abroad might be my next logical step.

But Stephanie had other ideas. Since leaving the Ivy job, she'd been working at a restaurant called Stir for a chef on the Boston food scene I'd always known about and admired from afar—Barbara Lynch. That day, Stephanie told me to wait on the international move. Instead, she asked me to come to Stir and work next to her again.

This was the first time a job was offered to me not because of what I promised to do but because of what I had already done—my reputation, what I'd proved, the relationships I'd built for myself. I had been running for so long, always trying to jump ship before I could be left behind, adrift.

I learned so much in those early East Coast days, but nothing was as valuable as the relationships I made. There's no way to quantify what it meant to me that even as I thought there was no possible life worth living for me if I didn't run, there was a person giving me a reason—and asking me—to stay. Valuing me not for my cooking but for my company, my presence in her life.

I was relieved to have an option not to leave. Boston had come to feel like home to me because of the people I met, who welcomed me and made me feel appreciated and wanted, and because of the relationships I'd built on my own, for myself as an adult. These were early steps in constructing a sense of self that would be sturdy enough to support me when I came out, to know for certain that I could be loved by people who weren't my parents.

So I stubbed out my cigarette and, in that moment, made a new mental plan. I told Stephanie I would stay.

8

No matter who you are or how you identify, I'm pretty sure you are aware of a shared inarguable and universal human truth: Breakups absolutely suck. Which is why, when possible, I highly recommend coordinating them with your best friend.

For the entire time I'd known her, Stephanie had been in a relationship with one particular guy. They lived together in the town where they grew up, just outside the city. And it just so happened that around the time Scott and I were coming to terms with our limits as a couple, Steph was also reaching the end of the road with her relationship.

I was still living with Scott in his condo at the time—a home he'd purchased and that we moved into together after we left our first apartment. Our split had been amicable, and he wasn't kicking me out while I considered my next move. We wanted what was best for each other.

But I also wanted to be there for Steph. When I found out what she was going through, and because of this situation, all I could offer—with Scott's support and encouragement, since he knew and loved Steph, too—was a spot on the couch where my now ex-boyfriend and I were living. She accepted, grateful to have the landing pad despite the unconventional setup. And that might've been a strange enough situation for some people, but then Scott's best friend wound up splitting from *his* girlfriend, and Scott extended the same courtesy to him as I did to Steph. And just like that, our very grown-up, live-in-couple situation became a quartet of newly single twentysomethings crammed into a condo together. We called it Heartbreak Hotel, and if the rest of my career falls apart at any point, I'll be pitching this as a sitcom for my fallback.

We nursed our wounds collectively, helping make the pain more tolerable—or at least distract one another from it—and although the arrangement lasted only a few weeks, it was long enough to level up my already solid friendship with Steph. Although she was someone I considered family, seeing her every day, the both of us tentatively navigating what being newly single would mean for our lives, deepened our bond.

And while our friendship had already given me so much personally—a foundational sense of home and stability and mutual respect and love—Steph had also made good on the Stir invitation, helping lift me up to the next step professionally.

I knew of Barbara Lynch, just as anyone who knew anything about food and wine in Boston did during those days. Her empire included a number of renowned spots, from classic New England concepts like B&G Oysters to the pasta-centric Sportello to the Butcher Shop, a love letter to Italy and France. And then there was Stir. Stir wasn't quite a restaurant in the traditional sense; it was a cookbook shop by day and a ten-seat demonstration kitchen by night, one where the menu changed each evening. It was, to my mind, the restaurant group's crown jewel.

There were many employees in Barbara's operations who hoped to one day end up behind the counter at Stir, but only a handful could make it. The place was tiny, and not only was there not enough physical space to accommodate a large crew, new spots also didn't open up often.

The fact that Stephanie was working there after starting with Barbara at B&G was a testament not only to her own cooking skills and grit, which I'd witnessed at Top of the Hub and Ivy, but also to her ability to perform in this unique role and shine in such a large company with a deep pool of talent. There's something respectable to me about leadership teams who make strong choices, and the fact that this company recognized those qualities in my friend—someone who really deserved it—made it all the more admirable to me.

When Steph told me to come to Stir that day outside Dunkin', I had a range of feelings: gratitude for my friend and our friendship, excitement at the idea of a new career step forward, relief at not having to leave Boston and run again. But afterward, I realized I was also intimidated in a way that I hadn't been about most of my preceding job prospects. Barbara's presence was profound even in name and idea alone, and whether I was ready or not, I was about to be in it.

That first visit wasn't set up to be an interview or anything formal. I just popped in to see my friend while she was prepping for service. When I arrived, it was a warm spring day in the South End, and Boston was alive. The corners of the block were busy with people popping into neighboring restaurants, tourists and locals alike all shopping and eating lunch outside. This part of town had a charming *Mister Rogers' Neighborhood* vibe, and when the mercury was on the climb, it seemed like everyone was having their best day.

I knew a little about Stir from photos I'd seen online, and from the way Steph had described it, but I had never worked or even been a guest anywhere quite like this. Upon entering, I could easily see that the space was designed for efficiency. It was about 250 square feet—the size of some midsize primary bedrooms—with ten seats around an island that doubled as a cooking station. Still, it was charming. A floor-to-ceiling shelf of cookbooks lined one wall, while pots and pans hung from the stainless-steel hood above the range. It felt like it could be someone's home.

Steph was busy working—she had pots everywhere—and it was just her and a front-of-house person working on their own prep. And then there was Barbara, seated at the island on the far end from the door in what I would soon learn was "position ten." I was introduced, in a very casual way, as Steph's friend. The idea was just to meet Barbara. Steph needed a sous at Stir, and while I would still eventually need to go through HR, her recommendation would carry a lot of weight. It would be helpful for Barbara to have a frame of reference for who I was when that moment arrived.

When we exchanged pleasantries, I was nervous, but not scared, exactly. And despite the fact that she loomed large over the city's culinary scene, Barbara was considerably shorter than I am, with kind eyes and an air of wisdom, as if she'd seen it all. She was intimidating—direct and to the point—but I would come to learn that her affect isn't coldness; she just takes a beat to warm up to new people, a process that accelerates once you've earned her trust.

I hung out for a little while, shooting the shit. At some point, Steph—who is the first to tell you that she is not a fan of doing desserts—described what they had planned for that night's final course. It was a fig tart, and—leave it to Steph to subtly put me forward—she asked me to help her out while she prepped it. And suddenly there I was, working in front of Barbara. I paid close attention to what I was doing while participating in what had very naturally become a group conversation, since there were only four of us in the space. My cooking history came up, how Steph and I had met, that I'd been working at Sensing by Guy Martin. It was small talk and a very welcome way of getting to know one another without the pressure of being interviewed. We talked about the menu for the evening, and I loved the idea that each dish was totally new, that every day they changed the offerings based on inspiration, theme, or ingredient.

At some point, Barbara asked for a snack—peanut butter and celery. Steph was busy, and I've never liked just standing around without a purpose, so I offered to prepare it for Barbara. I'd already become so comfortable in such a short time that this didn't seem out of the ordinary, even though I wasn't an employee and had only just met this woman. Before I could go for the ingredients, though, Steph pulled me aside.

"You have to peel the celery," she said.

I'd learned a lot of skills in school and in restaurants over the years, but I'd never seen or heard this request in my life. It told me much of what I needed to know about Barbara: that she liked things a particular way; that she knew what she wanted and communicated it clearly to a team who complied without question or complaint; that she was consistent enough in her requests that her people knew how to execute to her taste. And there was no grumbling about this request in the resentful way of a team who didn't respect their boss or feel respected in return. It was just a simple fact: You have to peel the celery.

I peeled the celery. And I prepared it with the same focus and intention as I had prepared my seared scallops and risotto back at my Sensing audition. Despite the added step, it was a simple and unassuming snack, but it might have also been the most important dish of my life.

Money has never been the biggest motivator for me. It still isn't. As my paydays have grown from those early mall days at Twist & Shout, I've welcomed the increases and been grateful that my life and work have afforded me greater financial rewards. And, especially in my younger days, dollar signs were important to me as signifiers of a change in status, a type of recognition rather than a means of purchasing fancy things.

I'd had a salaried position under my belt by then, which had felt like a big step at the time, but when the offer came in at Stir, in one of those super-official-looking manila envelopes, with a description of very adult-sounding benefits and a number to go with it—$32,000—you'd have thought I'd hit the lottery. Never mind that today, that number could barely cover living expenses in a Midwestern suburb (including Kentwood, Michigan), much less a major US city. But it came attached to a coveted spot in one of the most respected restaurants in Boston—if not the country—and that was a benefit I couldn't quantify.

In addition, the schedule at Stir—typically, ten-hour shifts from noon to 10:00 p.m. as opposed to the fifteen-plus-hour marathons that could last into the early hours of the morning at other jobs—was exceedingly rare in the business and kind of a dream.

It was handy to have some cash, though, since Scott and I had finally officially parted ways and both Steph and I needed to find our own places. Fortunately, a building just a few blocks from Stir had recently opened, and there were several vacancies. They were efficiency units, meaning the apartments didn't have kitchens and were basically glorified shoeboxes, but it was a four-minute walk to work in the South End, which was hard to beat. Also, my standards had changed since that trip with Jonathan. Now I had a job I considered remarkable. I had friends I cared about and who cared about me, and I no longer needed my apartment to be some kind of representation of my personal worth.

Once we moved into apartments three doors down from each other, Steph and I got into a groove. We would wake up, stop at Starbucks for my daily doppio (a double espresso, black—pure rocket fuel), and walk the few blocks to the restaurant together. Even though working at Stir was a totally new experience for me, I took to it quickly. Everything aligned for me to be successful in that role: I had a renewed sense of dedication to my work after Scott, enough experience to feel confident in my cooking, and a supportive friend beside me.

I also had a full enough life that I wasn't distracted by my anxieties, although that's not to say there weren't some. Stir was a study in some ways of how far I could push myself socially. Kitchens are pretty safe from interactions with humanity at large; for the most part, we cooks can hide behind our stations and focus on what's in front of us without worrying about customer service or smiling or small talk. That was part of the appeal for me prior to Stir. I'd had some exposure to an open kitchen at Sensing, but that setup is more of a one-sided experience, allowing the guests to get a little show. Mostly, the important thing in that scenario is to keep your station clean and tidy and appear as professional as possible, but it's not exactly interactive.

At Stir, on the other hand, we were actually hosting an intimate dinner party every night. The space wasn't big enough to hold lots of employees, and clutter would not only be unsightly but could also be the undoing of an entire service. Because of the size, we needed to be carefully organized for things to go smoothly. We did it all ourselves: We were cooking and cleaning as we went through the meal, making sure there were no pileups of pots or plates and we were directly serving, explaining the dishes to our diners every night. And because we did so many themed nights and educational events, we were also teaching diners about food and technique—which was an incredibly tricky dance. These were maneuvers I knew well, but suddenly I had to be charming, smiling, responsive, and charismatic while I was at it. Beyond the fact that the restaurant simply couldn't have a huge roster, I could see why Barbara and the leadership team were so selective about who worked at Stir; not many food-service workers had this combination of skills. And early on, there was a moment that made me question whether I was one of them.

It was one of the nights when we were hosting a cooking class. I was doing my best to appear comfortable and confident, to communicate to the people watching me closely that I knew what I was doing and had the authority to be sharing my knowledge with them. In my normal cooking life, I had no problem performing the task at hand: deboning a chicken. But demonstrating it at the same time? That was a totally different animal. I was sweaty and shaking so badly that at one point, my hand slipped, and I nicked my finger. I felt it happen and knew the blood was coming, and all I could think was *fuckfuckfuckfuckfuck*. But somehow, maybe through the telepathic powers of our friendship or because we'd worked together long enough to know each other well or because she is simply that attentive, Steph caught it when it happened. She seamlessly and wordlessly stepped in while I casually wrapped my finger in a towel and ducked away to deal with it while diners remained none the wiser.

It might have made me second-guess things at another point in my life, but I was so supported in the challenge that was Stir, so clear that I could lean on the people around me, and so certain that this was an invaluable experience that I knew it was worth pushing through the anxious parts of me. There are times when personal growth comes as a result of pure want. I wanted to be there, and so I had to grow.

It's a good thing, too, because it wouldn't be long before those skills—to be able to teach and talk and engage with an audience while cooking and educating people about food—would be a defining part of my life and career.

Despite the discomfort of demonstrations, there were many things about the job that I loved, and almost nothing could have made me want to leave. Of course, I wouldn't change a thing about my life now, but if I had to choose a period of my life to relive, those early days at Stir would be a top contender. The work was like nothing I'd ever done before. We were making new menus every single day. I was never bored. This was truly creative work. It was collaborative. It was inspiring and inspired.

And although initially I was nervous about being in front of guests, I realized the beauty of being able to really connect with the people we were feeding every night. It was a new dimension for me professionally to see how the work I was doing was resonating, how it affected diners' experience and their lives. We got to be part of so many special occasions, and we had the ability to provide the backdrop for so many memories, designing the details of someone's unforgettable night. It felt meaningful and helped me reorient my own sense of purpose in social situations. The idea that engaging with other people could be positive— that was a game changer. In contrast to so many periods of my life up to that point, there was not a day that went by when I didn't wake up ready and willing and *excited* to get up, get ready, leave my home, and go out in the world, to a job.

It wasn't all work, either. I was able to have fun in those days with people I considered friends. There was a small crew at Stir, and we quickly became close. When the guests left, we poured glasses of wine and pored over menus for the next day while we talked about life and love and all the things that matter to twentysomethings just starting out. Early on, when the wounds from the split with Scott were still fresh, there was a period when all I wanted to do was listen to Adele and crank sad breakup ballads at top volume after my shift. I really leaned in to the sadness in a way that some people might have rolled their eyes at, but my friends let me do it—and then we laughed about it, which was more healing than any therapy session.

When we went out on the town, it was to an industry hang called Franklin Cafe, where I could stretch my salary to cover two-dollar bottles of Miller High Life and sometimes splurge on steak frites. And on occasion, we got into some cheesy, gooey chicken parm at a place called Anchovies. These hangs were a far cry from my hard-partying days in Chicago. After that period ended, I didn't find myself reaching for drugs and alcohol in the same way. They had been tools to help me survive stressful social situations. But with these people, in this world, I felt safe. I also had a job that kept me busy—a job I loved and wanted to keep—and this very full life curbed that intense craving for anything so destructive.

Another great thing about Barbara's restaurants is that we were in close proximity to other spots she owned, and so although our own team was small, there were always people within the "family" for us to spend time with, including Matty and Daniel from the Butcher Shop, next door, both of whom were very out gay men and who hung with us sometimes. They were handsome and adorable and so fun. There were moments when I envied them for being okay with the people they were (or at least that's how I perceived it), but mostly I admired them quietly, still not ready to join them out of the closet. If I had wanted to, Boston had plenty of opportunities for me to seek out queer spaces—the South End was known for it. But it wasn't at the forefront of my mind. I was surrounded by friends. I loved the work that filled the hours of my day. I was content, at least for the moment. My life was full.

When things are hard, it can be difficult to share your concerns or your pain, even with the people who care most about you. I have found that in some ways, it can be equally complicated to talk about good, positive things happening in your life. But while I still wasn't ready to talk about my queerness to anyone, I was very happy when I had a chance to share the goodness.

My mother came to Boston to visit me early on during my time at Stir, but I'd been there long enough to feel comfortable and excited to have her. I couldn't wait for her to see the restaurant. In addition to the tasting counter, there were two banquettes in the dining room: Those were the spots we reserved for VIP guests, and that was where we sat my mother when she came to dine at the place that was quickly becoming my home. I remember preparing the dinner and really putting my heart into it. My parents have always been incredibly complimentary of my cooking, sometimes to the point of hyperbole (the number of times I've heard "The best I've ever had..."), yet this felt different. Not only because of the food, which was indeed on a level I felt was more refined, more mature, more reflective of what was inside me creatively, but also because of what the place signified for me as a person.

I was so proud to demonstrate to my mom how far I'd come, and I felt so lucky to be able to share my experience, give her something special, to repay her in some small way with a good meal and the assurance that her daughter—about whom I knew she worried—was doing well.

We had such a good time together. When I had downtime during her visit, she stayed with me in my efficiency apartment. We shopped for and built IKEA furniture together, had a meal with Steph at Legal Sea Foods in the Prudential Center (a Boston classic), and shared my futon when it was time to call it a night.

Many times, I thought back and regretted the way I'd treated my mom back in high school. I still do, to be honest, even though she has absolved me more than once when I've apologized, always insisting that she knew I was just figuring things out. Having her in Boston was a chance to spend the kind of time with her that I hoped for in my heart, the kind I still cherish when on occasion we come together. It's the kind of time that comes with the shift in the mother-daughter dynamic once you become a true adult, when the relationship can be less about reliance and more about love, respect, and appreciation for each other's company—uncomplicated by certain needs and the stress of competing ideas about how to meet them.

More than anything, I was just happy to show my mother that I was growing up—that I was functional and part of something—and that I was okay, knowing that's what she always wanted most of all.

Having the presence of a parent has been grounding at so many points in my life, even—or perhaps especially—as I have been establishing myself in the world in a place far from home. I was sad to see my mom go after her visit to Boston, but although Barbara wasn't a maternal figure per se, she was a kind of matriarch, someone I consider a mentor.

That said, I realize now that hasn't been everyone's experience. More than ten years after my Stir days, reports emerged about Barbara and the work environment in her restaurants. I can only speak honestly of my own experience there. When we did work together, Barbara inspired me personally. She was a brilliant cook who cared deeply about women in the industry, and it seemed to me at the time that she consistently pulled other women into the limelight.

When I did a good job, I was recognized, always, and there was one instance that really cemented my sense of belonging in that restaurant and, frankly, as a chef in general. We were coming up on a themed night called Little Birds & Burgundy, which Barbara herself was set to host. The structure was loosely defined: It was to be a five-course dinner based on great big burgundy wines and little game birds. It was understood that the sous chef role for these events was one Steph and I would be trading off, and this was my first time at bat. These dinners were a major draw with Barbara as the headliner, and for me, as her main support, the stakes were super high. It was less than a week prior to the event when I waited for the scheduled call from Barbara to discuss the plan. I remember how I was sweating when I saw Barbara's name on my phone.

"I'm really busy right now, Kristen," she told me when I answered. I was outside Stir getting ready for another dinner. I stood there on the curb in my Birkenstock kitchen clogs, rocking back and forth and smoking furiously, doing a kind of balancing act—my nervousness manifesting itself physically. "I don't have a lot of time to work on this menu. Can you take the lead?"

Of course I said yes. Partly because, well, what was the alternative? And partly because I wanted to. I wanted that chance. She went on to explain the general vision, and the whole time, I listened and nodded, making notes in my head, saying, "Yes, Chef; I got it, Chef; definitely, Chef."

Inwardly, though, I was freaking out. Not only was I going to be helping her out during service, but taking the lead also meant that I was going to be making the menu for a class and meal that Barbara herself would be hosting. Beyond concocting a list of dishes that would speak to the caliber of chef that Barbara was known to be, there was the practical part of the job. I was going to have the mise en place prepared as well as various iterations of the dishes we'd be serving, because when you're demoing, you need elements at all different stages so you can show them to the guests while you're preparing the meal, just as they do on food television shows. You want to be able to show and tell.

For example, you might say, "This is what the sauce looks like when you first start out," then show what it looks like forty minutes or an hour later, so guests can get a look at what they might expect at home as they progress. Plus, there was the added layer of making sure we had a finished meal to enjoy during dinner service at the restaurant. I was going to have to plan all this, brief Barbara on everything, and make sure we were organized on a nearly military level—because in a restaurant where there's very little space, there's no room for error.

I worked hard on every detail of that menu. Every dish had to reflect the theme, so even my dessert was a cake that had melted foie gras incorporated into the batter. I knew it would be a challenge, but it was so creative and fun and inspiring that it almost came easily. It wasn't a stretch for me to create and execute this menu. Fortunately, for that meal, we were in a wheelhouse of food I knew. When I finished, I was proud of what I'd put together and confident in my ability to get us ready, but also so, so nervous to cook with—and for—Barbara. There was a ton of pressure. What if the menu bombed and people hated it? It was going to reflect on her most of all, since she was the one at the helm.

I mapped it all out in my head leading up to that night. I checked and double-checked our mise en place in advance of service. When we finally got underway, I was laser-focused. Barbara ran through the menu for the diners, and we got started on the first course. I was already staging components, working around her so she could entertain and talk, putting pans on, pulling out deli containers, making sure that when she turned around, she had a component to talk about and display. I was orchestrating everything. I was behind the scenes but also right in front of everyone—and she was fully trusting in me. With that vote of confidence, I got in a flow and realized that night that we worked in similar ways. It didn't feel like I had to learn how to work with Barbara; it was intuitive. We had a shared goal—both of us simply trying to efficiently pull off a beautiful dinner for our guests. A few courses in, she turned to me and asked, "Chef, how do you want this plated?" I answered before I even realized that there I was, telling Barbara Lynch what to do.

Diners were, to my great relief, super complimentary for those first courses, and at some point after Barbara had been praised again for the meal, she stopped.

"You know, I can't take credit for this," she told the guests. "This

is all Kristen," she said, gesturing to me. "She made the menu, prepared everything—this is truly her meal."

This simple statement, this brief remark made by such an influential figure, left a lasting impression on me in many ways. Not only
did it make previous praise feel like a sweet little pat on the head, but
because of the setting we were in and the source of the recognition,
it also had the unexpected benefit of creating a sort of small fan base
for us at Stir. We had regulars who came back to the restaurant to
see us, who developed relationships with us—and in that moment,
when Barbara put me forward with her endorsement and acknowl-
edgment, I became a figure they connected with and wanted to
return to see again.

In all my years of cooking, moments like this, of shared—or
transferred—credit, even in cases when it was unquestionably due,
have been rare. And while that does not invalidate the experiences
of others in Barbara's orbit, this is my own memory of working with
her in those early days at Stir.

Often we are faced with questions about separating art from the
artist. How we answer includes evaluating what that artist's work means
to our own lives. Regardless of Stir's origins and ownership, for me, that
restaurant was about more than Barbara. My time working there was
marked by moments like the one in which Barbara acknowledged my
work, as well as many more, involving art created by others, relationships built and strengthened, fundamental lessons learned, and memories made—personal and professional. The place was a platform for my
personal growth in ways I never thought possible.

And I would soon find out just how much I would rely on that
foundation, on every bit of skill and grounded confidence I developed in those days, because I was about to be launched into the
stratosphere.

9

There's something about airplane turbulence that I appreciate. Let me be clear—it's not like I want my flight to feel like a thrill ride. But it is about a sense of aliveness. Without those bumps and rolls, a plane can feel as if it's not moving at all. Which for some people is the ideal scenario—arrive at point B having hardly noticed you departed from point A.

But for me, stillness sometimes feels less like safety and more like stagnation. And without a clear sense of forward motion, I can feel like I'm not really getting anywhere, no matter what might be promised in the future, on the other side.

I'd found my groove at Stir, and it was smooth sailing. I was happy and appreciative, and I really did love the work. We were challenged and stimulated, thanks to a menu that changed daily and an invitation to contribute to those concepts, ideas, and strategies (a sign of strong leadership in my mind, keeping your people creatively engaged). But still, I started to feel a little like my life not only lacked turbulence—evidence of progress—but was also on total autopilot.

I had a routine in place, right down to my time at home. Steph and I would regularly make our way back from work and, when the weather permitted, take a beat before heading in. We sat outside our building on the narrow maroon steps, smoking cigarettes and recapping the day, squishing to the side when someone else had to squeeze through us and make their way past. In the beginning, that ritual was a great way to do a little people watching, to let our eyes adjust and observe the world beyond our long shifts behind a range at Stir.

But I remember beginning to see a repetitiveness even in this little reprieve, which at some point was symbolized by an unexpected object—a plastic bag caught in the tree in front of us. I don't know when I first noticed it or how long it had been there by the time I did, but it became a thing for Steph and me. We would sit, taking drags and wondering out loud how that bag got there, speculating when and how it would ultimately take its leave and move on. But there it was, every day without fail, and I started to wonder if—as comfortable as it seemed to be in those branches—it was ever really going anywhere.

It feels difficult to imagine now, when streaming services deliver just about any series, episode, or clip with a click or a tap, but in those days, options were limited for television viewing. The concept of recording TV shows was still relatively new and a pricey addition to cable packages, and between my entertainment budget and work schedule, plus occasional social extracurriculars, I didn't have a place in my life for TV.

Still, if you worked in the culinary world and didn't live under a rock, there were certain things you just knew. Particularly as celebrity chef culture had begun to take hold, it was inevitable that some of the names, brands, narratives, and touchstones would make their way into the collective consciousness. And one of those was the Bravo juggernaut *Top Chef.*

The show was one of the few cooking franchises that wasn't airing on the Food Network, and it had real reach, with its high-stakes competition-style format, not to mention an extremely charismatic triad of figures—Tom Colicchio and Gail Simmons as judges and Padma Lakshmi as host—with whom home audiences seemed to deeply connect.

I was clued in enough to know these facts and details about the show, and occasionally I would catch wind of a particular contestant or winner, but it wasn't exactly a phenomenon that felt close to home. All that changed, though, in 2012, when Barbara was asked to participate in the finale of the show's ninth season.

In a 2015 interview with the *New York Times,* Barbara told reporters, "We need more women on television." But by the time she had that conversation with the nation's paper of record, she'd already proved her own commitment to that ideal, because back in September of 2012—six months after her appearance as a guest chef—both Steph and I found ourselves in front of a camera. Our presence was a direct result of her influence, and while it might have been a relatively small contribution to the grander vision Barbara voiced in that conversation with the *Times,* for me it changed everything.

When the idea to audition to be a contestant on *Top Chef* was first presented to me, the notion that being on television could be life-altering never crossed my mind. To be honest, I didn't even completely understand the assignment. As my boss, Barbara had expected me to do many things at Stir, but this wasn't an expectation: It was an invitation, into terrain that was completely unfamiliar.

I now know a bit more about the pipeline of contestants for *Top*

Chef, and the sources are varied. You can apply, attend a casting call, go through the standard procedure, but as in most casting scenarios, production companies look for referrals and recommendations as well. While Barbara was in Texas filming season 9, the producers of the show asked if she could suggest anyone from her restaurants as a future contestant, and she took the opportunity to put forward some of her female team members. When she returned to Boston, three of us were approached. One was a woman named Michelle who worked at a different property and who declined respectfully and quickly.

The other two names in the *Top Chef* hat belonged to me and Steph. Given that the crew at Stir was four people at any given time, and that Steph and I were its two full-time chefs, this meant that Barbara had essentially offered up half her team from one establishment. There were plenty of employees in the company who would have been thrilled to have our gigs, but in retrospect, I wonder if it ever gave Barbara pause that she gave up a major part of her core team at Stir in order for us to have this opportunity. It was a vote of confidence that couldn't have been conveyed with words of praise.

And while I was humbled and surprised, I was also very uncertain. I knew what the show was in essence, but at the time, I had no context for the reality of making a television show, nor did we have much to go on as far as what it could mean for one's career. It could just as easily have been viewed as an unnecessary—even a detrimental—detour, a step away from a carefully mapped-out plan. But for me, the timing was perfect. A disruption wasn't just something I could digest; it was also what I craved.

Steph and I had sat on our stoop beneath that plastic bag many times, discussing the state of our careers, our occasional frustrations, our hopes and dreams. But this wasn't something that would ever have crossed our minds to want. I'm not sure if I would have given this invitation serious consideration had it not been a journey I could take with my best friend. But together, Steph and I had each other, and at the end of the day, the stakes actually felt pretty low. I can get on board with most anything if it doesn't feel like there's a full commitment involved—especially if it allows me to satisfy a curiosity, learn something new, explore the idea of a parallel life—and saying yes to the audition didn't lock us in. We would still have a process to go through with numerous steps and zero guarantees. At any point, it would have been easy enough to say, *Never mind; no, thank you,* and resume life as usual. We agreed that we would step away from our daily life, go through the motions and have an adventure together, and just see what might happen if we said yes.

After an initial call with Samantha Hanks, the show's casting producer, the next step in the process was to compile some introductory materials. Today I'm so fortunate that I get to work with some seasoned, talented crews for making TV. But my very first filmmaking experience was with a particularly scrappy team of collaborators, of whom I am no less proud: Steph and her legit cameraman dad, who arrived at our apartment building one afternoon armed with his clunky (but iconic) camcorder to record our audition tape.

And since we'd been recommended for the gig together, Steph and I created our submission as a pair. It was handy, since it not only took some of the pressure off us as individuals and allowed us to combine our resources (namely, Steph's dad), it also supplied a narrative to work from. We had a *thing:* We were best friends who worked together and lived in the same building and could banter with the best of them, our conversational acrobatics having been honed during years of being behind the line together. Later, it became clear that this was part of what made us attractive to producers, too, because they also had to land on stories for all the contestants on the show: Even in the absence of scripts, documentary and reality TV rely on "character-driven" storytelling. But at the time, we only knew that we could use it to our advantage.

We invited our "viewers" into our building for a tour, volleyed some clever dialogue back and forth, and tried to lay on the charm. It was all very DIY, but I did devote some resources to wardrobe. I had one pair of True Religion jeans—the kind with the horseshoe stitching on the back pockets—which I paired with an American Apparel V-neck T-shirt and slip-on shoes. I was going for cool but comfortable and felt confident in that outfit.

When it was polished and complete (and obviously Oscar-worthy), we submitted the video along with the rest of the requested materials. When you're deciding whether someone can not only handle a televised cooking competition but also carry a compelling enough storyline to keep viewers invested—and on top of that, be emotionally stable enough to live in a house with seventeen strangers—there is a *lot* of due diligence to be carried out. That included everything from asking for family photos (speaking to personality and backstory) and menu samples (speaking to skill and competency) to conducting psych evaluations (speaking to stability and providing general evidence that you're not totally unhinged). I remember pulling all this together and stuffing pages into manila envelopes to send to LA—a faraway land to which I'd never been—and envisioning the fancy TV executives awaiting them on the other side.

But I wouldn't have to use my imagination for very long. Steph and I soon found out that our little film and submission packet had earned us a ticket to the next phase—and a boarding pass to the other side of the country.

⸻

These days, airports have become like second homes to me. Some I've been through so many times that I can practically navigate from Hudson News to the gate with my eyes closed and have a mental catalog of where to find my favorite travel snacks in every terminal, especially the kiosks that sell Bugles and candy—gummy, chewy, fruity, and sour. But in 2012, at twenty-eight years old, despite my original plans to be a jet-setting, power suit–wearing business lesbian, I hadn't traveled much beyond visits to see my parents in Michigan and some trips to Disney World as a kid.

And while this wasn't my first-ever plane ride, it was the first time I was handed a free ticket and had a ride extended to me entirely on the merit of my own accomplishments, in recognition of my skill. Regardless of where or how it all went on the other side, I was astonished. When you signed up to be a cook in the early aughts, perks like free trips were few and far between. Maybe you got enlisted to do a travel gig somewhere, but this kind of thing was unfathomable to me back in my days at Le Cordon Bleu.

Steph and I took the journey together, wide-eyed and lightly packed for the brief trip. And although to a degree I understood that this next step indicated a level of seriousness in the vetting process— that the show probably wasn't flying just anyone three thousand miles for a casual chat—I didn't feel super nervous, because it still didn't feel real. I think fear and nerves really come into play when you so clearly, so deeply want something. When you become attached to an outcome without the promise of it. When there's a threat that you may not get it for reasons beyond your control, or that you could somehow do something that will cause you to lose it. I was somewhat at ease because I didn't have those expectations or hopes; I was simply trying something new.

That said, as I have with everything I've done in my life, I committed to it with focus and intention. I believe that's why, to this day, I can't really tell you much about that LA trip. I don't remember my first impressions of the city; can't recall the moment I saw the Hollywood sign (or *if* I saw the Hollywood sign); don't remember any cool culinary experience that informed my cooking down the line. To my memory, there was no aha moment of personal growth—or even an extravagant room service order on the company's dime. I was there with one purpose: to attend our scheduled meetings.

I do vaguely remember the production company's offices, though, which were situated in a converted warehouse and populated by a *lot* of brown things. Brown furniture, including a brown desk, a brown carpet, brown accents—it was not unlike my therapist's office from years before, except with an entirely different, creative energy. After I arrived, there were a few hours of casual conversation with casting folks followed by an in-person psych evaluation. The agenda was very similar to what I'd already provided via paperwork from afar but in greater depth and face-to-face.

I didn't know back then exactly what they were looking for, so even if I wanted to, it wasn't like I could put on airs or play a part in the hope that I could persuade them to select me. I had no insight, and in a way, that ignorance was comforting. I wasn't trying to live up to or be a TV-ready version of Kristen. I could only be me. In retrospect, though, I see what was working in my favor. I do believe the package deal of Steph and me made a difference. The built-in buddy comedy would become a clear focus of the first episode. I did worry that my relative lack of experience on paper—my résumé was filled mostly with cooking jobs—might be a strike against me, because the show was typically populated by professional chefs and not cooks or up-and-comers. (Although it might have been a benefit in the long run; what a cook does bring to the table is the ability to execute quickly and accurately, and that was something for which I was well conditioned.) I still believe there was a chance I might have been passed over based on my résumé alone, and it wasn't until years later that I learned from some of the folks in casting that Barbara had advocated for me, telling producers that she really believed I could win.

Of course, there's no secret formula for being chosen, even with a strong endorsement. Some people bring deeply honed skills or have a stellar combination of personality and talent. Some come with remarkable backstories or grand hopes for the future. These days, given the legacy of the show and its winners, there are people for whom simply being selected at all fulfills a lifelong dream.

I left LA not knowing where I'd fall in the overall consideration for season 10. But when Steph and I headed back to LAX, I felt good about the conversations I'd had, the way I'd presented on behalf of my mentor and myself. I'd at least accomplished what I'd come to do.

And although the trip was very much a focused one and at no point did Steph and I have the time or the interest in boarding a celebrity sightseeing bus, we did have one very Hollywood moment: As we stood in the security line en route to the plane that would carry us back to Boston, a siren began to sound. The blaring and flashing lights were frightening and confusing, but we were told to remain calm and be patient as the situation was resolved. Since we were in the economy line (this was long before I'd have TSA Pre-Check or any kind of priority boarding privileges), I wasn't about to get out of the queue and lose my spot.

Steph had already passed through and was on the gate side, so we made eye contact from afar, a telepathic check-in. Steph and I could communicate pretty well without words—the secret language of close friends who'd clocked untold hours together, a quirk that would prove useful in just a few short weeks. But in that moment, amid the chaos, Steph chose to telegraph an important message to me by another means. She was frantically mouthing something, clearly gesturing to someone a few spaces ahead of her. It took me a minute to realize what she was getting at, but as I watched her mime guitar playing and make some seriously overexaggerated facial expressions, I finally got the gist. There in line, not five feet from my friend, was the 1997 Best New Artist Grammy Award nominee and songstress Jewel. Steph was singing "Who Will Save Your Soul" silently from afar when the sirens finally ceased. To this day, I can't hear that song without losing my shit. While we boarded that plane not knowing exactly what to expect from our future, my very first trip to Los Angeles would go down in history as the day we shared a very dramatic airport experience with Jewel.

We told the Jewel story to our friends at Stir, but that was about all we could talk about from our trip and our lives at that moment. Because not long after we returned to Boston, we got the news that both of us were being invited to yet another city. This time it was Las Vegas, to film the very first episode of the new season of *Top Chef,* as official contestants.

Though I'd been somewhat ambivalent about the show up to that point, that call was the turning point. The moment I really started to feel something. This was it—the thing that was really going to shake things up, that was going to get me and Steph off that stoop and far from that plastic bag. It was a ripple through the routine—evidence of forward motion.

When I was a kid watching *Great Chefs of the World* from the comfort of my parents' Michigan kitchen, daydreaming about the foods of far-flung locales and coming up with my own concoction to mimic chocolate mousse, I wasn't considering what went on behind the scenes to create those dishes—who was buying and supplying the ingredients, proposing the menus, preparing the sets and lighting, and making sure the chefs showed up for their call time. To be fair, the budget and production quality of the program were probably closer to my audition tape than anything you'd find by flipping channels today, so they were probably working with *slightly* different conditions from those I experienced during my first brush with food TV.

The scene was a far cry from some coastal restaurant in 1980s France—like something I might have seen in an episode of *Great Chefs of the World*—when in the summer of 2012, Steph and I found ourselves sitting in silence on a sweltering concrete bench, smoking cigarettes in a strange place (Las Vegas) with a stranger, a producer on *Top Chef* named Neomi, who was essentially our chaperone. It was our first day in town, about a billion degrees, and not exactly the kind of weather in which you want to be doing anything, let alone filling your lungs with smoke. And yet this was the only way to get some not-so-fresh air. By that point, our phones had already been taken from us, and we'd been installed in our hotel rooms, to which we did not have the keys. If we needed food, it was delivered. And while casino revelers roamed the Strip below, we weren't permitted to interact with the outside world.

If this sounds intense, it's important that I share some of the behind-the-scenes context. This is how it has to be in order to create the show that viewers know and love. It prioritizes fairness among competitors by ensuring that everyone has the same resources across the board and won't be reaching out to others or researching advantages independently. It's critical to the show's authenticity as well, because exchanges between contestants—even ones who happen to be best friends—need to be caught on camera in order to capture the purest and most real emotion. It was also not a surprise to those of us who agreed to this endeavor—contestants know exactly what they're getting into when they sign on. For me, an introvert and a person who reaches full charge most efficiently when I'm left alone with my thoughts, stepping out for a smoke was a welcome break, but the isolation was honestly helpful to staying centered and focused on the task ahead.

The task, however, wasn't something for which I could truly prepare, because it was still totally unknown. Some viewers speculate that contestants are given a hint ahead of time as to what the challenges are so they can begin strategizing in advance, but that is not the case. The only instructions we were given was to dress in our chef whites and be ready for an early morning call time, so long after that last cigarette was stubbed out and I returned to my room, I climbed into my hotel bed with infinite possibilities swirling in my mind, attempting to somehow mentally prepare for all of them.

The next morning, we were collected and silently met the other contestants on our way to the challenge. At this point, there were only five of us, because similar qualifying competitions were taking place around the country. Through bleary eyes, we quietly took stock of one another. There were two men and three women, including me and Steph, and I remember noticing that some of the others had perfectly tailored, personalized coats with their names embroidered on the chest. Steph and I were coming from a large restaurant group that prioritized economy over style and provided free uniforms from a linen company—standard-issue black pants and oversize chef coats. This was before companies finally went beyond the then ubiquitous idea of a hulking male chef and began offering a variety of sizes for different bodies. It gave me a little flash of intimidation, but I reminded myself that culinary skill couldn't be communicated with a needle and thread.

And while I tried to stave off any distracting factors from our fellow challengers—fashion aside—there was no escaping the pang of fear that rippled through me when I realized for whom we were about to cook.

Like most Americans, I'd seen Emeril Lagasse on television probably a million times, enough to hear the expression *Bam!* reverberating in my head as soon as I saw his name on the marquee above the Table 10 restaurant in the Venetian hotel. Emeril was one of the first, beyond cooks and industry types, to generate popular interest in food; even my parents knew of and watched his show. But I was quickly learning that things move very fast in TV, so before anyone could even consider asking for an autograph and a selfie, we were lined up before him in the bar of his establishment.

"Welcome to my restaurant," Emeril said in his signature Louisiana–New England lilt, about to finally deliver the challenge we'd all been anticipating since we'd received our official call. Then he laid it out.

"Before I hire any chefs at my restaurant, they take a simple test," he said. Then he informed us that we would be subject to that same trial. He expected us to prepare a soup, because, he explained, as seemingly simple and humble as this dish can be, a soup can actually provide quite a bit of insight as to a chef's ability. I agreed with him then as I do now and saw the simplicity and beauty of this assignment. Soups can be layered and expressive and deceivingly difficult to execute.

"You have one hour," he concluded, and from there, what viewers see is contestants taking off like a shot to gather ingredients, knowing that the clock has begun ticking. What folks at home don't know is that this moment is a false start. We do indeed take off running, but there's an interruption during which the crew yells, "Cut!" This is not designed to be disingenuous. Rather, it's a very important pause in the action, during which the crew takes a few moments to give contestants the lay of the land and make sure everyone understands the rules. They want a fair game, informed contestants, and a safe environment. Once we were all clear and briefed, filming resumed, and we were back in the thick of it.

After we were unleashed for real, I did my "shopping." While Emeril was explaining the challenge, I had been listening and giving my full attention and respect, but my mind was already off and running. Back in my Sensing days, we served a spring pea soup—a dish I had prepared so many times it was basically in my bones. I decided I could do a variation on that theme, and when given the go-ahead, I quickly snapped up the peas, some crème fraîche, and bright yellow lemons. I had been thinking I'd gild the soup with some crabmeat, but then I saw the scallops and changed course, knowing that the seared shellfish would bring contrasting texture and a bit of complementary sweetness. Plus, the crab was canned, and although it was good quality and would have been convenient, the scallops required real cooking, which gave me a chance to demonstrate another layer of skill. I was feeling confident in how well I knew how to make this beautifully vibrant, complex green soup that showcased both ingredients and competence—plus a bit of my personality and style. I had unknowingly practiced for this moment so many times and could envision it all coming together—going through the paces—relying on muscle memory even if there were unexpected distractions.

What I didn't account for, because I had zero experience in television, was that we'd be expected to perform not only our culinary act but also one for the camera. It's not that producers were expecting us to dance while we cooked, and it wasn't an attempt to mess with our heads or disrupt our process, but the point was to make good television, not just good food. They didn't want a silent kitchen, because audiences at home couldn't read our minds, and that wouldn't give them a reason to stay tuned and thus provide us all a reason for being there in the first place.

Naturally, Steph and I set up our stations side by side. We hadn't yet spoken to each other since we arrived, and for all the things I wanted to discuss with my best friend, this wasn't exactly the ideal time. Still, the producers *did* want us to talk. They prompted conversations, encouraging us to ask each other the questions that viewers might want answered about what we were preparing, why and how—that sort of general commentary.

There is a world in which this might have thrown me off my game. Many cooks are creatures of habit, accustomed to repetition and reliable ritual. In fact, it's part of the appeal for a lot of people who—like me—prefer solitude and a relative distance from real social interaction. But Stir changed all that. There we cooked while we chatted with guests and answered questions, smiled, and made small talk and invited people to feel right at home in our company. I hadn't imagined a world in which that skill would serve me beyond those four walls—in part because I hadn't honestly looked that far into the future. But in that tight corridor in that Vegas kitchen, surrounded by stainless worktables and ranges, as I cooked beside my best friend and answered questions about what we were creating, for a few moments the only unfamiliar part was the weight of the microphone pack I was wearing.

Our dynamic as a pair was on full display at this point, too, and later, when footage of our cooking process would be cut with behind-the-scenes interviews, our storyline was almost entirely about who we were in relation to each other. In fact, one of the first things to ever come out of my mouth on national television was in reference to my friendship with Steph: "We bonded over the fact that we were getting boob sweat, because we were the only two girls on the line," I told cameras in an interview. (I regret nothing; it was the truth!) And when Emeril came through our area and commented on our friendship, asking whether we lived together, too, Steph clarified—only in the same building.

It was a fun framework for our story, but as I look back, the implication was evident. Particularly during that time period, it was common to assume or even just make "jokes" about two women who were close—they must be romantically involved. This undermines the validity not only of true gay couples but also of close female friendships. To be clear, as much as I have always loved Steph with all my heart—right from the early boob-sweat days—I have never been *in* love with Steph. I have always been one hundred thousand percent gay, right from the start of my life. This can be shocking to people who can't seem to wrap their minds around the fact that queer people can be friends with other people of the same sex without wanting to sleep with them.

Of course, Steph didn't know I was gay and was preemptively responding to that usual speculation in one of her behind-the-scenes interviews. She pointed out that people often mistook us for lesbians and emphasized that we were not. When I saw the clip later upon the airing of the show, I got the joke, but it also made me wince a little inside. Not because Steph did anything wrong. It was funny, and she was simply giving voice to what other people were probably wondering, but I didn't want to be part of perpetuating that idea. And beyond that, when you're closeted, you want to stay as far from any discourse about queerness as possible, as if simply having your name uttered in the same paragraph as the word *lesbian* will out you immediately, thus destroying your entire life.

Fortunately, there was far too much going on to focus on anyone's sexuality in depth. The dance of *Top Chef* and any show like it is to skillfully present enough of a backstory through which viewers can connect with contestants, which raises the emotional stakes when it comes time to see their cooking skills put to the test. It's a balance, and Emeril didn't linger long on our personal lives; he kept up the pace, moving on to what we were planning for our dish and then to the next contestants.

I worked hard and fast and with focus, and for all the chaos and uncertainty of the day, I found my groove at that stove, with my tools and ingredients and ideas. But no matter how lost I could get in the creative process, once we were through, reality returned, and I was reminded that we weren't in Boston anymore. Here in this flashy fine-dining oasis in a literal desert, our next step would be to face judgment.

In a restaurant environment, chefs are accustomed to letting their food speak for itself, but here, we were required to give a rundown to Emeril, explaining our respective dishes. I can't say I'd been dreading that moment because I had barely given it any real thought, focused as I was on executing. But as someone behind the scenes worked on photographing "beauties" of the dishes for the screen, and as we were being lined up in the kitchen for our evaluation, I felt the inevitability of someone's elimination. All I could do was trust in my dish and know that I'd done my best.

When the cameras rolled, Emeril began his tasting process, and the first up was Steph. And for all the intensity of the cook, the momentary concerns of the last hour—whether I was getting the perfect sear on my scallops, achieving the right level of acid in each bite, ensuring I had texture and depth in my soup—all those little details that, when added up, would define my performance, and even my own imminent presentation—what scared me most was that Steph and I might have different outcomes. Whether she or I would be going home, being split up in any configuration was terrifying, which is why I winced a little when, after an agonizing moment in which Emeril was sampling Steph's lobster-and-cauliflower soup, he pointed out that it was light on cauliflower flavor for his taste. I hoped it wouldn't be more than a minor note, and while I would have loved to have stopped the clock to reassure Steph in some way, he was quickly on to the next contestant, Tina.

I was third in line. When he arrived at my station, I felt ready. I knew my dish, my techniques, and my inspiration well. Being confident and prepared is the best way to combat anxiety, and while communicating socially has always been a challenge for me, expressing myself through food had become second nature. As I described my spring pea soup to Emeril, explaining the apples and crème fraîche and seared scallops, he and I might as well have been speaking our own language. The cameras and lights and producers could fade away, and in that moment, Emeril wasn't even a famous celebrity chef, just a fellow cook who understood the shared culinary vernacular. Even when he posed a probing question about my process—why I poached my lemons three times—I didn't falter in answering (to pull out the bitterness while preserving the lemon flavor). I knew my craft and my dish, the mechanics and the chemistry, and I knew he'd understand.

It was a relief to have my moment come and go without negative feedback from Emeril, but still, as he continued down the line, I knew I wasn't the only one fluent in this parlance. This group was varied and vetted and experienced. I could count on myself, but these other people were variables, wild cards, and I didn't know what they would bring to the table. Apparently, a chef named Jeffrey was also speaking Emeril's language. We all knew that on the other side of the wall, on the bar top in the dining room, there was a stack of folded chef's coats bearing the *Top Chef* logo waiting to be collected, each one a pass to the next step in the competition, which would take place in Seattle. And immediately after Emeril tasted his soup, Jeffrey was awarded a chef's coat on the spot—the only one of the five of us to have that honor so quickly.

When the kitchen tasting wrapped, the remaining four of us were ushered into the dining room, where—within full view of that stack of coats—we awaited the news. Emeril made it clear from the outset that there was no predetermined number of contestants he intended to send through to the next round. It was entirely up to his discretion—it could have been one or all four—and it was even more unsettling not to have that information.

The anticipation in those moments was every bit as dramatic and high-stakes as it is depicted on-screen. I was already exhausted from the trip, the emotional toll of the uncertainty, and the physical energy I used in preparing my dish. By that point, standing and waiting was almost as taxing as the stoveside acrobatics of the previous hour.

With the cameras rolling, Emeril began by addressing me and Steph together.

"One of you hit it out of the park, and one of you missed the mark," he told us, making it extremely evident that only one of us was staying. Then, after a beat that might as well have been an eternity (during which I recalled the way Steph's soup had been dinged for the lack of cauliflower flavor), both Steph and Tina were told that their time on *Top Chef* had come to an end.

Although I always knew this was a possibility, much like the rest of the experience, it didn't seem real. I couldn't wrap my mind around it in the lead-up, and I definitely didn't want to wrap my mind around it in reality. My heart plummeted, and in the split second before I could read between the lines and realize that this meant I would be among the contestants to advance—before I could feel any hint of excitement or apprehension or surprise for myself—I was crushed. I wanted more than anything to comfort Steph and talk her through it, the way I would have for anything else in her life. We weren't just a TV storyline; we were best friends. The truest kind, and our bond was, well, like a well-developed soup—layered and complex, representative of thoughtfulness, diligence, and an investment of time and love. But I didn't have a single second to process her feelings or my own, because just as quickly, my best friend was exiting the set and I was being addressed by Emeril again.

"Kristen," he said, "that was one of the best soups I've tasted in a long time."

To call the emotional whiplash intense is a severe understatement, and to say that I was experiencing competing emotions doesn't even come close to doing it justice. For so much of my life, I looked for external validation—in classrooms and sweltering kitchens, on catwalks, and even in dingy Chicago clubs. From friends and parents, teachers and bosses, and occasionally some less savory sources. Now there I was in this fancy restaurant in a flashy casino, surrounded by formidable competitors and cameras, with one of America's most beloved and respected chefs praising my food. My heart was already breaking for Steph, and it was swelling with pride at the same time. Under the most ideal circumstances, it was so much to parse, but no one was waiting for me to sort it all out, because, *right*—we were also making a TV show.

There was a quick round of congratulations, and before I knew it, I was being whisked off to conduct the interviews that would be cut in with the cooking footage. I sat in a chair with so many of my own questions running through my head while trying to answer the ones being posed to me. I needed to describe every move and decision I'd made during the cook, sometimes in several versions and tenses (i.e., "I'm *making* a spring pea soup"; "I've *made* a spring pea soup"; "I *will make* a spring pea soup").

At the time, it felt a little chaotic and redundant, but I've come to understand the importance of these repetitions. *Top Chef*, even in those days, was a well-oiled machine, and above all, it prioritized the experience of the viewers. This doesn't mean that anything was, or is, fake or contrived. I can assure you that the cook, the competition, the stakes—all of it is very real. Producers don't tell you what to say: They just understand that once the contestants and celebrity guests leave the set, it will be up to the production team and editors to cut together a compelling and clear story that authentically conveys what occurred on set to audiences at home. They need those who lived it to articulate the experience and reality, and for me, that reality was emotionally explosive and resulted in total sensory overload.

As I boarded the plane back to Boston the next day, shell-shocked and exhausted, exhilarated and mentally bewildered, I knew it'd be a while before my personal audience—my friends and loved ones—would see that footage and know what went on in that hotel. I had no idea how it would look on-screen and wasn't even positive I understood my own feelings yet. All I knew for sure was that whether or not we hit turbulence on the way back East, my world had been seriously shaken up.

———

There are times when I can manage my energy, especially when I can recognize how I'm feeling and am able to adjust accordingly, with intention and some control. But especially when I was younger, I experienced moments when there is a kind of dissonance between what I know I *want* to be feeling and the reality of my emotions. That sensation is involuntary and frustrating, and it can really, really suck.

After Emeril's decision, Steph and I didn't have a chance to have a debriefing session in Vegas. When we'd done our parts and it was time to go, Steph and I were picked up in a van for our airport transfer. We were silent then, but it's not like we were deliberately not talking to each other—being around producers and strangers just wasn't exactly the ideal scenario for a heart-to-heart. I don't recall much about our time in the airport together other than the fact that we were surrounded by people drinking and gambling at casino machines while we waited at the gate. It was a strange vibe that just added to the surreal nature of the whole experience—including the unusual awkwardness between my best friend and me. After we boarded, we were separated by a few rows on the flight home, and to be honest, that space was probably a good thing, because it gave us both a chance to process a bit.

We'd been so accustomed to talking about anything and everything, but back in Boston—at least initially—there was an obvious tension that we just couldn't sidestep. I knew Steph was happy for me in some way, because when the subject inevitably did come up, she told me so, and she always made it clear that she supported me.

But still, there was an unease that was so unusual for us. Nothing prepares you for your friendship to be tested on national television in such an unthinkable way, and there was a beat—probably not more than a few weeks, but it felt like longer at the time—during which Steph and I both faced this internal contention.

Fortunately, the layers of our relationship were deep. Our lives were intertwined in so many ways, and it's not like we could take a break from each other even if we'd wanted to. So we went back to work, went back to being neighbors, went back to sitting on the stoop smoking cigarettes. We both wanted the weirdness to go away so badly, but we couldn't control how quickly that would happen. In retrospect, it was probably the best thing for our relationship that we had to get right back to work and life, going through the motions as we would otherwise. It forced us to be patient and taught us an important lesson—that time would help soften those feelings when the foundation of a friendship is strong enough, and for perhaps the first time in my life, I wasn't worried about irreparable damage. I knew that at the end of the day, I'd have dropped everything if the situation called for it, and I knew Steph felt the same. We just had to figure out how to be with each other again, and eventually, almost without realizing it, we did. One day, it just started to feel normal again. It was evidence that time does heal, that some love *can* be unconditional. That it was possible for a person to love me even through her own pain and still want me in her life when the pain passed.

Before the end of the *Top Chef* season, Steph would be one of my biggest champions. In the meantime, she got another role: cover-story generator. I couldn't tell a soul where I was going, not even my parents, so Steph had to run interference at Stir, where she was the only one (besides Barbara and the management) who knew what was going on. As always, Steph got creative with her responses ("Kristen is becoming a Buddhist monk," "Kristen ran off with the circus," and "Kristen is training to go to space" among them).

I, on the other hand, got serious. I signed paperwork and had conversations with my employers. I filled a suitcase based on the packing list I'd been provided, which also included a list of forbidden items, from hard drugs and alcohol to cookbooks and recipes—in maybe the only instance when those items have appeared on the same list—even while knowing there was a chance I might not be gone very long. Now my feelings were clear: excitement among them but also fear—of being eliminated myself. I would later understand that there's no shame in being sent home. There can be countless reasons for this, and it's no reflection of personal value or even culinary skill in some cases. But more than anything, I feared embarrassing not only myself but also Barbara and everyone else whose opinions I valued. It was that fear of letting others down—the one I'd harbored so often over the years.

But there was another feeling related to the people in my life, too. This was one of solidarity and support, which comforted me and which I hadn't known to seek before. Although my journey with *Top Chef* was just beginning and although I'd be embarking on it alone, in the brief process up to that point, I'd come a very long way in understanding the importance of a network of people championing and encouraging me. I recognized that I was part of a powerful group of women, including Steph and Barbara, who truly believed in me and would stand by me. I can't say I initially signed up for the *Top Chef* experience with the intention of making space for more women on television or in the culinary world, but I did go forward hoping to make the women in my life proud by holding my own, and in doing so, in retrospect, I hope our combined efforts did in fact help make room for more women like us.

To be honest, I'm not even entirely sure what my hopes and dreams were for the show at that point; I only knew that I had set out seeking something new and different. And while I know now that I never could have been prepared for what this journey would enable me to accomplish, when that fasten-seat-belt sign lit up on the plane to Seattle, I knew for certain that the winds were about to seriously change.

10

've often heard that first impressions are everything. I have also heard that they're very hard to change—that once they're made it's nearly impossible to revise what we think of someone or what someone thinks of us.

Once I got back to Boston and resumed work at Stir, there was little of that pressure to present myself in a new environment. I had been there a couple of years by then, and although I met other cooks and guests regularly, the core people in my life were recurring characters. I knew them, and they knew me. And aside from that moment when national audiences back in Las Vegas heard my brief dissertation on boob sweat, it had been a long time since I'd had to think much about first impressions.

Naturally, anticipating the next stage of competition in Seattle, I had nerves about everything from the culinary execution to the social exchanges, none of which I could plan or prepare for. That said, not once after grabbing that coat off Emeril's bar in Vegas did I reconsider. One thing about me has always been true: When I commit to something, I'm in it, and I'm going to see it through. Particularly when I feel I'm doing it for someone else. In this case, it was for

Barbara, for Steph, and for the people who put me up and held me up. I was not about to let them down.

Like anyone going into a competition show, I worried about being the first to go home from the moment I signed on. No one wants to be told to pack her bags out of the gate, but I buried that fear as I loaded my luggage into a van at the Seattle airport, where a production assistant was waiting to whisk me off and where we'd be put up in a hotel in town for the first few days before the competition started. I can't say it was the swankiest place, but it still felt like five-star treatment.

Although there had been many steps involved in getting there, it really all happened so fast. One day I was sitting with Steph on our stoop, and the next I was being fitted for my very own custom chef's coat branded with the show's logo.

There were a lot of fun and novel elements to this experience, and perks I never considered as a cook or chef, but when wardrobe came to my room to take my measurements, there was a distinct feeling of something close to luxury. In those days, finding chef's coats for women was almost impossible, and I was always swimming in the uniforms at Stir. Of course, the motivation wasn't just to provide a high-end experience for contestants; it was also to make sure we didn't look schlubby on television. But still, I thought back to my school days—my baggy pants, my friends giving me a makeover, my own cycling through styles trying to find something comfortable. Having a tailor-made piece of clothing felt so significant, no matter the reason.

This was the kind of prep that took place during the first few days in Seattle, before we officially started filming the show. We were placed in our respective hotel rooms, separate from the other contestants, where we wouldn't run into or interact with one another.

Periodically, producers showed up to conduct checks: Each contestant is allowed to bring a specified number of knives and smallwares and specialty food items, a stipulation intended to ensure a level playing field. They also check suitcases for contraband and anything that might be a danger or liability when you're living with seventeen other people. There were some preshow interviews as well, during which they asked about my family and my personal history, whether I believed I could win, and how I was feeling in general, all of which would be dropped in to add depth to the overall story. And all this takes place while you sit waiting in anticipation for the first challenge, before you meet your fellow contestants, before you really get started. It's a waiting game, with time-outs to sit with this decision you've made, to wonder and speculate what might be coming and whether you're up for it. At times, filming *Top Chef* is as much an exercise in patience as it is in urgency.

In those quiet moments early on, maybe there were people who wished they'd chosen another path or could opt out. But I was strapped in and ready for it, and with my brand-new perfectly tailored chef's coat, I was prepared to make an impression.

I always remembered the first day of school as electric. Even when I didn't want summer break to end, it was hard to deny the energy of it all, the vibrant sensation of nerves-slash-excitement, whether that was from seeing new and familiar faces, getting to know teachers, or sensing the promise of learning and being challenged to prove myself.

That first day on set in Seattle had that energy. Following a few days in our respective hotels, we were transported to a location, miked up, and finally—after much buildup and time spent in relative solitude—released into a large room lined with shiny new ovens and gleaming stainless prep tables. This would be the scene of our initial Quickfire Challenge.

Season 10 had eighteen chefs—a large group for the show (by comparison, season 21 had sixteen)—and there were a *lot* of personalities. It was like those first-day-of-school situations: It seems that no matter the age or grade or background or ability, some group dynamics never change. A pecking order is quickly and almost imperceptibly established, although an observer can usually see immediately who will play which role and what everyone is hoping to present as part of their identity. It's a fresh start for some, a chance to invent or reinvent themselves in front of a new cohort, the crew, and the audiences at home. The extroverts always take center stage, finding one another and feeling out the crowd. Those people may seem intimidating at first, but their confidence can be misleading, sometimes falsely indicating skill or experience when in fact it's a facade.

I don't claim to be a flawless judge of character (in fact, my own initial reads of a few fellow contestants turned out to be quite off), but I can smell ego a mile away. I think this is an ability born from my own bluster during my younger days, when I tried to be something I wasn't—or something I wasn't *yet,* at least. And I knew ego could be an Achilles heel in competitions like this, so I was on alert for it. That said, I wasn't trying that hard to identify the strengths and weaknesses of my fellow chefs or build a mental dossier of my opposition. But I do think my nature as an introvert is to hang back and take note, let everyone else jockey for a spot, show themselves either through how they behave or what they choose to express out loud. So while everyone milled about, all wearing the same tailored coats but trying to differentiate themselves in some way, going through the small-talk motions and working out their own nervous energy, I mostly listened. Then, after a few minutes of this very familiar getting-to-know-you circus, a ringleader was introduced.

At the time, I had very little knowledge of Padma Lakshmi beyond *Top Chef.* Not only was my engagement with the show fairly limited before my auditions began, but my pop culture awareness in general was also pretty low, because I had very little time for and interest in such things.

What I did know was that Padma represented an element of the show that scared me most of all: judgment.

It became clear upon her arrival that playtime was over and we were about to get down to business. We were instructed to line up and look alive. Some contestants made an effort to position themselves closer to Padma or the cameras, whether in the hope of more screen time or attention from the judges or simply for their own personal reasons, but I mostly tried to blend in, not unlike the way I had at so many points in my life: I wanted to avoid that spotlight, to select positions from which I'd be less likely to invite judgment and criticism. In retrospect, my approach not only put a desirable distance between me and the powers that be, it also allowed me a vantage point from which I could survey the others.

Padma explained our challenge, a seafood-based task to "highlight local shellfish," for which we'd organize ourselves into teams and ultimately be evaluated by three contestants from previous seasons. We'd later find out that these chefs would join us as competitors—a surprise unveiled after they concluded their judging.

Top Chef is ultimately an every-person-for-themselves exercise, but there are also moments when—for logistical reasons—the group is organized into teams for a challenge, and particularly because of the sheer number of contestants that season, it's unsurprising that we started out with this format. Some chefs bristle at the idea of teams, just as many students don't like a group project: Maybe they don't like to share ideas or responsibility, or they want the glory for themselves should it come. But I appreciated it. At least in getting started, there was comfort in being able to disappear a bit within a group. It was a welcome way to ease into what had quickly gone from a vague invitation from my boss back in Boston to a full-blown but totally unbelievable thing.

In retrospect, the reality of the show snuck up on me. Even though the process came together relatively quickly, in a matter of months, it was still a bit of a slow build. I never had the shock of being thrown in cold water, and I was able to warm up to each level, from filming an audition tape in our apartment building to having conversations in Los Angeles and even cooking for Emeril.

Still, standing in that room, discussing with my new team members how to prepare our geoduck, knowing that Padma and the guest judges would be delivering feedback imminently, and surrounded by rolling cameras, I suddenly knew there was no turning back. Even if I lost my nerve and wanted to jump ship, that decision would be captured and documented and broadcast. Not that the thought really crossed my mind; I was 110 percent dedicated to the challenge. And so I focused on what was in front of me in that moment, as I had learned to do so many times in my life and career, taking it step by step, giving each ingredient my attention, layering one flavor over another and another. I'd learned by then that doing my best with individual details, building upon what I had learned and done rather than being distracted by the big picture—whether I was peeling celery as a snack for Barbara or cooking on a national TV show—was a personal strategy for winning.

At various times in my life, I'd come to appreciate living with or near other people. I'd lived happily with Scott for several years, and Steph and I loved having the common experience in our efficiency building, so I was no stranger to being a roommate, being a neighbor, and cohabiting. But even the bizarre circumstances of the Heartbreak Hotel days—with an ex-boyfriend, his best friend, and my own best friend under the roof of one condo—couldn't have prepared me for the living conditions of *Top Chef*. In fact, I'd venture to say that very few people have experienced, or will ever experience, anything quite like it.

The living space alone was worth writing home about: a stunning penthouse on the top floor of a Seattle hotel with a view of the Space Needle and the sparkling city below. The version of Kristen from back in Chicago who was living for that high-rise life and its implications of success, as well as the one who balked at the first Boston apartments back in the day, would have died to see the place.

But of course, what was truly unique was the roommate situation. Eighteen people is more people than a football team puts on the field at any given time. It is more than occupy some college classrooms. And there were a *lot* of cooks in that kitchen, or the penthouse, as it were. On that first day, when we all were finally let loose to have some conversations without the expectation of cooking and competing (at least not formally), it was evident that, as we would in a restaurant, we'd all play different roles.

With the first Quickfire Challenge behind us (my team landed firmly in the middle—which I counted as a win), we were running on a ton of excitement and adrenaline. We'd successfully made it through our first day of cooking, received the details and done our grocery shopping for the challenge the following day. The next major step was to get settled.

Much as I had hung back in the room when Padma arrived, I maintained a measured approach when we got to the penthouse. There were a handful of contestants who took off running, to explore, to pick out a room they felt was best for whatever reason. I think everyone had different criteria for what they considered a prime spot—maybe a view or proximity to a bathroom or the kitchen. But I wasn't the type to fight for a particular place; I figured each would have its pros and cons, and I'd learn to live with whatever spot became mine.

What I wound up with was a room with three other women, including Brooke Williamson. I could speculate whether we became friends because we were roommates or whether we became roommates because our similar energy and approach drew us to the same space, but today, I believe things happen as they're meant to, for a reason. Then, though, I just saw an open bed among many others being snapped up. I dropped my stuff and staked my claim. Then I meandered around the space, taking it all in, and stepped out onto the balcony to bask in the spectacular view. I briefly thought about this unfathomable thing that was happening to me with the limited time and brain space I had to dedicate to such reflection, then joined a group of contestants in the kitchen.

While I remember everyone to a degree, the high-pressure environment combined with the passage of time has edited down some of the details. But I do remember a few who stood out. There was Bart, who earlier in the day instructed Padma to "Google me" if she wanted further information about his background. And while I'd later come to consider Bart to be a really lovely person, I initially bristled at what came off as intense arrogance.

On the other hand, there was Jeffrey. He'd been the first to receive a chef's coat in Vegas, so I knew a bit about him by the time we got to the house. I did not know, however, that he was gay and engaged to be married to a man. This was information that emerged when someone asked about the ring on his finger that first day, then referred to his partner as "she." In a most unassuming and casual but poised kind of way, Jeffrey corrected the pronoun to "he" in between bites of his taco. And just like that, Jeffrey was an out gay man on national television.

I admired this so much about Jeffrey. It reminded me of how I felt about Matty and Daniel back in Boston and Vinny in Chicago. And while he didn't last long on the show, Jeffrey made a very powerful and lasting impression on me.

So arrogance and admiration—those were the qualities and reactions I either detected or felt and that made someone stand out and stick with me in those first moments. And while somewhere deep inside I wished to be less like Bart and more like Jeffrey, to be humble and honest yet confident and self-assured, I was still far from ready to be a representative of the gay community.

I would later come to understand so much more about television and how it's made, how stories are captured and told, but I was already aware from my brief stint in Las Vegas that producers can only work with what you give them. At times, I hear people object to their own portrayals, blaming their dissatisfaction on manipulative or even devious editing. But the reality is that no one can make you say or do something that doesn't align with how you want to be seen or how you see yourself. It's up to you what show you put on.

Being closeted for so long, I already understood how to draw attention toward or away from certain parts of myself and rely on some less-than-authentic behavior to prevent others from questioning or really seeing me. These were self-preservation strategies I'd relied on through my time in Chicago and even Boston, to a degree. And the thing is, no matter what the setting or intention of a gathering, human beings can be very interested in one another's love lives. Jeffrey wasn't the only one fielding questions about this subject, and when I recognized how many discussions centered around relationship status, I again leaned on the tried-and-true strategy of diversion.

An early episode features a scene in which Stefan—a contestant brought back from an earlier season to compete—rubs my feet on the balcony. As it frequently does in situations where lots of people are together under intense circumstances, little flirtations developed among some of the contestants, and one of them was between Stefan and me. When I realized that the show's producers had caught on, I not only allowed them to follow the storyline, I also provided the fodder. It didn't go any further than some well-placed scenes for the camera, but as foreign as the *Top Chef* competition was in the grand scheme of things, this was a game I knew how to play.

If I'd been itching for action back in Boston, *Top Chef* presented it relentlessly. From the moment you wake up to the time your head hits the pillow, you are *on*. On those early seasons, you're either cooking or doing interviews—or both—and there are very few occasions when you're totally free. Even in those moments, it's not as if the cameras stop, so true downtime is basically nonexistent.

For any human, this can be exhausting, to say the least. For an introvert like me, it is depleting in the extreme. I had to find my routines, little pockets of time during which I could be and feel myself.

Somehow I had the foresight to bring along a watch with an alarm clock built in, and rather than allowing the cameras to wake me, I set it for super early in the morning (since call time was usually a moving target) to make sure I could get up on my own terms before the crew arrived.

I used my mornings to recharge. Sitting on that balcony in the predawn light, quietly smoking a cigarette and taking in the view of Seattle—the snowcapped mountains in the distance, the real-world sights and sounds of the city below—was the closest I came to meditation, a sense of peace, for the entire six weeks I was there. And although I can't imagine going through that process now, it did give me a grounding sense of control, allowed me to mitigate anxiety and the risk of not feeling like my best self, which would have been a distraction.

Still, as hyperscheduled and chaotic as the whole thing was, *Top Chef* actually provided me with unexpected relief. I didn't have to plan a single thing about my life, and never once was I obligated to sort through logistics—the processes that always dominated my brain back in the real world. I didn't have to do anything but cook. That removal of day-to-day pressures was so totally unique, so surprisingly wondrous, that to this day I can't say I've experienced anything like it.

Somehow we even managed to find a groove in the thick of the competition. Despite the fact that the challenges were always changing, the day-in, day-out of it all was "rinse and repeat." Although the production crew hoped we might have big family meals and cook at the penthouse, absolutely no one was interested in getting behind the stove after a long day of grueling competition. Instead, we requested certain tools and ingredients that made it borderline effortless to feed ourselves and find our little comforts. The show had a partnership with a frozen-food company, so the microwave was in frequent rotation, and I distinctly remember jars of dill pickles being a hit among many in the house (some things are just universal). Another contestant, Sheldon, had asked for a rice cooker, and I was grateful, because I spent many so-called mealtimes simply eating rice and kimchi, trying to decompress.

I'd decided early on to abstain from drinking (not a difficult decision, given that I'd never been huge on booze outside of those Chicago days), so my biggest hurdle was just trying to catch some shut-eye. That was sometimes as difficult as the daily challenges themselves, because the night owls of the house stayed up attempting to quiet their own adrenaline overloads by drinking and loudly debriefing.

Even though there are a lot of people around you at all times, *Top Chef* is isolating in so many ways. It's not like I could have called up Steph or my parents and told them about my day. It is, however, very bonding for the people in that bubble. The only humans you see or talk to have something to do with the show. Even when personalities clash or emotions run high—which they absolutely do—there's an appreciation of that shared experience, and you find your people. For me, my roommate Brooke was one of them. We both preferred snippets of quiet and solitude to partying in the evenings, which provided the basis for a friendship that endures today.

And although there were routines during filming, there were also plenty of opportunities for excitement, and I had some highs of my own. For all that was ambiguous about the show, money was something that barely crossed my mind when I signed on. It was an element discussed during every challenge, and the prize money for the winner always dangled in the distance, but cash remained more of an abstraction or idea—until the first time I won some.

It was the fourth challenge that—thanks to some double-cooked mushrooms, a side dish for which I may still be best known today—I took home $10,000. I'd never seen that kind of money in a single payout before and could never have dreamed of such a thing as a cook.

As I look back, the cultural implication that the show was funded well enough to bestow such awards throughout the season was evidence of its popularity and evidence that the industry I'd chosen—for completely different reasons—was one in which the general public had begun taking a serious interest. I can't sit here and say I understood the implication of that interest and what it meant for myself and my peers, in terms of what would be possible for our futures far beyond food and cooking, but it is evident to me in retrospect that there was a major sea change in the air, building upon the success of the Food Network and so-called celebrity chefs.

In that moment, I certainly did not see myself in such a category, nor did I have any grand plans for those dollars beyond the possibility of paying down some student loans. The win was, more than anything, a major boost and a validation—the kind I'd thrived on since way back in my culinary school days. And most of all, in the *Top Chef* bubble I was living in, it meant another small step forward.

As unrelatable as a competitive reality television show can be, these series resonate because of some universal themes—among them, a fear of instability. We all worry whether we'll have a home, a job, our health; if we'll be able to be surrounded by loved ones during our life. The nature of the competition (and really any high-stakes storytelling; think *The Hunger Games*) is that you're 99 percent guaranteed to *not* "survive." It makes for great TV, but it's exhausting to live with that underlying worry, and at the end of every episode, there are contestants who for various reasons face the idea that they may have to be one of the ones to pack their knives and go home. Sometimes, it really is the end of the road for them. Others are spared and live to see another geoduck.

Fortunately, I never had to deal with this stress—not a single time was I in the bottom group of challengers on the chopping block—until the day I was actually eliminated. The moment was fraught and came at the end of an extremely intense day during which we essentially "built" a restaurant from scratch, and because I'd won a previous challenge, I was put in charge of that effort. I can spare you the gory details (bouillabaisse and big personalities were involved), but needless to say, I was disappointed. It was a moment, though, when my own reaction surprised me a bit. I believed I had done my best—I was thoughtful and worked hard; I planned as well as one could under the circumstances, and I considered my performance both behind the stove and in collaboration with my fellow contestants to have been conducted with integrity. I was at peace, and the belief that I'd done everything in my power saved me from an intense state of despair—and that's a lesson I carry with me today and attempt to impress on younger cooks.

I was also saved in a way through the extended universe of the show. I was given a shot at redemption through *Last Chance Kitchen*—a web series extension in which eliminated challengers face off in head-to-head, all-or-nothing rounds with other eliminated chefs who are also vying to get back into the competition. One loss was all it took to be out. This was a gauntlet of its own, because I had to compete in two rounds before leaving Seattle as well as another two rounds in Alaska (where the show moved on after I was eliminated) and would have to later participate in one last round, months later, in Los Angeles, where the show would ultimately hold the finale. That last round would determine whether I would return to the show. And although there was so much riding on these challenges, it was all actually much less stressful for me in a way. *Last Chance Kitchen* had a smaller, more contained production footprint, with fewer cameras and crew and without the chaos of a dozen or so other chefs circling me. I was cooking only for Tom Colicchio, so it was much calmer and less overwhelming despite the high stakes.

For a number of reasons, the show is no longer filmed this way, but at the time, those of us who still had a shot at the title entered into a seven-month purgatory waiting to film the finale. This means that by the time I headed home from Alaska after the second-to-last round of *Last Chance Kitchen,* I had no guarantees of a win, but I at least secured a chance to continue to compete. In the meantime, it was back to Boston.

This meant a temporary return to the real world—back to our old routines and our respective jobs, which for me meant reuniting with Steph and Barbara and the team at Stir. The reentry was strange, coming as I was from a parallel universe that no one could possibly understand even if I explained every detail. And while I had to readjust to the logistics and nagging routine of real life, the physical reprieve from the grind of shooting was very welcome.

I was still under a legal obligation to keep the outcome (as far as I knew it) under wraps, but I could finally have some conversations with family and friends about where I'd been, because the show began airing during the hiatus. My parents' reaction boiled down to: *I knew it!* (And apparently my aunt and uncle had guessed.) But they were no less proud and congratulatory, as they have been my whole life. I could have been informing them that I got a great night's sleep or won a national television competition, and their reaction would have been the same. My joy is their joy, no matter the source.

And then, of course, there was an opportunity to share the experience with my community, the one that helped me get to Seattle in the first place. Once episodes began dropping, Barbara made a point of hosting beautiful, convivial viewing parties. Every week, she invited employees and friends who were closest to me into her home, and we all sat around watching the challenges unfold, with the sole purpose of rallying around me. For so long in my life, I'd hated being the center of attention. I did everything I could to avoid it. But for the first time, the focus on me was for something solidly, indisputably positive. I wasn't fearful of judgment or criticism from the people in the room. Instead, I felt seen and supported and loved. Plus, my participation in the show gave everyone a good reason to get together regardless of how I performed, and that alone filled me with a sense of pride. I observed this totally different group—their smiles and laughter; the way they cheered and became so invested in every scene and story; the way they were sharing a moment together regardless of my role—and those moments made every stressful interaction and sleepless night worth it.

During those initial screenings, right up until my elimination episode, I also didn't have to worry about letting anyone down. I had the sneak peek, the behind-the-scenes blow-by-blow in my mind. I knew I was going to make it at the end of those episodes—and in some cases, I knew that I'd totally crush it, which made everyone so excited and proud. The anxiety only set in toward the end, when everyone began speculating.

"You're going to win, Kristen, I know it," people would say, and I could smile and play coy, informing them that I couldn't divulge a thing. The reality was that even I didn't know how it was going to shake out—and I couldn't let them in on my own uncertainty, either.

But that limbo period was an unexpected gift in some ways. It provided moments in which to enjoy my accomplishments in a very pure way, without the crushing fear of failure. I worried a lot less about whether I'd beat my fellow contestants in Los Angeles when I was sharing glasses of champagne with my closest friends in Barbara's home. And it allowed me to see that no matter what happened, I was surrounded by people who believed in me and loved me, regardless of any title. It was a message I sometimes wish a younger version of me could have received, although I'm not sure she would have been ready to accept it without the lived experience. But those are the moments I try to hold on to in life so I can revisit them when I'm knocked down or feel low. For all the events the brain has to consolidate over the years, uplifting memories deserve all the mental real estate we can spare.

I was able to enjoy recognition from other sources as well. Diners who watched the show came into Stir to cheer me on and congratulate me—some regulars I knew well and others who had just seen me on TV and decided to come for dinner. I was honored to have the backing of people like Barbara and my parents—the ones I hoped to make proud—and this extended community was a delightful surprise.

But the most moving and ultimately life-changing sources of support were the messages I began receiving from Asian Americans and adoptees thanking me for representing them on TV. These were communities I never really sought out, ones to which I never realized I belonged, but they considered me their own. Before *Top Chef,* I didn't realize the impact of representation, not just for the audiences who needed to see themselves on-screen but also for those doing the representing. I'd so often craved a sense of acceptance and belonging in my life, and this was the first time I recognized that I could find it in ways that had not occurred to me before. I decided then that this was only the beginning of my engagement with these groups and these parts of myself going forward.

It was a heartwarming and overwhelming time, and in those interim months, I could almost have forgotten that there was more to come with the show, because as far as I was concerned, I could already consider the whole thing a win.

But of course, there *was* still more. I just had no idea how much.

There are so many ways to define success. It can be evident in simple and unexpected ways—in delighting your doorman with a frangipane pear tart or achieving the perfect sear on a scallop for your spring pea soup. Or it can be in simple and unexpected ways, like typing the words *executive chef* on your résumé.

Early on, during that first Quickfire Challenge on day one, I listened to fellow contestants talk about their accomplishments and accolades, and I grappled with my own personal value. I had none of those credits. I was a cook, and in my mind the most notable thing about me was whom I worked for. But week after week on the show, I dedicated myself and focused and endured. After a little while, I started to realize that my devotion and perseverance had value, too, not just my culinary ability or the entries on my CV.

I had qualities—my commitment to efficiency and order, the self-awareness of what I needed to do to be my best self—that helped me excel. My dedication and my being hyperfocused on what was in front of me helped me take one step at a time. I ended up approaching many of the challenges with a similar mentality, and in retrospect, I think it served me well. When I could surprise judges by creating a memorable dish from what others left behind, it seemed like I was recognized for creativity and resourcefulness.

I had brought some of those qualities with me to *Top Chef* and took a lot of new ones away with me. The show helped me confront some of the social anxieties I'd struggled with all my life, because I simply had no choice but to face them and learn to manage them. It helped me make friends and find ways to interact with others under unimaginable pressure in extraordinary circumstances. It forced me to relinquish some control—to accept, to collaborate, and at times even to delegate. And seeing yourself on television definitely has some surreal moments and can make you question certain things (i.e., *Is that how my voice sounds in real life?*), but overall, I was comfortable with how I was portrayed, because the way I came across on that screen really *was* me. The show helped me appreciate some of my own features after I'd seen them reflected in this new way.

Eventually, the time came to complete the journey, and I headed off to Los Angeles for the second time in my life. There I'd have to compete in a final round of *Last Chance Kitchen*. This was the one last step before the semifinals. If I won, I'd be reintegrated back into the primary show, as if merging back onto the highway after a brief detour. Still, although the stakes were higher than the Space Needle back in Seattle, I knew that no matter what happened, I was returning to friends and family and a full life back in Boston. With my people in mind, I took it one ingredient, one breath at a time, and when I cleared that hurdle and earned my way back onto the main stage, I was prepared to stand on it proudly front and center.

With my final *Last Chance Kitchen* win, I competed first against Sheldon and Brooke in a semifinal, then against Brooke in the finale after Sheldon's elimination—in yet another *Top Chef* face-off with a friend. It was tough, to say the least. Brooke was talented and thoughtful and a true competitor, and it was by no means a sure bet that I'd beat her. But I put my head down and did my best, summoning everything I'd learned—in school, on the line, at Stir, and in life. It took every ounce of skill I had, and it was a close match that could have easily gone either way. But somehow, thanks to combinations of hazelnuts and chicken liver mousse, celery root puree and bone marrow, red snapper with leeks and tarragon, I impressed the judges. I created dishes that represented me and my journey, and I worked with a level of calm among chaos that I couldn't have imagined just a few months before. And—spoiler alert—I *won.*

The moment I heard the words "Kristen, you are Top Chef," I was overcome. It was a tidal wave of emotion—not to mention adrenaline—and after trying to keep the ship steady and on course during the competition, I let it wash over me.

This was the culmination of so much work, so many small details and sleepless nights—not only in those six weeks of competition and seven months of hiatus but also over the course of my life to that point. It was layer upon layer of intention, from my foundations back in Michigan to the personal and professional trials in Chicago and Boston. I was buoyed by the love and support provided by those around me, all of whom had demonstrated that they cared for me in so many ways, big and small, personally and professionally. I was ecstatic, elated, overwhelmed, and overjoyed to have earned this honor, and even more so to share it with those people—some of whom were right there in the crowd that night.

But the win was about so much more than a title or the prizes (although the $125,000 was not nothing) or even the professional and culinary growth that came out of the competition. Before I had set foot on that LA-bound plane after the break in Boston, and before I ever went head-to-head with Brooke, the experience had already reframed my idea of success.

Top Chef was obviously a turning point for me, but maybe not always in the ways that I expected or that others might imagine. My whole life, I'd been judging and editing myself, trying to create and control my own narrative and write my own story. On the show, I was subject to all kinds of judges—professionals and peers, the cold gaze of the camera, and, of course, the public eye, and I was surprised at times to glimpse the positive lens through which others saw me. I was paid compliments and given encouragement and constructive criticism—not to mention, for the first time in my life, real money. The show taught me so much about the person I was as well as the one the world perceived me to be. With those lessons, plus the title under my belt, I would be stronger, bolder, and more self-assured in my next steps.

But maybe most important, I recognized for the first time in my life that I was enough. Not just as a chef but also as a person—a *good* and worthy person. I started out doing the show for others. For Barbara, for my friends and family. I was doing it for them every step of the way, right up until the moment I won. Now, looking back, I know that I did it for me. And after so many years spent questioning my value in the world, wondering whether I really deserved good things—or anything, for that matter—I was able to stop, to reflect, and to feel it. I was able to think and to tell myself, *I am enough.*

Prior to the competition, I thought I knew who I was, but this? This was a totally new experience. And while I'd have to go back to the routines of reality—my reality, without cameras or judgment but with all its messy real-world challenges—having that information would change everything.

11

Every day, people from every corner of the world go about their lives in search of joy. They look for it in ways big and small—by taking up a hobby such as cooking, by listening to a self-help podcast, or by just enjoying the simple things in life, like the spectacular colors of a butterfly's wings, Sunkist Fruit Gems, or a beautiful sunrise. And, of course, they look for it in relationships with others. Joy is not always easy to find, especially since it's not always easy to define, but it doesn't stop humans from trying to experience it.

I'm very fortunate to have known joy early and often in my life. As a child, I felt it when my dad wrapped me up in warm sheets on laundry day and in high school when I was twisting pretzels and serving mall customers. I felt it in culinary school when I received praise in exchange for my efforts and later in the kitchen at Stir, where I could cook and learn and live alongside my friends and my mentor. And then, of course, I felt it on that *Top Chef* stage when I heard the words sealing my win. And yet there was one dimension of joy I still hadn't allowed myself to seek.

I have always believed deeply in love. Like so many queer

people, I applied those feelings toward friends and family before I was out. But I had also always longed for a love like what my parents have, what I'd heard about in songs and seen on-screen, and what Julia Roberts and Hugh Grant found in each other (despite my still believing that her *Notting Hill* character and I had a missed connection). For such a long time, I had a deeply internalized fear, unsure I deserved that kind of love, and so it felt scary to pursue.

When I was young, so much about life felt high-stakes. I worried that if I lost one job, one person, one opportunity, I might not have another chance. But for me, one of the greatest things about growing up is that with experience, at some point, I began to trust the process. To trust that I can and will do the work—whether of repairing a relationship or creating opportunities for myself. To trust that because I have already worked hard and treated people well, those opportunities will present themselves. And slowly, almost without noticing, I began to see myself move forward with less fear that one false move might make my world crumble. Sometimes pursuing real joy required me to take a leap, but knowing even in the worst-case scenario that I will be okay gave me confidence in taking that risk.

After *Top Chef*—and after so many people demonstrated their own love for me in ways that were surprising and strong, and after realizing my own value in terms I'd never imagined—I started to see that maybe I was worthy of love of all kinds and that maybe it was time to enter that new, joyful dimension by opening myself up to possibilities.

I can't say that I flipped some switch and immediately began the search for a partner or that I went into full dating mode. And it's not as if the show ended and I suddenly started hitting gay bars and going on the prowl. In fact, to this day, aside from those Chicago years, I've never really been a bar person. There were other options: Dating websites existed (although they were nascent and limited in 2012), but that's just not where my head was. As has always been my nature, I was hyperfocused, and I was entering a new professional phase. I was finding myself with opportunities and invitations to industry events, meeting iconic figures in the culinary world, and fielding press requests and interest that had been totally unfathomable to me before. I was considering possibilities for my future that I never knew to dream. I was simply, for the first time, just enjoying the ride.

Still, there was something different about how I felt. The self-consciousness of my past was not gone by any means, but it was at least partially supplanted by excitement, a sense of possibility and awe at this new life. There was also an expansive and generative feeling of gratitude. Doors were opening for me, and I entered them wide-eyed, thankful and curious and even proud that I'd helped create those portals. It was a far cry from the days of hiding in my own apartment. I didn't want to miss a thing, and maybe there was a subtle new confidence in the way I carried myself.

I've always found some of these qualities attractive in others, so even though I look back at moments of awkwardness as I entered this new world and era (like trying to choose the right outfits for all those fancy shindigs), perhaps I was presenting a new kind of energy. Because the very same year I walked off the *Top Chef* set with the title, I also fell in love for the first time with a woman, and she loved me back.

I believe in protecting the privacy of others, so I won't get into the fine details of how this happened, especially because this first relationship—although very real and true and critical to my formation as a romantically active queer person—did not last forever. But what is relevant to my story, and what I believe is universal, are the feelings. And if you don't recall the first time you had a crush, experienced an infatuation, or fell in love, I can remind you that there are *many* feelings.

So frequently, people in my life had told me about their feelings in relationships. It might have been a thirteen-year-old friend on the baseball field in Michigan pouring her heart out about a crush or a Chicago friend venting between shifts in a restaurant or Stephanie crying about her breakup in the Heartbreak Hotel days. I had heard it all. From the butterflies to the first kisses, the virginities lost and hearts broken, the engagement rings and birth announcements, I had witnessed the full spectrum in my almost thirty years. As I listened, supported, rooted, and lent a shoulder (or Scott's couch) to cry on, I performed the role of a friend who could relate, embellishing my own experiences to amp up my romantic résumé (not unlike acting *as if* for those executive chef jobs). I assumed the part of someone who understood what others were going through. But even though I could imagine and empathize—and I did that, mining what I could from my own life and what I'd absorbed from others—I was always missing a critical element: experience.

By the time I was having my own very first real romance, with all that exhausting-slash-exhilarating-slash-obsessive intensity, most of the people in my life had been there and back again, sometimes many times. But it was all so new to me. I was seeing the world in Technicolor after living so long in black and white. There was no question in my mind that I was in love—I just knew. And finally, I was the hero of my own rom-com instead of just a supporting character.

I had enough experience by then to feel secure, to know I was surrounded by love and community. I had also seen people—like Jeffrey on *Top Chef,* Vinny, and Matty and Daniel—living out and proud and enjoying their lives. Barbara's restaurant group also had plenty of out queer people, and I was in a city that had a thriving gay community, not to mention a state that was the first to legalize gay marriage, all the way back in 2004. The last hurdle was convincing myself that I deserved to be on the other side, among those people. Now that I'd found love, I finally had clarity that any risk would be worth the reward of sharing my joy with the people who had shared their own with me.

And so, on the one-year anniversary of my very first real queer relationship, and after being in the closet for almost three decades, I made a decision not only to live my life but also to share it.

Every coming-out story is entirely unique, and no queer person ever forgets their own personal journey to that moment or the ones that follow. You can agonize and rehearse, imagine and project; you can speculate and try to prepare for every possible response and scenario and outcome, but at the end of the day, it's a decision and moment that is only your own. And the truth is, coming out usually isn't a single sentence or exchange tied up in a neat little bow. It's a process, one conversation at a time, and you can't approach every relationship the same way, because not every person is the same. For me, although the matters of how, when, and under what circumstance were less clear, I was very certain about who really mattered and the people I wanted to tell.

The first person was not my mother or father or even my best friend. It was Barbara. She hadn't yet publicly come out herself, but there was a sort of unspoken awareness that Barbara was dating women. And although that certainly gave me a feeling of comfort in a sense, there were other more important factors for me in making this choice. First, she had already demonstrated her support of me in so many ways—professionally, when she gave me the spotlight during that Little Birds & Burgundy dinner so early on, and then with her vote of confidence in putting me up for *Top Chef*, and personally, with the parties she threw in my honor and the way she celebrated me, always treating me with respect and like a person worthy of her time.

For as much as she meant to me, Barbara was also not my family of origin. She couldn't disown me, and if she didn't accept me by some chance, it would be a blow—but one I knew I could handle. For those reasons, I had a sense of safety with Barbara.

I knew I had to find the right time for the conversation, when she'd be free of distractions and able to hear me. But I also had a sense of resolve once I decided to come out and, with it, an almost sudden impatience and urgency. It may seem strange after living with a secret like this for so many years, but once you start to sense the possibilities and relief, all that nervousness takes on an element of excitement, too. You can't wait to get to the other side, because you can see good things there.

Fortunately, I had an opening with Barbara. I knew we'd have some one-on-one time when we were driving back from an off-site event—the kind with which I helped out from time to time. During these little road trips, we'd listen to music and chain-smoke cigarettes. That day, we were in her SUV with the windows down, Lyle Lovett crooning through the speakers, and speaking to each other only when we had something to say. Silence with Barbara was always peaceful and comfortable, but when I climbed into that passenger seat, I knew that before I set foot back on solid ground, I would have said my piece—and I would no longer be the only one with the information that I was queer.

When I finally did tell Barbara, I didn't make some major declaration. There was no script and no drumroll. Instead, I told her in the simplest terms: "I have a girlfriend."

I think for many queer people, this is a sort of soft launch. In this way, you're not only saying that you are gay (without actually saying it), you're also preempting a lot of "How do you know?" types of inquiries. And you're confirming that someone out there loves you, and sometimes that feels helpful and validating. In addition, for me, coming out in the context of a partnership meant indicating that I was happy about this information, happy in my life and my own identity—and with any luck that would encourage the person on the receiving end to feel that for me, too.

Barbara was never the most effusive communicator about anything. She wasn't shocked; she didn't yank the e-brake and pull over to make some major deal about it, and she didn't ask me a million questions. She had only one:

"When do we get to meet her?"

After so much buildup, Barbara's response was so *normal*. And there I was, just a totally average person having a totally average conversation about a person I was dating. She told me what I most hoped to hear, which was that she was happy for me, and after that, we went on with our day as if it were any other. And the biggest difference—the subtle sensation of my heart beginning to open up—would have been imperceptible to the outside world.

⸻

That moment with Barbara gave me a sense of confidence and relief, but I knew every conversation and reaction would be unique. It's also not always possible to find the exact right moment, and a long stretch of uninterrupted road-trip time with everyone in my life was obviously not going to happen. Sometimes you just have to allow circumstance to dictate the scenario.

I had a trip on the books to go home to Michigan for an event shortly after this conversation with Barbara, and—as he once did so many years earlier, when I arrived from Korea—my brother was planning to pick me up from the airport. This was the guy who was the first one to hold me when I got off that plane back in the '80s and, later, the one to really hold my hand when I made the transition to life in Boston, the unofficial advent of my adulthood. Jonathan had proved so many times in my life that he only wanted what was best for me, and I had to trust that would still be the case.

I had already invited my girlfriend to come home with me, so while we were discussing the logistics of my airport pickup over the phone, I casually let Jonathan know we'd have an extra passenger.

"I just want you to know that I'm bringing someone home with me," I told him. Then I added: "It's a girlfriend."

I couldn't see his face or gauge his reaction in any tangible, visible way, but he didn't make me wait long before responding.

"That's great, Kristen," he said, cheerfully and seemingly unfazed. "Can't wait to meet her."

Like Barbara, Jonathan didn't ask questions, and we finished our call, finalizing the details of our arrival without any big fanfare. It was, again, so totally normal. In the course of my life, my relationship with my big brother has changed and evolved so many times, from when we were kids living in the same house to our adulthood, during which he became a sort of adviser on everything from financial decisions to the kind of car I drove. And I took comfort knowing that my pragmatic, detail-oriented brother, upon whose guidance I'd relied so many times over the years—now had a full picture of my life.

Telling Barbara and Jonathan gave me a chance to test the waters and ramp up in a way, but every time you say those words to a person you love, it's the anxiety and adrenaline all over again. And to this day, there is nothing more important to me than the regard, acceptance, and love of my parents.

I knew my parents loved me; they had proved it and made that clear every day of my life. From the moments when I felt I'd truly earned their pride to the ones when I was decidedly less proud of myself and my behavior, they never wavered. Which is part of why telling them felt so fraught—I just never wanted to let them down or disappoint them in any way or make their lives anything less than perfect. I always wanted to be a source of pride and light for them; I had to hope that my happiness would provide that in this case.

I vividly remember lying on the futon in my little room in Boston, staring at the ceiling with the phone pressed to my ear. When I had both my parents on the line, I could picture them. It was March, springtime in Michigan, and they were probably in their bright, light-washed sunroom. These days, when we're on a video call, my mom sits in a chair with my dad standing behind her. In my mind, this is how they were positioned on that day, too, my voice coming through the speakerphone.

We spoke for a bit about general life stuff, as usual, but I was anxious to get to it. And so, just as I had with Jonathan, when we arrived at the subject of my impending Michigan visit, I let them know I'd be bringing someone with me. Someone I was dating.

"Great!" my mom said casually, followed by the question, "What's his name?"

The pronoun she used was valid; after all, my parents had met Scott, and I had given them no reason to believe anything had changed. I inhaled—trying to channel the courage I'd accumulated in telling Barbara and Jonathan, reminding myself of their reactions, reassuring myself once again that my parents loved me—and I gently corrected my mother.

"*Her* name is..." I said, finishing that sentence but not elaborating further for the moment.

In my family, acts of service have always been our primary love language—we rely on actions to express how much we care about one another. But I was far away; I couldn't offer or receive any kind of nonverbal affirmation. I wished so badly that I could gauge their expressions or feel the energy in the room, but there was also safety in having distance, so that if it didn't go the way I hoped it would, I wouldn't have to see it on their faces.

The beat after I said those words was probably the space of a breath but felt like an eternity. And while so often in my life I've moved around, fidgeted, bounced, smoked, sweat, or sniffled when I was nervous, in that moment I lay totally still, as if by doing so I might be able to maintain some level of chill. The only thing that moved were my eyes, tracing the recessed lighting on the ceiling.

Finally, my mom asked another question: "Are you happy?"

This wasn't something I had to think about or consider, and I told her yes, immediately and firmly. I wanted her to know that she could feel that happiness, too.

"Well, okay, then there's nothing to worry about," my mother said, and I exhaled.

As my parents had demonstrated so many times before and so many times since, my happiness was more important to them than anything else in the world. And when, after a few moments, my mom asked me a last follow-up question—whether I was sure—it didn't feel like she was asking because she was worried that I didn't know myself or because she wasn't ready to accept my queerness as a truth. She asked because the world in which we were living wasn't so hospitable to people like me (frankly, it still isn't in many ways), and she knew that. It was an inquiry born from a mother's concern, because she wanted the world to treat me kindly—because she did want my happiness more than anything. And when I answered that I was definitely sure, my mother heard me and never asked again.

"We can't wait to meet her," she replied, before my father—a man of few words—added his two cents.

"We're looking forward to it, Kristen," he said, echoing my mom's sentiments.

And just like that, I was out to my whole family. I beamed to myself on the other end of the line in my little room, sitting on the futon I'd once shared with my mother, allowing myself to finally move, and smile, and breathe. And although I couldn't hug them or look in their eyes and thank them for providing the foundation of love I needed to eventually love myself, my heart swelled at being able to finally share a complete, unedited version of myself with the people I loved more than anything in life. It was a moment of joy so small and so monumental all at the same time, so overwhelming and yet entirely anticlimactic in a way, and it is a feeling I have never forgotten.

With Barbara and my family behind me, it was time to tell my friends—my extended, created family.

Over the course of my time in Boston, I'd become close with a woman named Kim, who lived a few doors down from Stir. She would frequently pop her head in to say hi, always making a point to get to know the team. Kim was brash and warm, funny and bold, fierce and loving, all at once, and she took care of us.

It wasn't uncommon to accept an invitation to hang out at her place after work, when I would rummage through her fridge for leftovers so often that she joked I was her "human garbage disposal." Kim was older than I am but younger than Barbara. I can't share her exact age here (for fear that she may excommunicate me), but it was advanced enough for her to fall comfortably into the "auntie" category. Because I was far from home and my family, she kind of took on that role in my life. And because she was so generous with her love and support of me, Kim was on the list of people with whom I wanted to share my full self.

Kim was always very perceptive, and I had wondered at times if she already knew. I honestly can't recall the exact circumstances of the exchange, but I will never forget the conversation. I explained that I had something to tell her, and I hesitated, faltering a little around the words, and I hoped she'd mercifully fill in the blanks. But Kim wasn't letting me off that easy. She admitted that she *might* know what I was about to say—but she wanted me to say it out loud. We went back and forth for a while, which was truly comical and helped lighten the mood a bit, before I finally relented and told her that I was dating a girl.

"I *knew* it," Kim said with a smile. And then she, too, told me she was happy for me, and it felt like I was collecting little shimmery bits of support with every one of these conversations.

I checked the box in my mind beside Kim's name, knowing there was only one person left. After those six people, I didn't feel I needed to personally come out to anyone else. Whoever knew from that point forward could find out in their own way; I wasn't going to attempt to control the narrative or put myself out there any further.

But the last one on my mind was Stephanie. There wasn't a particular reason for her to be the final person I told; it was largely circumstantial based on timing. When the opportunity presented itself one afternoon, Steph and I were outside smoking cigarettes—a familiar interlude in our lives, just like hundreds of others since we had met at Top of the Hub. Apart from the weather or season or location—work or our building, Boston or Vegas—those moments could all easily blur together. But that day I knew what Steph didn't yet, which was that this scene was going to be different.

The following is a loose transcript of the conversation.

KRISTEN: "I have something to tell you."

STEPHANIE: "What?"

KRISTEN: "Guess."

STEPH: "Are you gay?"

KRISTEN: "No!" (Nervous laughter)

STEPHANIE: "Are you pregnant?"

KRISTEN: "No."

STEPHANIE: "Are you going to jail?"

KRISTEN: "What? No!"

STEPHANIE: (Shrug)

(Drags of cigarettes and momentary silence)

KRISTEN: "Actually, it was the first thing you said."

(Beat)

STEPHANIE: "Are you saying you're in love with me?"

KRISTEN: (Gently smacks Stephanie on the head)

(Both laugh)

STEPHANIE: "I'm so happy for you."

And that was it; we went back to our lives as usual. And I felt like a totally different person but also the very same one I'd always been—because both things were true.

I've noticed the thing about depictions of coming-out stories is that they usually end one of two ways: The first may include varying levels of rejection and heartbreak and is generally pretty awful. The other is the complete opposite, in which coming out ends in total acceptance, open embraces all around, a big, life-defining love, and maybe a ride off into the sunset.

The reality is that most queer relationships are just as complicated as any other, and rarely does anyone—gay, straight, or otherwise—wind up with their first love (my parents aside). Instead, coming out is usually followed by a series of partnerships that have elements of joy and pain, that are sometimes perfect and sometimes a total mess, that start and end and sometimes even come back around again. They are nuanced and complex and filled with questions. They end or evolve with very few firm answers and are entirely without a road map. (See? Gay people—just like everyone else!)

I had several significant relationships over the course of those first years being out, and I went forward in my life with priceless takeaways that informed the person I have become and each relationship I have had since.

For one thing, I really learned how to date and how to be with someone. I finally had a chance to exercise my romantic side, to perform the grand gestures that I'd always daydreamed about, like whisking someone off on a vacation, blowing paychecks on big, lavish scenes you might see in a movie. But I also discovered that sometimes small and thoughtful things—writing love notes, holding hands, carrying the load during the times when a partner is stressed—could be hugely impactful, too. I learned how to read a person and intuit what they might want and need when they don't say it out loud as well as how to ask when I need clearer communication and how to be more communicative in return.

I learned how to support someone I care about when they're experiencing some really hard things, and in doing so, I also learned about responsibilities—to your partner and to yourself. I learned how to recognize when it's time to walk away from something that isn't healthy, which required me to really understand and appreciate my own personal worth. I learned that no matter how badly I might have wanted to fix something about a relationship or another person's life, doing so may not be in my power. That was a hard lesson to learn but an important one that applies to all kinds of relationships. I learned that I want to be seen and cared for in return and that I want openness and authenticity and a collaborative love. And I learned that we all deserve a chance to have what we want and to feel that our individual hopes, desires, and needs are valid.

After a few years together with my first girlfriend, I also had my very first heartbreak. A few more followed—all of which were as tough as I'd always heard they could be from my friends. But I learned how to endure that pain, how to connect with and seek support from others, how to lean on the people in my life in a new way, and ultimately how to heal and come out stronger on the other side.

Each of these discoveries was a little takeaway to put in a relationship tool belt, to reflect on, refine, and retrieve when the time came along. Falling in love was a gift in itself, and allowing myself to feel it in full measure opened me up to the greatest gift of all: the motivation to pursue a life of authenticity, of happiness and joy, to be uncensored and utterly myself. And that changed my life forever.

To me, being out isn't about whom you sleep with or next to, or whom you kiss good night, or whom you long for when you're alone. It's about being able to breathe—fully, substantially, with space—and the ability to process that oxygen into a life force. It's impossible to explain to people who haven't experienced this, because for most people, breathing is something easily taken for granted.

Being out also doesn't translate to a life of pure elation and big gay pride parades at all hours of the day and on all days of the year. Adversity doesn't disappear when I open that door and step into the light. It is very much ingrained in our experience. When I came out, gay marriage wasn't legal; I had to accept that it might not ever be available to me. And while I did get to revel in the moment the Supreme Court ruled in our favor in 2015, guaranteeing same-sex couples the right to marry, I still fear, like many queer people, that this may be revoked. From a political standpoint, our rights, like those of all marginalized groups, remain precarious, subject to the public's whims and vacillations. Today I do my best to participate in making progress in the ways that are available to me. I donate time and money, advocate for and alongside organizations with which I share values, and make my kitchen a place of welcome for everyone. I do my best to see people in the way they want to be seen, even if they're not quite ready or sure how to express it.

I have been out for just a little more than a decade now, and someday I will wake up and know that more years of my life have been lived in this authentic and open way than not, but I remember those feelings well. When I see queer youth today, I know that no matter how many courts recognize our right to be seen as human beings or how many allies champion our causes, there are still many challenges for them and that every journey is valid and different. But I am also encouraged that young people have language and resources and role models, that they are out and proud in new and inspiring ways. Their bravery awes and encourages me.

When I came out publicly on Instagram in April of 2014, it was overwhelming to be so embraced, to be on the receiving end of so much gratitude, which felt unfounded at times simply because I was just being *me*. But the messages and stories moved me so deeply back then and continue to every day. I know how fortunate I am to have had such a joyful life as a queer person and have tried to fortify the community through my presence and platforms in whatever ways are possible, because that sense of belonging and shared experience is a lifeline for so many who do not have the resources and support that were available to me.

Coming out allowed me to seek and find real joy, in all the messy and fun, challenging and rewarding, complicated and thrilling, sometimes terrifying and always fully human ways. It took many years, and a lot of people supporting me and showing me their love, but now I know joy when I see it and feel it. It is an unbelievable, alchemical thing that can change your whole life, rewire the way you see the world, and reorganize your priorities. Joy can supersede so many feelings and make your fears suddenly feel totally irrelevant—or at least a little less intense. It may be complicated and nuanced and deeply personal—and the same can be said of coming out and the experience of being queer in general. But to me, pursuing love and being able to share the joy—and all those other emotions and lessons that come along with the journey—make it worth taking a risk, trusting the process, and opening your heart.

12

n food, we talk about the idea of contrast a lot, and when you're
creating a dish, it can be an important ingredient all its own.
Sameness, bite after bite—whether in flavor or texture—can
result in palate fatigue. Essentially, it's boring. Contrast keeps
each bite interesting, but it also highlights and emphasizes differ-
ing flavors and elements. As chefs, we work to build that contrast,
adding crunch to something that is otherwise soft—like a sear to a
creamy scallop—or adding acid to balance sweetness.

Contrasts in life are important, too. It's what I was seeking
before *Top Chef,* and the show helped deliver some sweet high notes.
But contrasts can occasionally be bitter, too, and a little less pleasant.
Life was as smooth as I could have dreamed in many ways: I had my
friends and family and a job I loved and even a first real relationship. But I was about to encounter some major contrast—and not
the pleasant, keep-things-interesting kind.

Initially, being back in Boston was manageable, even if there
were adjustments. I had been working at Stir for years, but there
was without question a totally new kind of pressure. Often it was
self-imposed, like the pressure to live up to my own standards, but

now there was a new sense of outside expectations, from strangers and fans. And honestly, the idea that I had fans was itself such an adjustment. Since Stir was also a cookbook shop by day, we'd often keep the door open when it was nice out, enjoying a little fresh air while we did our work to get ready for service. But guests started to pop their heads in during prep time just to ask questions, say congratulations, profess their love of the show, or offer support or praise.

It was fun at first to meet friendly new faces who were so genuinely interested and admiring, but it was also a little overwhelming; I still wasn't used to being the center of attention. On the show, the spotlight was different—I was there to do a job, and the camera crew didn't feel like an intrusion; they were just there to capture what was happening and do *their* job. While the outpouring was flattering and appreciated, it was also distracting. I had work to do at Stir—real tasks that needed to be completed to execute our nightly service—and it was difficult to field the attention with a smile while also remaining consistent and dedicated to my work. At times, I had to just shut the door and shut out the world so I could focus.

Still, the recognition was rewarding after so much effort, and I felt like I was also able to return a favor to Barbara in some way. To this day, I don't believe that she put me and Steph up for the show as bait for business, but I like to think that in a small way, contributing to the draw at Stir was a way to thank her, so I did my best to be cordial and welcoming of any attention. Whether or not she intended to, Barbara absolutely, completely, and profoundly changed my life, but I had no idea just how significantly yet.

The thing is, after the win, it takes a beat for the big returns to begin to reveal themselves. Sure, there was prize money, and there was press. The Top Chef title came with a *Food & Wine* feature—plus notice from many other media outlets that covered the show—and I was invited to events hosted by the magazine and adjacent industry gatherings. Beyond that, the attention at Stir was the biggest indication that there had been a shift, though, and I wasn't thinking it would be anything more than that or that it would last very long.

Prior to the show, despite the fact that I'd been itching for something different—for some contrast—I still loved my job and didn't really have any plans to make major changes when I returned. My world had been shaken up plenty, and I enjoyed the change of pace, but I expected to get back to business as usual, as if not much had changed. Except there *were* changes, and some of them were a bit isolating, too. I was coming out of this experience for which no one else had any context, trying to dive back into a former life with the team and knowing they couldn't really understand what it was like. And then on top of it, there was this layer of relative fame for which I was being singled out. It was lovely and strange and disorienting all at the same time.

For whatever it was worth, though, I did believe it would pass— that the attention wouldn't last long. As it turned out, I wasn't the only one who felt that way.

I had already learned so many times over the years that kindness and mutual respect are critical to any kind of functioning work environment, and being made to feel bad about success in any way is hurtful and, frankly, unnecessary. Today, I try to emphasize to others that when someone makes strides, it doesn't take any runway space away from you.

That said, it's possible that women have been conditioned to feel this in a way—as if there are only so many spots at the top we'll be able to occupy, and so instead of cheering one another on and lifting one another up, some give in to reactive jealousy. I hadn't really given it much consideration when I was on the show because I was intent on the challenges in front of me, protected from the general public's impressions by the insular, almost hermetic environment. You can kind of forget that you exist as part of the outside world in those weeks of the competition, and the true reality check of being on TV is reconciling your television life with the one you live in before and after the cameras roll.

Those patrons stopping by Stir were a reminder that I hadn't actually been in a vacuum and that there *had* been people—many of them—who had seen and witnessed what I was experiencing in that *Top Chef* bubble. But there was another layer, too. While I was happy to see the response to the show in terms of business, not everyone in Barbara's company was as pleased about the attention. It was disruptive—I admit I felt that, too. But I have always believed that a rising tide lifts all boats, and it seemed it was beneficial to everyone involved.

Still, while friends like Steph were genuinely happy for me, I started to become aware of murmurings within the ranks. When Steph overheard one girl gossiping and assuring her boyfriend (a chef at another restaurant) that "Kristen's fifteen minutes" would be over soon, she told me about it. I had been fortunate to get through most of my life without major brushes with bullying. I had thought those days were behind me—the *Mean Girls* mentality of middle and high school. And while this person and I had never exactly been friends, we had worked together for a couple of years, and I was still hurt to find out that she was talking about me in such a way. I did my best not to engage, to stay focused and live up to the new hype around my cooking, for the sake of my own reputation and that of the restaurant. I had to manage my response to this new kind of pressure on my own for myself. I didn't want to let on that I had hurt feelings over this kind of shit-talking, not to mention the fact that it was coming from another woman.

Stir had always been a safe place for me, one of happiness and positivity, and I didn't want to imagine it any other way. But one sour voice among many supportive women was nothing compared to what I was about to experience with a group of mostly men.

***

I want to be really clear that I have worked with many wonderful men over the years. From chef instructors at Le Cordon Bleu to Gérard at Sensing to some of my fellow contestants (and Tom!) on *Top Chef,* I have learned from and been lifted up by and laughed with a whole lot of well-meaning, great guys in my life. That's to say nothing of my father and my brother and Scott—the men who cared for me on a personal level. I feel lucky to have had them all in my life.

But in my experience, there is some validity to the notion that male-dominated environments can become so-called toxic. I can't say if that's because we live in a society that encourages hyper-masculinity and male "strength"—one that doesn't promote or reward emotional education for men; that doesn't even really allow them to feel softness or vulnerability. But in the food industry, the trope of the screaming, demanding, tyrannical chef is absolutely ingrained in the culture and public perception, and though I hadn't really witnessed it before, I knew that the idea stemmed from someone's reality out there somewhere.

At Stir, which was owned and run by women, I had been blissfully separated from this kind of kitchen. We generally treated one another with kindness and respect, and since we were continually onstage for guests, it's not as if we could be screaming and throwing pans at one another even if we wanted to.

But while I had always loved working at Stir and recognized that the environment was a rarity, I couldn't help beginning to wonder what else was out there. I was still making a salary that hovered in the low $30,000 range, which was not totally uncommon for the culinary world. But *Top Chef* slowly started to open some alternative opportunities for me. I remember the first time I was asked to participate in an event outside the restaurant, on my own. It sounded fun, and I figured it was in my best interest to take advantage of it—who knew how many offers like this would come along? Then when the paycheck rolled in, and it was a whole hell of a lot more money than I earned on an average day at Stir, my jaw dropped. I was working so hard at Stir, and I loved it, but wow—game changer.

Still, it's not like I was ready to hang up my apron, exactly. I didn't feel like I could rely on that kind of thing or expect to continue to connect with people without a kitchen or a show. Tom Colicchio always said, before my season and to this day, "Stay in your restaurant." That's what I intended to do—in part because that's what I knew how to do. But once again, a few months after my *Top Chef* win, Barbara approached me with another opportunity.

Barbara had opened Menton under the umbrella of her restaurant group in 2012. It was a chic restaurant with a luxury experience and a French- and Italian-inspired menu. But this wasn't just run-of-the-mill fine dining; this was Boston's very first Relais & Châteaux restaurant. This is a distinction given to establishments that exemplify a very particular vision of excellence. Each candidate for this designation undergoes a rigorous evaluation of its philosophical and technical qualities measured against strict criteria. The honor—which is conservatively and rarely bestowed—is a beacon to a class of travelers and diners who seek out these properties and dining experiences for the assurance of something truly exceptional.

In short, it's a very big deal—and it so happened that in mid-2013, shortly after *Top Chef* ended, a position was opening up for the chef de cuisine at this restaurant.

In the food industry, there are several structures by which a restaurant or restaurant group might operate. I had previously been fixated on executive chef jobs, but in Barbara's group, there was an EC for the entire company. That was the figure to whom the head chef of each restaurant would report, and those chefs in turn were called chefs de cuisine, or CDCs. Essentially, these individuals had the same roles and responsibilities as an executive chef in a single restaurant, so while the title was slightly different, chef de cuisine was the equivalent of what I'd been gunning for since the earliest days of my career.

And it was a sunny afternoon at Stir when Barbara personally told me that she wanted it for me, too.

"I want you to have this on your résumé before you turn thirty," she said. And by "this," she meant chef de cuisine of a Relais & Châteaux restaurant. I could feel the excitement bubble up through me. I had never stopped wanting that for myself, and this was even more illustrious than anything I'd dreamed of.

I can't imagine how many people in the company wanted that job. I was floored that she was suggesting it for me, but even with Barbara's vote, it wasn't a done deal. What I had learned in my career to that point is that just because your name is on the company letterhead doesn't mean there aren't other voices and personalities in the mix. Barbara didn't make every judgment call, and the management of the company had divided opinions about my preparedness for this role. Barbara, along with the company's director of operations and its wine director—both of whom were women—were pulling for me to have the job. But there were also two men in the upper echelon of the organization who were not in agreement and didn't buy that I was ready for it. I can't speak to all the behind-the-scenes conversations or how it was ultimately decided, but for better or worse, the majority ruled, and I was formally offered the position.

When I received it, though I was appreciative and excited, it wasn't exactly the offer of a lifetime. For one thing, my starting salary at Menton was hardly mind-blowing, particularly as I continued to receive substantial offers for external gigs. I'd later discover that the chef who succeeded me at Stir was hired at a higher rate to take my position, despite the fact that I'd been told there was no room in the budget for me to have a raise.

That said, money has never been a major motivator for me. Naturally, I was always happy to see my income increase, and had always dreamed of being able to do special things for my parents, but in this case, there was still enough that was attractive about the job for me to take it. I still wanted the prestige, that line on my résumé, the chance to make my mentor proud.

I also saw the value in Menton as a learning opportunity. Previously, I'd always worked according to someone else's vision and menu, and while Menton was very much an established restaurant and not my own, I believed I'd get to begin experimenting and have more control and autonomy. When I received the details, though, it was made clear that this was not going to be the case—at least not right away. It was evident that compromises had been made among the management team in creating my offer, and I was going to be subject to an initial formal training period during which I would not be allowed to make menu changes. I was to begin my tenure by cooking the existing menu set by the chef who preceded me, with some additions made by the overall-company EC.

I had gotten to grow and explore my own culinary identity a bit on *Top Chef* as I was cooking my own food within the parameters of those challenges. And at Stir, I was also frequently cooking a menu of my own design, because we changed the offerings nightly and I was very much involved in that process. Had the executive chef of the company ever actually tasted my cooking there, maybe he would have felt differently, but as it was, he had not, and he decided I wasn't ready to take over the Menton menu yet. It felt like being invited to dinner and getting seated at the kids' table.

I doubled down anyway. I was prepared to be patient, to go in with a completely different attitude from the one I had at my jobs before Stir, when I was younger and felt somewhat entitled. It all meant so much more now. It was a major responsibility to be running my own kitchen at that level and making a mark for myself—one that would be amplified now that the world, or at least the viewers of *Top Chef* and the industry, was watching.

Leaving Stir would be bittersweet, and I knew there was so much about it I would miss. But I had been ready for a change prior to *Top Chef,* and it felt like the moment I'd been waiting for in my career. It was a bonus to be able to make this move within Barbara's company, where I'd been so happy for so long. I was nervous about running a kitchen on my own, but with the support and encouragement of those women at the top, I felt ready. And so, on June 3, 2013, less than a year after winning *Top Chef* and almost six months before I turned thirty, I accepted another new title: chef de cuisine. No matter the contract's fine print or parameters, it felt like a major step forward. Unfortunately, I was about to learn quickly that not everyone was interested in following.

***

For much of my life, trying hard was a major part of my identity. I believed that working at something with dedication and diligence would eventually yield results. But I also believe that most success takes a village, which is especially true of a restaurant. You need people who lead and follow, people who cook and clean, people who source and supply ingredients, people who see and hype, and people who sit in the seats. If you don't have all these elements in harmony, you don't have a restaurant.

When it's all working well, everyone knows and understands their roles and recognizes that when they aren't up to the task, everyone suffers. It's a delicate ecosystem, vulnerable to one false move. It's why kitchens make great TV and drama—it truly is that high-stakes. If someone is off their game, it can create a cascade of problems that stack up faster than dirty dishes. The same is true for morale. One bad attitude can be infectious. It can come from the bottom—someone feeling dissatisfied or underappreciated—or from the top, in which case it trickles down and can set the tone for the team. It can be difficult to pinpoint, and it spreads quickly, but it is almost impossible to eradicate no matter where or how it begins.

On day one, though, I showed up at Menton as most people do when they're starting a new job—I was optimistic, excited, and ready to work. I was nervous for sure, but at least part of that felt normal and to be expected, especially for a major move.

That said, my nerves were compounded by a few factors. For

one thing, I was intimidated, pure and simple. I knew these guys were truly great cooks and that they'd been running a celebrated restaurant really well. My credentials were solid but a little uneven. Winning *Top Chef* made for a great headline and indicated a certain competence as a cook, but the show was about individual competition—a totally different skill set from running a restaurant. As far as recent work experience goes, Stir was another impressive résumé line, but it was run on a ten-seat tasting-menu format with four employees on the clock at any given moment. Again, a very different ball game.

Still, I trusted in myself and my ability to cook, but I also knew I couldn't run the place alone. No one could. I needed guidance from the crew, who knew the place well. I needed for them to show me the ropes and make space for me. I needed positive attitudes and people who brought ideas to the table, who wanted to participate and collaborate. But what I found was that there was already poison in the water.

I knew that not everyone in that kitchen felt I should have the position. I was also aware that at least one key player in that kitchen wanted the job for himself and was disappointed that he didn't get it. So while I stepped into that restaurant bright-eyed, excited, and hopeful, I was also wary—and it turned out I was right to be. It's not that anyone was immediately rude to my face that first day, and there were even a few people who seemed genuinely excited and were kind to me. But there was just an energy that felt off; you can tell when you walk into a room where you aren't wanted, and the few good vibes didn't stand a chance.

Still, I wasn't about to accept defeat right out of the gate. I tried to play it small and not ruffle any feathers. I tried to read the room, thinking that if I could get a handle on what the crew needed and genuinely get to know them, eventually we'd find our groove. I thought of what I would have hoped for from a leader—someone who would make an effort to understand the culture and systems before trying to summarily change them—not that I had the authority to make significant changes yet. I did my best to be accommodating, offering to help with prep, always hoping to ingratiate myself whenever and wherever I could. I cross-trained at different stations to learn the ways the kitchen operated, to understand each role and its challenges. I knew that would be valuable in helping me find ways to improve or provide better support to those stations eventually.

But I was limited, too, because I was "training." That meant that my schedule was written for me. Any kind of oversight period can be a little nerve-racking, but this one felt more so, given that not everyone was convinced I was the right person for the job.

Still, having an assigned schedule and tasks helped me maintain a tunnel vision of sorts, and that prevented me from spinning out too much, just as having my days on *Top Chef* planned by producers helped ease some of my anxieties. I showed up every day prepared to work while trying to earn respect from those around me, believing that it was all just an adjustment period. I wanted to live up to the expectations, the job, the Relais & Châteaux designation. I wanted to lead, learn from, and, I hoped, inspire my team. Honestly, I just wanted to go in and do a good job. But I wasn't even given a chance to demonstrate my competence or given a safe space in which to ask for guidance in order to grow. If I were to run down the list of reasons why I look back at this period as one of the most difficult of my career—and my life—it would fill this book. At the end of the day, though, it boiled down to one fundamental truth: I was not at all respected from day one. And that lack of respect was revealed in little ways that I noticed over time, like a string being pulled slowly.

It was always evident that there was no love or support for what I was trying to do even if no one was outwardly challenging me. That made it even worse in some ways because it was difficult to address. It was a kind of gaslighting—to know I wasn't being treated well, but I didn't have firm evidence of how or why.

The team, mostly men, probably had a range of their own reasons for being recalcitrant at best and more often perniciously undermining. Maybe some believed I didn't have the talent or skill to be in charge. Maybe they were jealous that I was coming off a successful *Top Chef* run and thought I didn't deserve the win or the attention that came along with it. Maybe they felt like *they* deserved my job. Maybe they just didn't like my food, the way I looked, the way I walked or talked or breathed. But they made it clear in a variety of ways. Sometimes I was disregarded or ignored. Other times, they preferred to spread corrosiveness in more cowardly ways, like talking about me behind my back. I found out about their disrespect even when I wasn't on-site, thanks to the fact that I did encounter at least one empathetic person at Menton.

Robeisy Sanchez had been at the restaurant for three months by the time I took the position. She was a skilled cook, and it was apparent that she cared about the work. And in contrast to the negativity, her kindness and maturity—despite the fact that she was among the youngest members of the team—were all the starker and more deeply appreciated. Robeisy was—and is—a good person who didn't feed into the toxicity, and we developed a rapport quickly. She also wound up becoming, at times, my eyes and ears. She clued me in when, on my rare days off or when I was traveling to external gigs, the guys were talking shit or, later, when I'd finally begun to have some influence on the menu, they were changing dishes without my knowledge. This wasn't about Robeisy being a tattletale or currying favor; there were good reasons for me to have this information. It was important that I root out the issues and attempt to get everyone on the same page in order to create a safe, generative, and positive work environment and culture.

This divisive behavior created a tension that not even the sharpest knife in that kitchen could cut. The atmosphere was miserable, and I can't imagine that was true only for me. It was a sort of psychological warfare for which I wasn't prepared. Not a single cell in my body wanted to engage in this kind of mind-fuckery and conflict. It was demoralizing and exhausting. And in those early days of social media, I even started to experience a type of passive-aggressive digital torment previously unavailable to bullies. Once, one of the sous chefs posted a picture on Instagram of a dish he prepared according to my recipe. When someone made a nasty comment about the dish not looking good, he simply replied, "Not mine." The implication was clear, even if he didn't call me out by name.

It was humiliating on the daily and made it impossible to lead effectively, but it was even worse when I knew there was a VIP in the dining room. Early on, before I had a chance to work up my own menu, I got word that Emeril was planning to visit the restaurant. I had a rapport with him after my time on *Top Chef,* and I made a point to be there even though I'd been traveling for an out-of-state event. I didn't want to miss a chance to see him. Emeril had become a friendly face, and that was more than welcome to me in those days. Beyond that, I honestly didn't trust the crew to take care of him the way I wanted them to.

After his meal, I checked in with Emeril, and while he was cordial and complimentary, he added, "I look forward to when it's *your* food."

It was a subtle way to let me know that he didn't see my influence on the menu, and hearing that was both embarrassing and extremely validating in ways. On the one hand, I had been made to believe that the food at Menton was the best of the best. And yet here was a chef whom I respected immensely telling me that he believed that my cooking—which he had actually tasted, unlike many of the men in the company—had the potential to be even better. It was eye-opening, and I realized then that I should trust my gut and my own standards rather than the ones being set by the powers that be at Menton.

There have been moments in life when I was subtly aware that I was learning and growing but not able to really live by those lessons just yet. During the time that I was at Menton, I still had to operate within the existing systems, and when I could catch my breath and think clearly, I attempted to take note of what I did—and more often did *not*—want to carry forward with me in my life and future leadership opportunities. But in those months, I was focused on survival, which sometimes meant adaptation.

I did my best to work with the guys in the kitchen and even gave in to their tactics. In fact, one of them told me that the best way to get through to him was to yell at him. I'd never really done that before, in any part of my life, and I hadn't been on the receiving end of such aggression, either—not even in the many male-run kitchens in which I'd worked. I honestly don't even know *how* to shout to this day, and yet there I was, raising my voice or punching stainless-steel tables rather than actually yelling, trying to get their attention and prove that I was a boss—the kind to which they were accustomed, the kind to whom they would respond. I found myself behaving in ways that were totally unnatural to me, desperate to try anything, and I just hated it.

At some point, Barbara started coming to me with invitations to be her on-the-road sous chef for off-site events, to help her with the work and represent Menton at the same time. It was also a way to lean in to the *Top Chef* afterglow; I believe Barbara saw it as another chance to support me in my career growth and as a way to garner additional interest in the restaurant. I welcomed the opportunities to learn and network, but without question, those gigs provided me with increasingly critical moments of relief from the environment at Menton. That said, those absences—although not a regular occurrence—definitely didn't help the building resentment within the kitchen at the restaurant.

Communication was an all-around nightmare, since it seemed clear from the start that I didn't speak the language of most of the other people in the kitchen. I did, however, hear rumors—in plain English—suggesting that the only reason I had the job at all was because I was having an affair with Barbara. Even if she wanted to, Barbara wasn't in a position to offer me much protection; she was dealing with stresses within her own life, professionally and personally, and although I never felt abandoned, I knew I couldn't expect her to save the day—nor did I want that to be part of my narrative. It would only have made things worse.

With all this going on behind my back, it's a gross understatement to say I was crushed, beyond frustrated, and furious with the situation all at once on most days. I felt so tired and so unwanted, and so unbelievably beaten down. I didn't know what to do. I was at the end of my rope and was trying anything and everything. For a while, my instinct was to show up earlier, stay later, and work harder than every single person in that kitchen. I figured that way, they could never accuse me of coasting and favoritism—certainly not anything untoward with my boss, since I was always on the line. But that strategy couldn't work forever, because burnout is real. I was basically face-planting into bed at night, my back sore and my feet swollen beyond recognition. But I could have handled all that. I could have managed the physical labor and pain if I had a shred of spirit left—if there were any contrasting highs to complement the hard work. But it was the emotional drain that really took me out day after day. I was also trying to maintain some kind of relationship with my girlfriend at the time, to not entirely neglect the ecosystem of people who had just done so much to support me throughout the show and that I had worked so lovingly to develop.

I missed Stir all the time, which was rainbows and butterflies in contrast to the snake pit I felt like I was descending into every day. I had worked so much in my life, all the way back to the mall in Michigan, and while some days over the years I'd felt tired or a little less motivated to get to a job, I never actively dreaded it the way I did every single day at Menton. I felt totally trapped and knew I needed out, but I didn't know how to pull myself up just yet.

After *Top Chef,* the on-the-road jobs with Barbara were some of the first times I was really getting to travel, to explore the life I'd dreamed about all the way back when I was watching *Great Chefs of the World* or planning my international business degree. Sometimes, they were local gigs, and New York City was in regular rotation. But there were also times when we got to really get out there. We took a trip to London that I'll never forget, in part simply because it was the first time I'd ever flown business class—and on my own dime.

I could not believe this was a possibility for me. I had heard people talk about this kind of luxury, but I never really imagined it for myself. The event was a gathering of Relais & Châteaux chefs, and we also got to stay at the Corinthia, which was swanky and posh—although honestly, I was just so excited to see anything beyond the walls of that restaurant.

That said, I also learned that some attitudes are universal. At a dinner on that same London trip, there was a German R & C chef whom I don't care to name, but suffice it to say he was a white male of a certain age and disposition, the kind who seemed to think his very existence made him better than we were. It started right from the get-go, as we were all setting up our individual stations in a massive ballroom for the event. He got himself prepared, put out his course, and walked away. He'd finished his part but left his shit all over the place—taking up way too much space and making it a mess for those of us around him. We had no choice but to clean up after him so we could get our own work done. I tried to mind my business and do my work, but at one point he returned and approached us, in a blustery way offering help as if we *silly women* must be lost without him. Barbara brushed him off, but before he walked away again, he stopped me.

"You're too pretty to be a chef," he said to me.

I was instantly annoyed but didn't even have a chance to react. I'd never seen Barbara lose her shit so fast. She told him in no uncertain terms to get the fuck out of there and leave us alone. And while I felt protected, it also made me sad. It was very clear that this was something Barbara had probably been dealing with her whole career. There was an almost rote reaction that many women in many fields would likely recognize—one they needed to cultivate in order to survive and succeed. Always playing defense, working harder, storing up responses to pull out when some entitled, over-bearing dude shows up, seeming to think he matters more.

Years later, we'd see the #MeToo reckoning reach the food indus-try. And in some ways, it was long overdue. I didn't stay at Menton long enough to witness that moment and cultural shift, although as rough as the situation was for me there, it was obvious that there were other places around the country in far worse shape. I'm for-tunate to say I never saw or experienced anything beyond this kind of psychological trauma—but I'm also sorry to have to call that for-tunate. I want to confirm for anyone who needs to hear it that this kind of distress can be extremely damaging, especially when it's pro-longed and relentless.

It is also isolating. Especially as a woman, and especially as a minority, I was under the impression for a while there that I just had to try harder and everything would sort itself out, so I didn't really tell anyone what I was going through. Only once, when truly pushed to the limit, did I go to the executive chef for support. It was not an easy decision to do that, knowing as I did how he felt about me and my abilities, but I had to do something. There was one chef—let's call him the ringleader of the bunch—who was deliberately insub-ordinate, and I very professionally and solidly made a case that he needed to go. But instead of trusting me and supporting me as the CDC of that restaurant, I was told to just sit tight and "wait it out." The whole thing felt like a bad joke.

I didn't really reach out to anyone in my personal life, either. The situation was too painful to rehash or relive in conversation. And I certainly didn't share anything with my mother, who might have wanted to comfort me. She was always worried about my work-ing in food. Primarily because of the physical dangers—the cuts, the bruises, the burns. But the emotional wounds can sometimes leave much deeper scars, and I have to look back with a measure of pride—not for staying and enduring or martyring myself in some kind of way but for ultimately realizing my personal value and knowing that I couldn't and didn't have to stay.

In winter of 2014, I told Barbara that I couldn't do it anymore. I gave three weeks' notice, and by March, I had put Menton behind me. I wasn't even there for a year, but I couldn't have lasted another minute. I had no ego about leaving Menton, as I might have in my younger days. I had lived enough to understand that I had value far beyond the way I was being treated, and no title or opportunity was worth the way I felt. I recognized that I had begun to backslide and see myself the way my team saw me. I learned from that experience that self-respect is a fragile thing, far too easily destroyed, and to this day I continue to work on rebuilding what was so damaged during that time. I can only be grateful to my younger self for walking away when I did.

Years later, I would run into the chef who preceded me at Menton. He apologized to me, admitting that he later realized that the culture when he left would have made it almost impossible for me to succeed as chef de cuisine. I tried to absolve him during that conversation—after all, he wasn't there anymore by the time I took over. But he had enough insight in retrospect to understand what he'd passed along. When he said that, I almost felt sorry for him. He really seemed to mean it, and enough time had gone by for me to make some space for forgiveness. But no amount of retrospective insight could erase what I went through or change the fact that I felt set up to fail. It's a lesson in legacy as well. Even though what we do matters in our day-to-day, it also leaves an impression when we move on. I always try to be present in the moment, but I am very cognizant of the energy my actions leave in my wake.

Before I left, in a February 2014 interview with *Eater Boston*, I had put on a happy face and tried to maintain that energy, for better or worse. I explained that "the team in the kitchen couldn't have been any more amazing during my time" at Menton, and that we had "become very close family members." I said thank you to the entire crew and naturally shouted out Barbara for her support. It's not a case of revisionist history. It was an early attempt at managing my own PR, giving things a positive spin, and doing what I believed would not perpetuate the rumor mill. I also didn't want to stoop to the level of shit-talking the team in the press when I had a microphone pointed at me.

I'm not sure I'd give the same interview if I were to go through something similar now, but at the time it felt like the right thing to do. For one thing, I was protecting my mentor—I would never have said a single word publicly that might reflect poorly on Barbara. Beyond that, I was also well aware that despite being in a major US city, I was dealing with a very small-town mentality. I felt I had to keep quiet about what went on at Menton if I didn't want to be painted as difficult to work with. As it was, I'd later find out that a prominent male chef had begun telling people that I'd slept with him to further my career—a rumor he maliciously started *after* I had already won *Top Chef.* It might have been laughable if it didn't have the potential to be so damaging. But imagine if that's the story I gave to the publication—I don't think I would have been taken seriously ever again.

It was a sad fact then, and one that persists now for many kinds of people, that you often have to wait a very long time before it feels safe to tell the truth.

There were almost imperceptible indications that my life was changing during that time, some of which I can only see in retrospect now that I'm not bogged down by the dread of the day-to-day. But then there are others that were really big mile markers of which I do remember taking note. After living in my efficiency apartment for a few years, I had decided to buy my first home. My friend and Stir regular Kim happened to be a real estate agent, so she helped me find a place, and it was a joyful moment in my life to feel so at home in a place and have such a sense of belonging after struggling for a very long time to feel that sense in my life.

I sunk my *Top Chef* winnings into a down payment and picked up the keys to my very first condo in Boston. I moved in on November 30 and woke up there the next day, on my thirtieth birthday. Although I was exhausted and deeply unhappy at work, a measure of pride and a flicker of happiness managed to peek through the darkness.

Once my days at Menton were over, though, I didn't really feel at home anymore. I look back at this period and realize I was about to enter a transitional phase—one that would be freeing and fertile and actually fun—but at the time I couldn't conjure any ideas for my future. I just needed to fill my lungs with fresh air. I didn't even have another job lined up. After Menton, restaurant work was completely unappealing; I was so burned out. And although I didn't know where I was going to go, I made the bittersweet decision to pack my things and put them in storage (keeping Boston as a home base) and sell that condo. I was prepared now to strike out for parts unknown.

One of the great things to come of being in the public eye was that I was being approached with offers for partnerships, TV guest spots, speaking events, appearances, and sponsorships. It was so unexpected and eye-opening, especially because I was coming from an era when it seemed like a chef would always have to be in a kitchen. Diversifying my work allowed me to make some major decisions, both professional and personal, and being open to creative alternatives and ideas meant I could be more nimble.

This kind of work required a different kind of consideration, though. It was unlike anything I'd ever done, and while the paychecks were attractive, I also had to really educate myself on the brands and companies that expressed interest. It would have been super easy to say yes to what seemed like easy work compared to standing on my feet for double-digit hours a day, but I was diligent in understanding the values of each of those businesses to make sure they aligned with my beliefs. And when I did make selections, I was very happy to use those partnerships as a platform. Beyond the financial scaffolding, there is so much value in being able to promote the work of like-minded companies and people and to represent my communities.

The concept of visibility started to become a theme in my life after that, because I was suddenly always on a sort of stage. Early on during *Top Chef*, there was a moment in which Padma was asking contestants about our backgrounds. When she approached me and asked where I was from, my response was automatic. It was the same answer I'd given hundreds of times in my life: Michigan.

But she looked at me sideways and asked again. "No—where are you *from?*"

It took a second for it to click, but I realized what she was really asking. "I was born in South Korea," I told her.

I didn't grow up with kimchi in the refrigerator or Korean-speaking parents. I grew up in a very white family with white grandparents who baked apple pie. I knew I was Asian—that part was obvious when I looked in the mirror—but I often forgot in a way. Growing up, I know my family would have given me space and support had I chosen to explore that part of myself, but for most of my life, it wasn't something I longed for. Once I was able to inhabit my identity more authentically as a gay woman and was embraced by the gay community, though, it emphasized for me the importance of representation, a sense of belonging, and it gave me a pivotal push to engage more deeply with my Asian identity. Of course, you never have to "come out" as Asian, but now that I had a platform, I recognized my responsibility to own it more fully and intentionally.

This was yet another result of my experience on *Top Chef* that changed the person I was and in many ways helped me become a more well-rounded and self-actualized person. As with so many things, I'm not sure I would have done the work just for me, but the idea that I was pushing myself in service of a community—that I was being trusted with a responsibility—was all the motivation I needed. I'd begun receiving messages from Korean and Asian Americans who were thanking me, telling me they'd been thrilled to see someone who looked like them on television at all, not to mention as a winner. The Asian community gave me a place. They came out for me in a big way; I wanted to be worthy of that support. Once I started to find a purpose within that world, too, I truly began to feel at home in my own skin.

And the more I opened up publicly about what mattered to me, the more relationships I developed with entities that shared my perspective and buoyed me in my passion projects, whether as a queer person, an adoptee, an Asian American, or as a woman in the food industry who believed strongly in strengthening our presence and network.

These projects gave me that platform, and diversifying my income in this way also helped me buy some time to explore the world and my options without having to settle on a place or role. In particular, one early partnership I entered into was with a luxury American hotel chain as an "insider." The job was to share some selected recommendations for Boston, since that was still my home base—what to do, where to eat, that sort of thing. Part of the compensation was given in hotel stays, which was especially advantageous because it allowed me to move around without an anchor. I was able to design my life around travel gigs for the most part. And one of the best feelings initially was that I started to make a subtle shift from mentee to mentor. For years, I'd been on the receiving end of support. I'd been uplifted and championed. Now I was in a position where I could be deliberate about whom I supported in turn. I hired Robeisy—who had also left Menton—to be my traveling sous chef when I needed a hand, which meant I got to take her with me on trips. We traveled around together for a while, cooking and experiencing all kinds of new places. We followed the work and our hearts, taking the jobs that felt right and exciting, and we made space for surprises. We had a very good time.

When I graduated from high school, I decided I needed a solid plan, something I could cling to and look to for a sense of security and hope. Culinary school gave me a blueprint for a while, and then in Boston I had the sure thing of a stable job. For the first time in my life, I was going off script. I wasn't totally sure what I would do or where I would end up, but it didn't feel irresponsible. It felt like finally having a chance to really open myself up to what the world had to offer rather than evaluating my options based on what I presumed was out there.

For many years before I started at Stir, I didn't know the person I was, and at times I wasn't sure I liked her or that anyone else would.

Now I was getting paid just to be *me*. It was exhilarating. For the better part of four or five years, I lived out of a suitcase, wearing a uniform of white V-neck T-shirts, black jeans, and boots and toting a knife, roll and backpack. I tasted things; I met people and made friends; I learned about the world and began to understand how to work professionally, not just as a cook but also as an independent business owner. I might not have ended up with the business degree I set out to earn straight out of high school, but instead I learned because I *became* the business.

Not everything I did was solo, though. At some point in my travels, I met the then New York–based chef David Chang, who owned a number of super-successful restaurants under his Momofuku umbrella as well as the magazine *Lucky Peach*, which shut down in 2017. He told me he thought I should have a cookbook and introduced me to a literary agent. It took a great deal of work, but *Kristen Kish Cooking* arrived in bookstores in 2017, and I had a tangible work of art to share with the world.

That project, happily, gave me an opportunity to spend time with Gail Simmons, with whom I kept in touch after *Top Chef* ended. In the years that followed, she began inviting me to visit her and her family in Gloucester, Massachusetts—which was easy enough to do, being that it's not too far from Boston. Then, when it came time to do the photo shoot for the cookbook proposal and there was no budget and I wasn't living anywhere permanently, she very graciously offered up her own beautiful kitchen as a backdrop. These were generosities that resulted from building our rapport, which I appreciated so deeply.

And Gail wasn't the only one from my *Top Chef* days who showed up for me. During my travels in those years, I was often going to New York, where Padma was based. When she knew I was in town, she emphasized that she always had an open door. She offered a room for me to sleep in or a seat at her table for a meal, and on the professional side, invited me to cook for a dinner she hosted in her home, and never hesitated to name-check me in interviews in a supportive way.

I couldn't have known when I was one of many contestants on the show back in Seattle that I would go on to develop real friendships with both women, but I didn't take my relationships with Gail or Padma for granted. And during that time, I realized that as much as I was learning and accomplishing, I still needed support. This time, I found it in new ways—not from fellow cooks on the line but from a management team who could help me stay organized and parlay some of my press into new opportunities, with an eye toward longevity for my career. Those fifteen minutes can last a lot longer if you have foresight, some guidance, a good foundation, and, as always, good people.

For those few years, I did all the living I hadn't gotten to do before. For the first time, I had some real money in my pocket, experience under my belt, and the deep, dark closet was far behind me. For nearly three decades, I'd kept everything inside. I had been a spectator in the life I wanted to live, keeping my hopes and dreams locked up. But when I put Menton behind me, I was ready to step out. I didn't need the salary, no matter the amount, because I finally believed in myself, and I trusted that others would see my value, too.

I was also starting to recognize a pattern in my life. That if I allowed things to happen rather than trying to force them, that if I was kind to others and committed to doing a good job, keeping an open mind as well as open eyes and ears and allowing good intentions rather than perceived expectations to lead the way, the right path had a way of revealing itself. And after I had followed my heart and honed this philosophy for almost half a decade, it was about to be confirmed once again.

13

n the years that followed my departure from Menton, I had been enjoying my independence immensely. I learned a great deal about the world, my industry, my abilities, and life in general. I wasn't in a rush to make major changes; believing in myself and feeling like I had a community that would be there for me if things took a turn made it easier to be more discerning when opportunities did come my way. I appreciated being approached by brands and companies that wanted to partner with me, but I didn't say yes to everyone. I didn't have to, and that was liberating, too.

During that time, I also had plenty of people asking me when I would open a restaurant. I could understand their line of thinking; it seemed like a natural next step. It's not that I hadn't thought about it. In fact, I'd been doing pop-ups and collaborations, and I loved getting to explore food culture that way. Even though it wasn't the purpose of those gigs, traveling and working in various kitchens and markets, and with various teams and cuisines, all gave me a chance to really get a sense of what was out there—a sense of what other chefs were doing and how as well as the way guests were responding.

I also had a number of people approach me about opportunities to partner or collaborate on opening a restaurant. It was always flattering and cool, even if some opportunities felt less than legitimate or serious. I would receive emails or phone calls and have an occasional casual conversation about the idea, but I never put too much stock in any of them, and either I politely turned them down or the discussion fizzled out on its own.

To be honest, even if some incredible offer showed up, I'm not sure I would have accepted it during those years. I wasn't ready. After Menton, I was extremely hesitant to get into another restaurant situation, and although there was a time in my life when I believed the pinnacle of a cheffing career was to have a place with your name on the menu, times had changed. I was working, and I had freedom and money and none of the stress of managing a team of cooks or worrying about the food cost or sourcing or updating equipment in order to execute some elaborate nightly menu. So when a direct message showed up in my Instagram inbox in March of 2017, I wasn't exactly clearing my schedule to pursue the conversation.

The message was kind of standard-issue as these things go. It was a corporate food and beverage director reaching out about a new project in the works. I'd received that kind of thing before, and especially when I saw that it was coming from a hotel group, I was initially ready to say "Thanks but no thanks" and send it to the digital trash file. If I was going to do a restaurant at all, a *hotel* restaurant definitely wasn't going to be it.

Also, the message was regarding a property in Austin, Texas, which wasn't exactly a city on my radar. I'd never been to Texas, and I didn't know much about the state beyond the fact that its political leanings might've been out of step with my own.

Still, something about this message did grab me. I usually at least take a look at the source when someone reaches out, and upon searching for further details about the company this guy was representing, I realized that while I knew next to nothing about Austin, Texas, I *was* very familiar with the organization—the Sydell Group. These were the people behind one of my favorite New York spots, then called the NoMad. I had been there many times over the years, at times with Barbara, at other times with women I dated, and I always loved that place. It was the epitome of hospitality, which is unsurprising given its pedigree. NoMad was at the time run by Will Guidara and Daniel Humm, the owners of New York's Eleven Madison Park, which was, incidentally, named the number one restaurant in the world that very same year. NoMad wasn't a hotel restaurant; it was a restaurant that happened to be in a hotel. And with its innovative, thoughtful food and classy, modern, but timeless vibe, it had a lot in common with the kind of place I aspired to for myself.

I'd been presented with the idea of dipping an exploratory toe into these waters before. That's exactly how I had approached *Top Chef*, too—just take the first step and go through the motions—and that turned out pretty well. I figured I could at least investigate the idea. It would cost me no more than a little of my time to take the trip to Austin. Besides, I was subletting a place in Boston at the time, and as anyone who has ever weathered a New England winter will tell you, March is a good time to seek out warmer weather.

I read the message a few times and considered the idea before responding to say I'd be game to hear them out—and pretty soon I was on a plane headed southwest.

When I arrived, the air in Austin was warm but pleasant—it reminded me of spring vacations to Disney World when I was a kid and was a major contrast to what I'd left behind in Boston. I gratefully let the warmth fill my lungs while I prepared to head to the hotel. My destination was a Radisson in Austin. The Radisson is a budget hotel chain for cost-conscious travelers—not exactly the swank environment I remembered from the NoMad hotel in New York. But this was the property I was invited to. When I eventually spoke to Jeremy—the guy who sent me the message—to arrange my trip, he explained that the plan was to convert this particular Radisson into a LINE hotel, which already had a location in Los Angeles and would go on to expand to DC and San Francisco.

And while the pre-renovation hotel didn't exactly have a lot of memorable features at the time, I do distinctly remember two things about my first moments at that property. The first was the valet at the hotel, a lovely tall gentleman named Daniel. He welcomed me warmly and took my bags, and for the next two days I don't think I ever had to reach for a door handle.

The second was a sign on the main door to the hotel. It read: OPEN CARRY PROHIBITED.

Because, *right.* Texas. It was a stark reminder that I wasn't in the very blue state of Massachusetts anymore.

I checked in and let Jeremy know I'd arrived, and we arranged to meet in the lobby for a tour. We'd had enough interactions from afar for me to feel comfortable with him, but when we convened, I liked him immediately. He was around my age and had an easygoing vibe—definitely not the stuffy corporate-suit type that a title like his (vice president of food and beverage) might indicate. He was friendly and warm and lacked the air of ego so common in dudes holding positions of power, an air to which I'd become highly sensitive. It was also quickly evident that he knew his shit and was very put together. In that way, he was my kind of people.

My trip wasn't going to be a long one, so we got right down to business. Jeremy gave me a tour of the restaurant space and pointed out the things that would be changing once Sydell began renovating. With a little imagination, I was able to get a good sense of their plans, and it was exciting to envision. The place had history—in the 1960s, it was a jazz club—and a gorgeous view of Lady Bird Lake, which is part of the Colorado River. I could see how under new ownership there was potential to make this into a really spectacular destination with a story.

What I couldn't see, however, was myself in the kitchen. When we made our way into the space that was the food-service epicenter for the Radisson, it was—to put it politely—in need of some updates. The walls had yellowed from years of exposure to steam and grease and all the other elements of a kitchen. The equipment was dated and in disrepair, and the layout was a complete mess in terms of flow. It's not uncommon for major corporations like Sydell to invest the lion's share of its renovation capital in public-facing spaces and leave pennies in the budget for crucial elements like a functional kitchen. At that moment, I was simply a visitor with no stake in the project, so it was easy to be extremely frank with Jeremy. I told him—hypothetically speaking—that there was no way I could work with that kitchen the way it was.

He was very receptive and curious about what I thought would improve the space. And although this was a no-strings kind of discussion, it felt good to have an honest conversation and know that this person was listening to me and that my opinion was being valued. Even five years after Menton, I was still so traumatized, still skeptical that I'd be taken seriously or given any respect, and a conversation like this signaled that this had the potential to be a decent working relationship.

We toured three food-service areas: One would become a cocktail-focused concept; another was a large dining room; and the third was a smaller, separate room with sixty seats. The latter was the one I was most interested in, the place where I could envision myself running a small, intimate, dinner-only fine-dining concept.

But we weren't far enough along to get into the nitty-gritty on that. We talked at a high level about the culinary needs of the hotel and the program they had in mind. Again, these were just conversations, nothing more, and I was happy to talk through it all, knowing no commitments had been made.

That evening, we had dinner at the restaurant of another former *Top Chef* winner. It was casual and comfortable, and while we did discuss the project at the hotel, we also had some time to just shoot the shit over an excellent shared meal of hamachi collar and roti with shredded chicken and a coconut sauce that I remember to this day.

Afterward, we took a walk back to the hotel, and I got a chance to see a bit more of Austin. My visit happened to be during South by Southwest, a massive music festival that has earned an important spot in the music industry as a way to find new talent. It's also become a major part of Austin's identity and today draws more than three hundred thousand people to the city over the course of little more than a week.

Even aside from the events all over town as part of the festival, there was such an *energy* to the place. It felt like things were happening. I can't say I was totally sold on the project, the city, or the partnership, and I knew how much due diligence would have to be done and how many steps would have to be taken, whether or not I got involved. But my wheels were definitely turning, and by the time my plane's landing gear hit the tarmac back in Boston the next day, I couldn't help wondering if things might be happening for me, too.

Right around that time, yet another influential figure came into my world, thanks to a network of women. This time, it was an attorney. A few years earlier, I attended an event run by *Cherry Bombe*, a magazine dedicated to covering women in the food industry. While I was there, I made the acquaintance of a hospitality industry attorney named Jasmine who introduced herself and offered me her card.

"Call me if you ever need my services," she said. I was pleased to meet her, said thank you, pocketed the information, and then very much went on with my life.

In the months following the meeting with Jeremy in Austin, after a number of conversations back and forth with Sydell and a *lot* of deliberating, things were getting more serious, and the time came to make that call to Jasmine. There were enough reasons to get excited about the possibility of moving forward, but cautiously so, and I knew I couldn't do it alone. Hiring a lawyer to help me negotiate was a natural next step in escalating the process, and I was grateful to have held on to her information. It was a pleasure and a comfort to have another knowledgeable, accomplished, and powerful woman in my corner.

For my part, I had much to consider. In terms of due diligence, to be honest, I relied heavily on Sydell's track record and its roster of collaborators. Simply knowing that Will and Daniel had worked with them on NoMad was a major plus. The group had already proved that they could do justice to a hotel-based concept, give their collaborating operators a chance to put their own fingerprints on the place, and create a guest draw in conjunction with the property.

There were a lot of considerations beyond the business, though. On the personal front, I'd have to give up the freedom I'd had working independently for several years, not to mention Boston, the city that had been my home for so long. I couldn't do this halfway—at least not at first. And that meant a major lifestyle change. Still, as hard as it was to imagine such major shifts in all parts of my life, the timing felt right. I felt ready.

I had learned repeatedly that timing is everything. While I had been happy with my nomadic situation, I also knew it probably wouldn't last forever. Even freedom like that can lose its novelty after a while, and although I was often on planes (or trains or in cars) going from gig to gig, and my life wasn't exactly static, my need for that sense of turbulence—that evidence of forward momentum—never left me. I wasn't searching, but I was definitely in a place where I was more responsive to ideas by the time I received Jeremy's inquiry.

Also, although a hotel restaurant didn't sound especially appealing at first, I had begun to see the benefits. I knew for sure by then that I absolutely did not want to be an independent operator starting from scratch. This project gave me culinary autonomy and so much more. It gave me infrastructure. A hotel group has human resources, engineering, marketing, tech—tons of built-in support.

Among other considerations, I realized there were things I'd have to reconcile myself to or concede. For one thing, during our negotiations, it came to light that the little sixty-seat spot I'd seen during my visit—the one that seemed ideal for a small dinner-only concept—wasn't going to work out for my potential project. Jeremy and I had spoken about it since, and he explained that because of logistical reasons, including the fact that it was closer to the pool, it made more sense for it to be a faster concept that could serve swimmers and sunbathers. It was one of the early lessons about operating within a hotel like this; there were so many moving parts, so much to consider for every decision.

While I understood the logic, it meant that the role I was considering for myself was something entirely different from what I initially imagined. If I agreed, the restaurant I'd be in charge of would serve not just a few dozen patrons for dinner but would provide breakfast, lunch, dinner, *and* brunch for 160 seats—plus room service. I was about to go from no restaurant at all to running the equivalent of a mini empire.

That was daunting and could have been a deal-breaker. That said, I understood that with more services and diners, there would be more revenue. My relationship to money had evolved as an adult, and on a personal level, in the time since *Top Chef,* I managed to pay off all my debt. I felt like I'd climbed a mountain I never again wanted to face. While this was a business environment and not quite the same, I was very aware of the power of the dollar and understood that if I wanted to be successful, we needed to be able to generate serious, reliable revenue. I'd seen restaurants undercapitalized and miscalculated, and the closure rate is enough to scare off even the most well funded and meticulous planners.

As I considered the pros and cons, both personally and professionally, there was another factor that I found attractive about finally opening a restaurant. In my travels, I'd been to other chefs' establishments many times; I'd been on the receiving end of generously comped meals and drinks and enjoyed really lovely special treatment. I wanted the chance to return the favor to others. I wanted a place where I could invite people in and take care of them. I wanted to be a host again, to have a home base from which to offer that kind of hospitality and care.

And so after months of back-and-forth discussions and lengthy negotiations, a deal was hammered out with my new attorney's help—and I handed over the keys to my sublet.

Saying goodbye to my Boston family wasn't easy. I wished I could have brought them all with me or collapsed the distance between Texas and New England as easily as folding up an accordion-style paper map so I wouldn't have to part with them. In a parallel universe, maybe Steph and Robeisy would have come to work at the new restaurant. But although Steph and I were both chefs and our careers had been so intertwined over the years, she had her own path going forward, and it was different from mine. We respected that about each other; I knew I had her full support, and she had mine. I did ask Robeisy if she might have some interest in joining the team, but she was at a point where she was determining her next steps, and while she was appreciative, it just wasn't the move for her at the time.

Still, as tough as it was to take this step away from them, it felt good to know that everyone was really excited for me, and a few months later, before I fully relocated to Austin to get things underway, I chose a Greek restaurant called Kava where I would have my last meal in town with my friends. It was in the South End, not far from where Steph and I had our efficiency apartments, and not far from Stir. There were six or seven of us around that table, including Steph and Kim. We ate fried zucchini, grilled fish, phyllo with feta and honey, a short-rib-and-orzo dish, and various fried potato items (my standard order even to this day when I return) while stories were told and toasts were made to our time together and to hopes for my future. It was so bittersweet. I thought about my early days—visiting with Jonathan to find an apartment; the shared house in Charlestown; Top of the Hub and the Heartbreak Hotel; the Sensing days and then Stir. I tried to forget about Menton for the most part, but couldn't deny that I'd learned at least a few things there, too (mostly what I didn't want in my life), but more than anything I thought about the people. Steph and Scott, Kim, Barbara, Robeisy, and the rest of the people who had such an impact on me. It wasn't easy to leave, but I left knowing I didn't totally have to say goodbye.

When I touched down again in Austin in March of 2018, this time it was for the long haul. Well, for the next year and a half, at least. My contract gave me a place to live at what would soon be the LINE hotel while we got the restaurant up and running, and I was obligated to stay in the city for a minimum of eighteen months. After so much freedom, I appreciated the fact that the deal wasn't boxing me in indefinitely. I know I can endure just about anything if I can count on having an out, and although I was optimistic about the project, it was a comforting thought to know that there was a door open in the distance.

Prior to the official move, I had started taking shorter trips to Austin to try to get the ball rolling wherever possible. I kept myself busy writing menus and recipes, meeting with local urban farmers, poring over hiring websites and pulling names for future interviews, sitting through meetings galore—all the administrative behind-the-scenes work that many people may not realize goes into preparing to open a restaurant.

When I got to town for good, in March, it was time to start

building my crew. This was especially exciting to me because I'd learned during so many of my jobs over the years—through experiences good, bad, and ugly—how critical it is to have solid cooks in the kitchen. And my first order of business was to find the person who would be the core of my team and my very first hire: my sous chef.

Given that I was new to town, I didn't have my own network of people I could turn to for candidates. And although we had an HR department involved in talent acquisition, I was happy when Damon, the opening chef for another outlet on the property, gave me a personal recommendation—particularly since this was going to be a pivotal role.

When Alex showed up, there was a good vibe immediately. He arrived with a positive attitude and was fully prepared. It was pre-renovation, so we met in that old Radisson kitchen, but even if our facilities had been fully up and running and we had brand-new resources for it, I wasn't going to put him through the wringer of a big ceremonious tasting like the ones I'd gone through. I felt like it wasn't necessary. My metrics were different; I was more interested in the way he carried himself, his practices, and his personality. So instead, we kept it very casual and worked together on some practice dishes.

With ingredients from the local Whole Foods and a badly warped pan, we attempted to make an omelet, knowing it'd be next to impossible to pull off the classic perfect French-style dish with such subpar equipment. Alex also made a pork chop in that same shitty pan. He was good-natured about the situation and resourceful—he clearly knew how to work with what was in front of him—and we got along great.

The truth is, I never really needed to taste Alex's food. I could tell by the way he set up his cutting board and his knives, folded his towels and labeled containers, that he had his shit together. I wasn't looking for perfect results; what mattered was that he tried. I knew that even if he didn't cook the way I needed him to just yet, he had qualities—including a sense of professionalism and levity, a personality that lacked blustery ego—that fit with the culture I was hoping to build, one that would be supportive and mutually respectful. I could also sense that he had no issue with his boss being a woman, and for me, coming off Menton, that was huge.

Between the positive meeting and the fact that he came with an endorsement, I was sold, and as soon as Alex accepted the official offer to become my sous chef, we got down to the business of designing the menu. We had to continue working off-site in a rental kitchen, since the hotel was still undergoing renovations and the kitchen was nowhere near ready, but we did our best with what we had. And what we had, incidentally, was a Rachael Ray nonstick skillet with an orange handle that I'll never forget and that we still laugh about to this day. But we also had *fun*. We got excited creating certain staple items (in particular, a burger that was fucking delicious) and talked through options for the menu based on all kinds of inspiration. I wasn't interested in making super-high-end haute cuisine or anything like that. I wanted to create dishes that were inspired by my life, like mafaldini with champignon sauce, pearl onions, and Parmesan cheese—a nod to my Midwestern roots and love of Hamburger Helper as a kid—and crispy rice with crab, bacon, and saffron aioli, a mix of callbacks to the crab fried rice I had ordered at times in college and my love of New England hot crab rolls. It was fun and playful food from my soul. Alex really got what I was going for and brought great ideas to the table. We hammered out concepts while also keeping in mind that we couldn't get too attached to anything because there were still so many variables subject to change—between our test kitchen and the real thing, between the limbo of preopening and actual go time.

Meanwhile, we calculated food costs and created spreadsheets. Even though I never did go to business school, at some point in my career I began to understand that I'd not only learned how to cook but had also picked up practical economics. I learned certain practices and gleaned knowledge in my restaurant work, and then once I entered that freelance period, I had to manage my own affairs as an independent contractor. Now I was getting to apply some of those lessons in a new way. I remembered being a kid who loved creative subjects—art and music and even some writing—but never really excelled or even felt comfortable with math. Now, through the lens of something I really cared about, it was all starting to compute.

Alex and I worked hard on the menu, but I didn't want him putting in more than eight or nine hours a day: A good rule is not to burn out your people before you can get the lights turned on. And as anyone who has ever opened a restaurant knows, there's so much more to be done than coming up with burgers and pasta dishes. So once Alex headed home, I would go back to the hotel and do the work of getting the dining room set up, making decisions about every single detail that would create the dining experience and give our restaurant an identity. And while we did have help in some of those capacities (see more on that in the next chapter), as we counted the days to our official opening, we still needed to build out our kitchen team.

HR hosted hiring fairs, and Alex and I met with candidates and reviewed résumés. When you're starting out, it seems best to go for people who have real, proven experience. It feels like a way to mitigate risk when you're hiring an entire team rather than filling a single position. You need a solid, sturdy foundation, and you don't have a whole lot of time and space for trial and error.

With that in mind, Alex and I assembled our line cooks. Every role in a restaurant kitchen is critical, but the skills required are varied. A line-cook position, like the one I had at Top of the Hub, is fast-paced and high-intensity. It is about executing, keeping an eye on tickets, and getting food up and out. Prep cooks, on the other hand, have a little more time to do their jobs. They typically come in earlier than the rest of the crew, often before service begins, and—as their job title suggests—prepare the elements that the line cooks will later assemble and fire, including pastas, stocks, and sauces. They will also break down ingredients so that they can be snapped up quickly for cooking later.

When you're hiring prep cooks, you can take a little more time with them if they need some training or support. Line cooks, on the other hand, have to be extremely solid—there are no spare moments for messing around or messing up. When you're opening an entirely new restaurant, this is extra nerve-racking, because it's not as if you're inserting a single new hire into an already solid and high-functioning line.

Alex and I looked for candidates with the deepest résumés—the ones who looked good on paper—because that was the most useful metric in that scenario. Perhaps it says something about the food industry at the time that those candidates were almost all men. This wasn't surprising, given that the pool of women in the culinary world was more like a shallow puddle and that even fewer of those women had experience in line-cook positions.

By contrast, our prep team wound up being composed of mostly young women. They didn't have the stacked CVs, but I hired them based on what I felt was a compatibility with the culture I had in mind and, honestly, just gut feeling. I really liked them.

It would take time for the lesson to emerge from this process—that instinct can sometimes override on-paper experience—but suffice it to say that the prep team long outlasted many of that first round of line cooks. I had gone into this project hopeful that I could start fresh, especially since we were building from the ground up. I wanted an environment that had the safety, support, and warmth I'd enjoyed at Stir, and even though this wasn't a ten-seat restaurant, I had hoped I could carry that energy into this new restaurant. But as we approached opening and then did a soft launch, I had some discouraging moments, running into the same issues as I experienced at Menton—some insubordinate cooks who didn't want anything to do with me, who talked behind my back, who refused to respect me, and who created tension in the kitchen.

For better or worse, though, I couldn't leave this time. That said, the advantage in this scenario was that, unlike Menton, the new restaurant *did* have my name on the menu. Although I didn't have carte blanche to kick people out—there was an HR process for that, and I had to adhere to a three-strikes structure—over time, we were able to weed out the negative energy. It helped that I had support there in the kitchen with me, too. To this day, I hear Alex tell the occasional surly cook, "If you don't want to be here, you don't have to be." He shared my values and priorities from day one, and I took great comfort in that.

Back at Menton, I had begun to learn an important lesson—that there is a difference between "nice" and "kind." In both restaurants, I tried to be the former, by which I mean I was accommodating, always wary of rocking the boat, and thinking that if I could keep the peace, we'd have a productive, positive kitchen.

But when it was my restaurant and my kitchen, I realized quickly that I had to put into practice what I'd learned—that leaders do not have to be nice. They have to be *kind*. Accommodating everyone does no one any favors, and part of being kind is holding people accountable. It's about being able to encourage but also guide and correct and even discipline at times, and to do so without being degrading. When I was being too nice, I wasn't really running the kitchen in a way that allowed everyone to feel safe and thrive. And that—creating an environment in which everyone can reach their full potential—is, above all, the job of a leader.

Although my goal was to get to a point where we had a stellar team and a united front, that was going to take some time, and when June of 2018 rolled around, we were going to have diners in seats—ready or not. Those months leading up were spent in deep preparation, trying to calculate and plan for every possible scenario and pitfall. And that required a *lot* of practice.

We started by conducting mock services in which our front-of-house team would punch a handful of tickets every fifteen minutes. The kitchen then put up those dishes, which servers carried and dropped to empty tables, then cleared and reset. It was a very controlled way to get our sea legs, a chance to evaluate and exchange feedback about every single element of service for both front and back of house, such as whether the configuration of the line was efficient, if the layout was working or could be improved upon, and how we could tighten points of communication. It was basically playing restaurant, the way kids might play with a toy tea set—except with, you know, real tools and fire.

The next phase was booking for "real" guests—in this case, hotel employees, including the engineering and sales teams. This was a way to develop a muscle memory by serving some actual human beings while still working out kinks in a relatively low-stakes environment.

Finally, we invited people to two nights of Friends and Family. F&F, as it's called in the industry, is a rite of passage for restaurants— part practice and part celebration—and it's the last chance to get a handle on any changes that need to be made before going fully public. We had a guest list that included people flying in from the corporate team in New York plus—as the name implies—friends and family. F&F is still controlled in terms of reservations, but it has none of the surprise variables like bar seating and walk-ins, and it raises the stakes to that second-to-last notch, the one just below real deal.

When you're in the midst of this process, particularly as you're closing in on being fully open, lots of people show up to say they're happy for you, to ask if you're proud and excited, and to express their enthusiasm. I was, without question, thrilled to be opening that restaurant in so many ways and for so many reasons. I knew that in my heart. But to be honest, it can be tough to take a step back and embrace it during those moments, when you're always catching something out of the corner of your eye that you want to fix, when you can't shake the feeling that you've missed something somewhere, when you think you could be doing just a *little* more to make it *extra* perfect. Preparation has always helped put me at ease and soothe my anxieties, but we could have continued practicing forever and I probably still wouldn't have felt ready to open. Even with all this lead-up—and with all the nights I stayed awake playing back every step in my mind, considering how and where to tweak things to make sure I'd seen every angle, anticipated every issue, and covered every base to set us up for success—I still didn't feel like we were where we needed to be after F&F. Some of what was on my mind were details no one else would likely have noticed from the outside, but I couldn't shake the feeling of wanting to be better.

The expectations felt stratospheric. It was the first time I'd done something like this on my own, and I felt that pressure to perform, to prove, to produce. But this wasn't just about my own name. I was no longer living the nomad lifestyle. I had a team and partners now—people who had invested in me and the restaurant in so many ways. This was an organization, and there were major implications for everyone involved if we weren't successful.

People in the service industry are fond of saying that everyone in the world should spend at least some time working in a restaurant for a number of reasons—from understanding food systems to the importance of tipping properly. But the work itself conditions you. It prepares you for so many challenges, and I know that I was able to handle some of that pressure in part because of the way I'd been trained in my many past restaurant jobs—when you're on the line during a rush and tickets are spewing out of that machine; when you have a brief moment of panic because you're so in the weeds that you're absolutely sure you'll drown there. But then very quickly, it goes away. That panic disappears because you know you're going to get it done. And you do, because there's no other option.

I'm not sure you can ever feel 100 percent prepared to do something like this. At some point when opening a restaurant (and, I imagine, other businesses) you realize that you can't possibly manage every single detail. Trust me: I've tried. If you wait for that moment, you will never open or serve a single thing. You have to accept that you've done your absolute best and let it ride.

I don't have children, but that's what I imagine it's like: You realize that you can't hold their hands on the bus or sit beside them on their first day of preschool (or college, for some parents). It's got to be so scary to let go, to be so vulnerable, to open yourself and your child up to the potential pains of the outside world. You just have to trust that you did your best and that you will continue to do so and hope that this extension of you—this piece of your heart—will be kindly received into the world.

I often think about my own parents and how they raised me. How even at the times when I'm certain they knew I was facing challenges, or when I *was* a challenge, they gave me the space to figure it out. Maybe they were terrified. I have to say that in high school, or in my Chicago days, like most kids and teenagers, I wasn't considering my parents' feelings as much. As I got older, though, I realized how rare and special it was that I always had their support with a generous amount of distance. Above all, I always had their trust.

I knew a long time ago that having kids wasn't something I wanted for my life, so I wouldn't have the chance to extend that kind of love and support in the same way to another human. But like a lot of people, I *had* considered what I'd name a child if I did have one, and somewhere in my mind, I'd filed away Arlo Grey. After extensive deliberating about what to call the restaurant, just weeks before opening, it came to me, and there was no second choice.

And although I didn't feel that Arlo Grey was 100 percent fully formed the day we served our first meal, I had no choice but to trust—trust myself to continue to adapt and problem-solve, trust that I'd made a sound decision to partner with Sydell, trust that I'd selected a reliable and like-minded colleague in Alex, trust that in time, the team would get sorted out and we'd find our footing. And I had to trust that because I had put something out into the world with care and thought, with good intentions and for the right reasons, Arlo Grey would be kindly received.

Most restaurants these days opt for a "soft open," meaning they don't make a big announcement. They just unlock the doors and let business slowly start to percolate. That's what we did after F&F, and frankly, it's the only way I'd ever consider opening a place—it's way too much pressure and too precarious to roll out a red carpet for a major grand opening when a restaurant is in its infancy. A soft opening lets the team continue to find its footing while business grows organically. For the most part, we let the news spread the old-fashioned way—by word of mouth. It was also a huge help to have a built-in clientele, thanks to the hotel. Eventually, when I felt we'd warmed to the water, I posted on Instagram that we were taking reservations, and my own followers began showing up for us. That felt really good. No matter how many people pat you on the back and tell you it's going to be great, no matter how much press you field or projections you review, it's impossible to shake the fear that when the time comes, no one will actually show up. We didn't have that problem, and to this day I'm so unbelievably grateful to the guests who choose our restaurant when there are so many choices out there.

We continued to keep a firm grip on operations, blocking reservations and slowly releasing more over the course of the first year, because as much as you want to be filling up the reservation books, it's critical to build in a way that's manageable, so you don't risk overwhelming a new team and system. That can only result in disappointed guests. That said, sometimes you can't avoid that scenario. Even if you're fully prepared and you ease into service, there are bound to be people who are dissatisfied with their experience. Any chef will tell you that reviews can be nerve-racking. That was true back in the day when only restaurant critics and major publications had the chance to weigh in, but once the general public got in on the game—first with websites like Yelp and Tripadvisor and then through social media—it created an entirely new layer of anxiety.

Our initial reviews had some frustrating commentary. In particular, we got dinged for portion sizes and pricing, which honestly isn't totally uncommon no matter what the restaurant is. But this feedback for me was a reminder that I wasn't in the Northeast market anymore. Austin isn't New York or LA or Boston. Austin is very much its own ecosystem, with its own identity and its own interpretation of dining categories and the value of food. To me, what seemed like an approachable concept—one that had elements of soul and whimsy, which was fun and relatively casual but executed with finesse, was considered "high-end" in the eyes of the Austin public. Maybe because the buzz was all about a New York hotel group with a "celebrity" chef at the helm (a term I still can't get on board with), there was a certain level of expectation. We had people who thought we were too fancy and others who felt we weren't fancy enough.

In retrospect, I'll be the first to admit that our opening menu wasn't right for Austin. It was a learning curve, trying to understand who our guests were and what they were looking for. Initially, our portions were a little too dainty, and the food and vibe *did* feel a little too high-end. It wasn't right for the space or for the volume we were doing. Whereas my natural cooking style is very subtle, this had to be a bit more assertive. I wouldn't say we capitulated or sacrificed our culinary point of view, but we had to find a balance.

I especially looked to Alex for this. He was born and raised in Texas, which was a huge help, and I leaned on him to help bring "more" to the menu but to do so through an Arlo Grey lens. Our relationship evolved in this way as we came to define the restaurant's cuisine in collaboration. Early on, he'd bring me a dish, and I'd give feedback, suggest some edits—ways to refine it to fit within Arlo Grey's aesthetic. These days, he has that pretty much on lock. He knows when to push and when to pull back, how to create something our guests will love while maintaining the art and technique that feels integral to the identity of our restaurant.

We course-corrected quickly after opening. Our portions got larger; we ended up eating the cost on some items and balancing the menu to compensate in others, and we started adjusting our offerings for our audience. We learned to adapt, to listen to diners and try not to impose upon them a concept that didn't fit their city or their lifestyle. We approached those efforts without ego, because at the end of the day, that's what a restaurant is—a place for the community, a place to gather, a place that provides hospitality. And even though we're not serving dishes the exact way we initially conceived of them, we found a happy medium—understanding Arlo Grey in the context of its city—that allowed us to retain our culinary identity while still serving the guests who were coming to see us.

I'm proud of our food. We didn't please everyone at first (I know we still don't), but we have found our people—the ones who want to dine with us and who inspire us to show up every day. They even helped us survive a pandemic no one could ever have predicted and welcomed us back when we reopened our doors—after many, many pivots.

I look back at those early days, when I was overwhelmed and overworked; when I had nowhere near the amount of sleep a human should have. Sure, there are things I'd do differently now: I'd take better care of myself, for one thing. But every step forward or stumble back came with an invaluable lesson and helped strengthen what started out as nothing more than an idea and a conversation and became its own little ecosystem of diners, kitchen crew, corporate support, and servers. Even Daniel, the valet who welcomed me to the Radisson that very first day, became part of the Arlo Grey story, taking a job on the bar team.

It has been a wild journey, one that started with baby steps, but I am immensely proud of what Arlo Grey has grown into. While it might have been my "baby" in the beginning, it has taken on its own identity, and the restaurant has become a home of sorts for so many.

In 2018, I received another direct message on Instagram about Arlo Grey, this time from the mother of a sixteen-year-old. She asked if we would consider taking her daughter on as a stage—an apprentice, in culinary-speak. She said the girl would work for free. I assured the mother that we would pay her, of course, and said we'd love to meet her. Then we welcomed her when she traveled to Austin for a weekend to stage for us. Two years later, when she was eighteen, this young person moved from North Carolina to Austin so she could work with us and has been part of the family ever since.

This is just one story of many, and today when I look around, I know that our kitchen team is a family, one that welcomes and supports people who really care and want to be part of it. This isn't the dude-bro drinking-and-partying culture of the old days. These are charming people who play video games together after work. They bring birthday cakes in for one another. A couple of cooks even have Arlo Grey tattoos because the place, the job, and the people mean so much to them—and that doesn't have to do with me, exactly. It has to do with the environment that has been fostered by the combination of people. What I'm most proud of now is having built a culture that attracts not only talent but also kindness. Collectively, we have a kitchen founded on congeniality, cooperation, and collaboration.

We also have diverse representation, not because we try to check boxes but because the more types of people we welcome, the more types of people we attract. The food business is famously homogenous, particularly in top positions. Having a restaurant and the power to help hire, promote, and foster diverse talent is a chance to make a real, quantifiable difference. As I've learned so many times before, being a vital part of a team is critical to my sense of self, too. After so many years of trying to find my place, having a vibrant, enthusiastic, and extremely diverse group of cooks and servers is exhilarating, and the fact that they came looking to join the team, that they trusted me, was proof positive that I'd made some good decisions in my life.

Arlo Grey was never about making my mark and getting stars or awards, although I do want those accolades for my team, because they're so talented, dedicated, and hardworking and because they deserve recognition. Instead, for me, it was about having a home base where I could invite people to come and enjoy a good meal and company. It was an exercise in building something entirely new, yet it was also constructed upon a foundation I'd been building my whole life. Sometimes you get a chance to really apply all the skills you've accumulated over time for a single major effort. Everything you've learned in personal and professional relationships, in various eras and contexts—you have to draw on that entire spectrum of experiences to accomplish a goal.

And while I always do my best to pass along some of that knowledge, Arlo Grey and the team taught me so much in return. Maybe more than anything, I learned lessons about leadership and responsibility to a team. By the time I opened Arlo Grey, I was a very different person from the one I'd been at Menton. I did not come in quiet or try to keep myself small, the way I had back in Boston, in part because I had had some time to build up my confidence through the experiences I'd been through in between. But also because I had to figure it all out so that I could teach others, so that we could operate as a unit, so that we could continue moving forward—because I was the only one with the authority to make those decisions. I've learned through their response to my leadership, and I have a deeper understanding now about what it means to lead, thanks to the people who want to *be* led.

I always knew I wouldn't live in Austin forever, so it was important to me to make sure they knew that and were prepared. By the time those eighteen months were up, I had no problem stepping away, certain that when I made my return trips, I would find the kind of healthy, happy environment I'd always hoped for in my career.

I sometimes think back to that direct message from Jeremy and about the ways that being open and curious and taking an almost playful approach to life changed everything for me. But while we both might have hoped that we'd create a successful, thriving restaurant together, neither of us could have predicted that the most profound, joyful, life-changing part of my time in Austin wouldn't exactly be about the restaurant at all.

14

've been fortunate enough to travel to a lot of places in the world—for cooking, for television, for press, for professional and personal reasons. But if you told me that the most magical place I'd ever go—where I'd experience the most meaningful, unforgettable, transformative hours of my life—wouldn't be a tropical fjord in Brazil or a Norwegian archipelago or any of the cities where I've lived or worked or called home but rather a small backyard in suburbia, I'm pretty positive I wouldn't have believed you. But in the spring of 2021, that's exactly where I found myself, standing under a blue New England spring sky and preparing to commit to the love of my life.

So much of my life has been about expectation. My own expectations of the world and of myself, my concern over the expectations others might have of me, and my fear of not living up to them. But one of the things I've learned is that magic and love are totally unpredictable forces, and finding them isn't luck. It's a blend of elements: place, people, circumstance, timing, hard work, openness, and an appreciation of the unexpected. And that was the combination that led me to my wedding day that April, on a journey that started years earlier and thousands of miles from that unexpectedly magical spot.

As a chef, I've seen so many couples having their meet-cutes, major life moments, and even falling in love over dinner. But for Bianca and me, it wasn't a special meal that brought us together. It was a plate.

It was early 2018, and I was about to open Arlo Grey. That moment was the culmination of so many projects and efforts, challenges and adventures that I could never have even dreamed of. Now I was as ready as I'd ever be. It was so close; I could practically taste the mafaldini with champignon sauce.

But as anyone who has ever opened a restaurant can tell you, *so close* can still mean so very, very far. It's a delicate dance trying to navigate what feels like a billion interconnected decisions, a web of causes and effects that must be obsessively managed all while somehow sticking to some sort of schedule. There were always so many options and opinions and interactions, and with very little time in between to recharge, it was hell on my social anxiety, which I'd been struggling to manage most of my life. But a major upside was that there was infrastructure built in, systems in place, and I was supported and encouraged by a whole team. I didn't have to do it all alone. I had been collaborating with so many people, all working on this one thing with me, and on one particularly freezing January morning, I was about to meet another one.

The day had gotten off to a disorienting start: Austin had experienced an ice storm—a total freak thing in central Texas. Growing up in Michigan, and then living in Boston long enough, made me develop a thick skin for the cold, but I'd gone a little soft by then. When I arrived in the ballroom where the meeting was being held, the hotel, which was still under construction, didn't have fully operational heat, and I was doing my best to look pulled together while still staying warm enough to function.

I was going to a lot of meetings in those days, and it could be a slog at times, but I had been actually looking forward to this one for a few reasons. First, I was there to meet the corporate director of food and beverage for the Sydell Group of hotels, who was flying in from New York for this and who, I knew, was a woman. Nothing against dudes in general, but I had been surrounded by *a lot* of them so far, and I was very stoked to have some female energy in the mix. I was also aware that the role of corporate director of food and beverage was a really important one for the restaurant. This person was going to be responsible in a big way for making sure we got this shit up and running smoothly, and it was reassuring to know that support was going to be in place. And lastly, after a whole lot of decisions that were about abstract, stressful, or, frankly, totally unsexy things, this one was going to be *fun*. The objective of the meeting was to review and pick out OS&E—industry-speak for operating supplies and equipment, a.k.a. plates, glasses, and serving ware. In layman's terms, it meant I was going to get to spend a few hours looking at pretty things, which was a happy departure.

Bianca Dusic, corporate director of food and beverage for the Sydell Group, was standing across the room when I arrived. Now, I wish I could paint you some grand romantic picture of this moment and tell you that I knew instantly, that it was love at first sight, and that I made some great gesture and swept her off her feet right then and there. But that's not what happened. Of course, I knew immediately, objectively, that Bianca was beautiful, but that's just not where my mind was. I wasn't thinking that way at all, and neither was she.

While my first impressions of Bianca weren't romantic ones per se, the thing that has really stuck with me from our first meeting was a hug. It wasn't uncommon in those days for women to exchange a hug instead of a handshake, even in professional settings, and that's how we greeted each other when we were introduced. Sometimes you can hug someone and just tell that it's a formality, maybe even feels forced or detached. And Bianca was a total professional about it—we both were. But what I remember more than anything was an overwhelming sense of warmth. I'm not just talking about the fact that the room was literally freezing and that another human being is inherently going to have some heat, but Bianca radiated warmth. And when you're stressed, bone-tired, and nearly at the end of your rope, that kind of thing can be comforting in a way you didn't even know you needed. I've thought about that hug a lot over the years, because Bianca hugs me now in the exact same way. To me, that is evidence of how genuine she is, how generous and present she is, whether that's with someone she's meeting for the very first time or with the person she's chosen as a partner in life.

That day, though, in addition to that sense of authenticity, I was also struck by her poise and professionalism and was so grateful that she seemed to have her shit together. I wouldn't find out until later, but Bianca was in a super-stressful whirlwind of her own. She was based in New York, where Sydell had a corporate office, but she had a big job and was continually on the road to open new properties. She'd come off a trip for two other hotels and had been only briefly at home in Manhattan, where her father was visiting from Australia, when she got the call to come to Austin. She had to leave him behind and hop on a plane super last minute, and now I look back and I can't imagine she was thrilled to be there that morning, but I would never have known she wasn't anything but one thousand percent in it.

After our hug and introductions, Bianca wasted no time getting down to business, which I appreciated. She led me to a series of fifteen-foot folding tables, all already set up with glasses and plates and silverware and water jugs for me to look at. Each item was more beautiful than the next. I'd developed a muscle for making decisions quickly, but I could see instantly that this was going to be extra tough. It was obvious that Bianca had incredible taste and had put a lot of thought into this, and even though she was just coming on board, it already felt like she really *got* the heart of our project.

I knew I'd been eager to look through this stuff, but it dawned on me then, while looking over these very tangible objects, just how meaningful this part of the job is. When you're in the thick of something like this, it's easy to lose track of the fact that it's a real thing. These dishes, at some point, would be a direct connection between our kitchen and our future diners, and *that* was a thrill. I envisioned the servers we were about to hire picking them up at expo (the station that manages tickets and the transfer of food from the kitchen to the dining room) and delivering them to the tables, carrying the dishes we'd been spending so much time developing amid the chaos. I sensed that Bianca understood this and took the task seriously; not one of those pieces felt phoned in or standard-issue. Each was unique and had personality.

It took a few minutes, but eventually, a charcoal-gray plate caught my eye.

"Oh, I love this," I said, pointing it out. "We need this here."

Bianca lit up.

"That's my favorite," she said. I was already sold when she reached for the plate so we could take a closer look. But then she turned it over, and our jaws dropped. There, stamped into the gray ceramic, was the word *Arlo*. I could not believe it. I could have chosen any one of hundreds of plates, but *that* was the one that spoke to me. *That* was Bianca's favorite. *That* was the one that seemed fated to sit on the tables at the recently named restaurant.

It totally surprised Bianca, too. We both laughed and made a few jokes about fate or the universe, whatever you want to call it, and about how it must've been meant to be. Of course, we had no idea that those greater powers had much bigger plans in store for us.

A romantic relationship was still a long way off, but that moment was the beginning of a period when Bianca became one of the most important people in my life. That was in part because we were both dedicated entirely to our jobs and needed each other to be successful. I trusted Bianca immediately, which surprised me, because trust has never come easily for me. I've reflected on that over the years, how quickly I came to trust her. Maybe it was because I knew we had this shared goal. But in general, Bianca's energy is something really special. She's someone of great empathy and kindness as well as tough love and hard-ass work. Those were qualities I valued most in any person in any capacity. I felt so lucky in those days that we were on the same team. It was evident that she *cared*, deeply, and that gave me instant confidence that she was gonna get shit done.

We were also spending a lot of time together and getting to know each other the way you do when you're in the trenches, and her openness in those moments not only cemented my trust in her but also made me just generally want to be around her. A lot of people were coming to me with problems, roadblocks, issues that needed my attention—it would deplete me by the end of the day. Bianca, on the other hand, was positive and proactive. Work, which had been so hard, so intense, so stressful, was feeling vibrant and fun again with her. We attended corporate meetings together and sat side by side. We stayed up and worked until two in the morning sometimes. When the deliveries arrived, we sat together, unwrapping glassware and those charcoal-gray dishes and running them through the new washer. We ordered takeout and told stories, and sometimes we didn't even talk at all. I was surprised at just how comfortable I was in silence with Bianca. In fact, being with Bianca calmed me in so many ways.

I can't say I was always at ease, of course. One night, during a run-through of service as we were approaching an official opening, it felt like everything was absolutely blowing up. I had really thought we were ready, but it was a disaster. I was losing my shit halfway through the night, and I tried to keep a lid on it around my team, so I went to Bianca instead. Bianca knew the stakes. Bianca understood how much it all meant to me. Bianca was the one I trusted most. I told her in no uncertain terms that this restaurant was *not* fucking opening. Now, anyone who knows me will tell you that I can be impatient and hardheaded at times. I have always hated being told what to do and have never known someone who can really reach me when things go south. That's why it still surprises me how quickly Bianca talked me off the ledge that night. Later, when I had the time and space to reflect on that moment, I was struck by how profound that was for me. Not only had Bianca inspired and motivated me during our time together, but she had managed to soothe me, too. And that was something I'd never experienced before. Being with Bianca was full of surprises.

I can't tell you exactly when my feelings started to shift. It happened so slowly and subtly that I didn't even recognize it. In retrospect, I wonder if I didn't know I *was* falling in love because I truly didn't know it *could* happen like that. In my life, and especially in the high-intensity food industry, so many connections were formed during moments of adrenaline and chaos, and in prior romantic relationships, there was never a slow build. They were immediately romantic, lustful, and intense.

I wasn't thinking about Bianca that way for a long time. For one thing, I was coming out of a relationship and could only make the mental space for Arlo Grey and work. Also, Bianca was essentially my superior, not to mention that she was straight-identifying. I had no idea if she'd been with a woman or would ever consider it. What I *did* know was that we had something special. I believe in soul connections, and she was squarely in that category. I thought we were just building a really beautiful friendship.

Slowly, though, some creeping feelings caught my attention. It began with the hugs. I was living at the hotel, and whenever Bianca was in town, she stayed there, too. At the end of our long, late nights, we'd walk to the elevators together and hug. Absolutely nothing was unusual about that, especially since that's how we started our working relationship from minute one. But at some point, there was a shift. I started to feel super awkward about those hugs. It felt like it happened all of a sudden, and I kept thinking, *What the fuck? Why is this so weird?*

It didn't take me long to realize that I was starting to have *those* kinds of feelings, and that scared the shit out of me. Bianca had come to mean so much to me, not just in my work but also in my life. I did not want to fuck this up. I think part of me wanted to avoid her and hide for that reason and because when you have a crush, you experience this weird mix of fear and excitement. But with Bianca, that fear couldn't possibly overpower how much I wanted to spend time with her. It was the excitement—the positive side of it all—that won the battle. We always had work to do, but there were some late nights when it felt like we were stretching it out, taking longer than necessary. I couldn't help but wonder, and hope, that it was because she just wanted to spend more time together, too. And that's what made me start to question whether Bianca was feeling things of her own. She's told me since about moments when she knew, like when I sat a little too close to her during lunch in the ballroom and there was a charge between us, or when she caught herself looking at me at an off-site catering event, when I was totally absorbed in the job and oblivious that she was feeling anything at all. I did my best to keep my questions to myself and play it cool, and I think I did a pretty decent job for a while there. Until the high five.

It had become our tradition to play games. We didn't go out to bars or party; this was how we could decompress and have a little fun. The games were old-school: pick-up sticks, connect four, stuff like that. One night, after a very, *very* long day, Bianca and I got set up to play a few rounds of jacks—the game with the little rubber bouncy ball. We brought tequila and sat on the pool deck, and we got situated while she set up the game. And I found myself staring at her hands.

I've always noticed people's hands—not in a creepy, fetishy way but just as a beautiful representation of a human, telling a story of their lives and who they are. I watched Bianca as she arranged these little game pieces on the ground and was totally captivated by her hands. It felt like this very vulnerable thing, and I found myself wanting to do for her, to take care of her, to protect her, to be there for her for anything she needed or wanted. I wanted to hold one of those hands. I wanted to be her person, and I knew it then so clearly.

I tried to focus on the game instead of the person playing with me for a while, and then, after a few rounds of laughing and talking and just enjoying each other's company as we always had, something happened that we now refer to simply as the high five.

The game was over, I know that much. I can't tell you who won, but we sealed the end of the match with a high five. And that high five—your average, run-of-the-mill meeting of two hands to celebrate something—lingered just a little too long. When our palms made contact, the air between us became supercharged. My heart was suddenly racing, and I totally panicked. I felt woozy, intoxicated not by the tequila but by Bianca's touch. But still, I was lucid enough to know that logically, this was not the time or the place. It was obvious that she was feeling it, too, and we were both flustered. We hurried back to the elevators, maybe both a little fearful of what would happen next if we let it. I wanted so badly to be next to her, but I needed to think and to make sure that if something was going to happen, we were going to do this right. That's not how I'd ever handled these feelings in the past, but this was too important. Bianca was too important.

Instead, we spent the rest of the night on FaceTime from the safe distance of our respective hotel rooms. In the course of that conversation, I suggested we take a drive the next day. I thought it might be a good idea to get off the property and spend a little time together in a different context. I still don't know how I got any sleep that night, but I do know I was bursting out the door by the time our meeting time arrived the next morning.

To this day, taking a drive together is one of our favorite things. We just jump in the car and pick an open spot or a body of water on the map and go discover something. Had I only known how many rides I'd get to take with Bianca in the future, I might've been able to keep it together, but on that first day, the ride was much more intentional. We wound our way out of town, and I suggested we stop at the home of one of my friends, about thirty minutes outside of Austin. I think we both knew something was about to happen and that we both wanted it to. Bianca had always made me feel steady and reassured, but this was a totally different story, and by the time we arrived and parked in the driveway, I could feel the tension manifesting itself physically. It's a well-documented tell that my nose sweats whenever I eat spicy food and sour candy or whenever I'm super nervous. In moments like that, you always have a version of yourself you want to present. I wonder if it ever goes that way for anyone. I knew it was about to happen. But all I could think was, *Be cool, Kristen; be smooth.* But I was wearing sunglasses and could already feel them slipping down my nose.

I took a breath, and finally, I leaned in. It's truly unreal in those moments how much one single human can be and feel and hold at the same time. I was in disbelief that this was really happening. I was nervous and excited, shy and confident, and it was all hitting at once. Cooking for a living has taught me to be aware of all my senses and respond to them quickly, but right then, it was total overload, and I was almost paralyzed by it. Until the sense of touch took over, and as soon as our lips came together, all those chaotic feelings melted away in a snap, along with the rest of the world. I was so in it, so completely wrapped up, that it was only when our sunglasses smacked together that we remembered we were still parked in my friend's driveway and that maybe it was time to move. *Yep. Super smooth, Kristen,* I thought. But it didn't matter anymore because all I wanted was to do that again. I lifted my sunglasses and then reached over and removed Bianca's, too, so I could look in her eyes, and now I knew she was feeling it all, too. I kissed her again, this time with all the confidence in the world that she wanted to kiss me, too.

After that, we spent the rest of the afternoon together, driving around and stopping for food (chicken skewers for Bianca, chicken tenders and french fries for me) and to sit by one of Austin's natural springs. We had spent so many days and hours and minutes together by then, but that whole day felt like a moment in time, one that was totally ours.

It couldn't have been more perfect, and to say I was on cloud nine could never do it justice, but that's not to say this was an effortless transition. Things were complicated, and we weren't ready to be super public. There was the restaurant and the team to consider. We'd both invested our hearts and so much of ourselves in Arlo Grey, and we wanted to make sure we didn't compromise any of our hard work.

There was also the fact that Bianca hadn't dated women. I had been with straight women before and been in secret relationships in the past. In those instances, whenever we were keeping it quiet, either because one or both of us remained in the closet, it didn't feel good. I know so many people in the queer community who can identify with this experience; it can be corrosive and cause deep shame. With Bianca, though, our decision to initially keep things under wraps didn't feel driven by shame in that way. It felt deliberate, intentional, like it was our choice, and we were making a mutually agreed-upon decision. We were being protective, trying to give our relationship time to grow and develop, to allow us to understand its needs and its nature before exposing it to the elements. The fact that I wasn't concerned spoke to the confidence I had in us. I felt totally secure in a way I never had before in my life, and I had no doubts about us as a couple. I knew we would tell the world when the time was right.

While I was undeniably in love and living all the joyful elements that come along with a new relationship, the restaurant had really hit its stride, too. I couldn't wait to share both my love and my baby with the people I cared about most, so when *Food & Wine* magazine asked me to participate in a Thanksgiving story for which I could invite the closest people in my life to Arlo Grey and cook a holiday feast for them, I was grateful for so many reasons.

Because of the lead time for the magazine, we had to do the shoot in the summer, and I was counting down the days, knowing I'd have all my loved ones around the table. My parents and Jon were coming, and Steph and Kim were traveling from Boston along with Robeisy, who even came in to help me cook the dishes that were so important to me. But I was also nervous. The stakes were so much higher than they were for the average press spot. My friends and family had never been to Arlo Grey and were coming to see it for the first time, which was huge for me. And on top of that, they were going to meet Bianca. I was asked to cook a Thanksgiving meal inspired by my Midwestern roots. I was hoping to create an environment where I thought everyone would feel comfortable and taken care of so I could focus on the relationships around the table. These were the people closest to me, so they were the ones who knew Bianca and I were together. I wanted my people to love the restaurant. I wanted them all to love Bianca, and I wanted her to love them.

I thought I had some reason for concern. My mom is one of the most loving, welcoming people I know, but she has a protective wall and never especially warmed to my previous partners. Maybe it's a mother's instinct (she really did know best in those cases), but I already knew Bianca was different for me. Even though I think in my gut I felt sure they would get along—that my mom would be able to see how special this woman is right off the bat—I couldn't help feeling anxious about their meeting.

In retrospect, I can see that I had nothing to worry about; Bianca has this indescribable way of getting people to feel comfortable around her, and my mother is an excellent judge of character. I didn't even have to intervene. While I was busy preparing a meal and handling the work part of the day and the hospitality for my guests, my mom approached Bianca on her own and asked if she would help her get ready for the meal and the shoot. Maybe the only thing that can make me love someone more deeply is to watch them care for and interact with someone else I love. Bianca helped my mom pick out an outfit. She applied her makeup for her. I had never seen that kind of openness from my mother. To see the two of them together nearly made my heart explode, and I could not get over how lucky I was, for so many reasons.

The rest of that day—the meal, the way everyone got along and laughed and joked and just got to know one another—exceeded my greatest hopes. Family, in all its forms, has always been so important to me. When I looked around and saw all these people I love in this one place—my parents and my brother, my best friends and my girlfriend among them—I felt so much hope for the future.

With Bianca, there were days of perfection like these, right along with the challenges of our daily life, and we didn't shy away from either. We embraced the moments that might be challenging and acknowledged and showed up for what was important to the other person. That was part of what made what we were building so beautiful to me. It wasn't peaks and valleys: It was a healthy evolution, moving forward subtly in so many ways. I think that allowed us to build a foundation and care for each other in a profound way. Having space and time to really learn about each other and from each other was the result of a slow, steady progression that started as a friendship and was evolving into family. And when the real

Thanksgiving rolled around, in November, we had another mile marker on the horizon.

—————

For about a year, Bianca and I had been sharing my Austin hotel room whenever she was in town. It was tight, but somehow even without a traditional home base, we always found a way to make space for each other and make it as much of a home as it could be. When we weren't together, Bianca was back in New York, and we made it work long distance, too. It wasn't easy at times, but we both knew it was always worth the effort.

Contractually, my end date with Arlo Grey was approaching toward the end of the year. There wasn't any deliberation about where we'd go next. Bianca had to be in New York for work, so that was always going to be the move. Austin was home to Arlo Grey and my team, but I wanted to build a life with Bianca, and I was more than happy to take that leap, so when I visited Bianca that summer, we started the process of beginning our life together in a more tangible way and signed a lease on a Manhattan apartment.

With that next step in sight, I had to start getting the restaurant prepared for my absence. I never wanted the team to feel neglected. Part of what made my relationship with Bianca feel so mature and strong was that we never lost ourselves in it. We made sure to keep our sense of priorities straight and not become one of those couples who blew off the world when we fell in love. There was never that sense of urgency to it because we knew our love wasn't going anywhere.

For the six months or so prior to that moment, I'd been preparing my people to take the reins. I worked hard on my end to make sure we were in good shape. I'm not used to giving up control, but for the first time in my life, the actual goal—the mark of success—was for me to be "useless." It was a hard thing to come to terms with, but Bianca helped me understand what an accomplishment it was when I had absolutely nothing to do during service and it was clear that the team was ready to run the place without me. For the first time in a very long time, I was also able to reallocate some of my thoughts and feelings, and now I had positive direction for my attention: our love and our future together.

For the following few months, while I was making sure the restaurant was in perfect working order, Bianca was doing her own job while moving from her apartment to our new home. I had a lot of guilt about this, knowing she was alone and I couldn't do much just yet, and so in addition to our daily FaceTime dates and texts about the domestic life we were planning together, I tried to find ways to contribute. When I was younger, I didn't have a lot to give, so when I finally started earning an income that ensured stability and a bit of economic freedom, the first thing I did was find ways to provide for my family and friends. Especially at times when I couldn't be with them physically, this was a love language that I felt needed no translation. In this situation, I leaned hard on that instinct, doing what I could from Austin to contribute to our future. I'd send things to the apartment that I thought might help her or that we would need eventually. Bianca was always grateful, but she quickly made it clear that she didn't need those things from me. What she wanted more than anything was for me to be there with her—as soon as possible. At the end of the day, her feeling was, "Kristen, I don't care if you can buy us a fancy vacuum. Just get your ass here as soon as you can."

I had been used to finding a lot of my self-worth in the ability to take care of things financially. But I was always learning lessons with Bianca, and I realized then that it was the emotional support and togetherness that she wanted most of all. It was in these small but meaningful ways that she changed how I perceive my own value in the world.

Transition is such a delicate thing, and I'd already experienced so much of it in my life. I remember recognizing it and reflecting on it in those days before leaving Austin, noting the changes that had come before and the ones that lay ahead, and maybe for the first time, aided by Bianca's encouragement, I really allowed myself to feel pride in what I'd accomplished with Arlo Grey and excitement about the future. It was bittersweet, but I wasn't afraid. I knew this was different. Now I was making a transition with great intention, confidently and with a clear purpose and sense of where I was going. And I wasn't doing it alone. I was moving forward with another person—with *my* person. Ultimately, the relationship was even the catalyst for me to finally end the one I had with cigarettes for decades. I quit smoking because I committed myself to a future we could build together.

I didn't have any anxieties or fears about taking a huge next step with Bianca. I never had to worry about whether she'd still love me if we got too close, if she saw too much of me, or if she saw versions of me that weren't my most perfect or "best" (read: bed head). There was never any second-guessing about whether leaving the life I'd built in Austin would be the right move. It may sound trite, but I do believe when you find the right person, everything that might be scary otherwise suddenly feels exciting, because you just know. It's impossible to overstate the value of trust in a relationship, and that was new for me. That trust was a gift that gave me confidence not only in us but also in myself. I didn't question whether I was making the right call or whether I could be "good enough," because Bianca made it clear how much she loved and was committed to me. I realized that by following this love, I wasn't at all worried about what could go wrong.

Bianca was in a period of change, too. She'd taken a new job, and her first order of business was a three-week trip to the Maldives for work immediately after my move from Austin, and she asked me to come. I'm sure many people would have been beyond excited to be invited on a trip like that, but the idea of a vacation was completely foreign to me. I've reflected on the idea of "fun" a lot over the years. People often ask me what I cook for myself, but the truth is, I don't, because doing things I'm passionate about is really only fun for me if I can do them for, or with, someone I love. Fun is waking up without a single thing on the calendar and being able to look at Bianca and say, "Let's go take a ride"—maybe to discover some cute little town and learn something about life together. More than anything, fun is sharing life and time and experiences with my person. To me, fun is freedom from the calendars and clocks and the fears those things represent: letting people down, not living up to expectations. When Bianca asked me to go away with her that fall, I realized I had done the work and had stepped away from the restaurant for the first time in two years knowing it was in excellent hands. I thought, *Fuck it.* I decided to take that time for myself, to relax, reflect, and have *real* fun with my person. I never would have done that on my own.

The strength of our love has always been in our steadiness, our ability to find balance and joy even in the small, day-to-day things. Going to the Maldives was different in that way because it was epic and grand and a complete departure. It was a moment of restoration and reflection, and I knew I was replenishing the reserves I'd depleted over the previous few years, when I'd worked so much and so hard. It was badly needed, and we had an unbelievable time. I was focused on restoring and making sure I had a solid foundation for building the best version of myself for what was to come next in my career and in my relationship.

Of course, at the end of 2019, in a paradise on the other side of the world, we had no way of knowing just how important that foundation would be.

As anyone living on planet earth might remember, 2020 was a *year*. But months before mask mandates and lockdowns and rapid tests were even a thing on anyone's mind, Bianca and I were experiencing our own period of mourning.

One of the things I admired about Bianca from day one was her dedication to the people she loved in her life. Family has always been so important to me, and that was something we clearly shared. Her father had been ill for some time with cancer, and it was January when she got a call from her sister in Australia, explaining that things had taken a turn, and Bianca flew there immediately. After she arrived and got a sense of the situation, we spoke by phone. I asked if she needed me to come, and when her response was simply, "I don't know," I knew that meant yes. Later that night, I was on a flight.

I was there with Bianca for the days leading up to her father's final moments, and though we were ready to a degree, nothing can truly prepare you for that kind of profound loss. I have always appreciated that Bianca is clear and communicative about what is most important to her, in our relationship and in life. I first came to understand how much she valued having me by her side during those days moving into our apartment. Then, in the devastating time prior to her father's death, I was just grateful that I was able to really be there with her. It was fortunate that I didn't have to worry about the daily restaurant responsibilities the way I had in Austin, but the truth is, it wouldn't have mattered. Nothing could have kept me from being there to support the woman I love so deeply when she needed it most.

Once we said our goodbyes and Bianca was able to spend time with family, we returned home to New York and to our own new reality, knowing her father was no longer with us. But reality was changing for the entire world at that point, as the global pandemic was just setting in. I'm not sure I can ever truly express how lucky I feel that we had each other in the time that followed. As anyone in the restaurant industry can tell you, COVID presented challenges that were absolutely crushing. It forced every one of us to reevaluate, to get creative, to pivot (and pivot and pivot)—to get angry, to get organized, to get together in new ways. It was relentless and a real test of the team in Austin. We were in contact virtually, managing it as it came.

Personally, though, for Bianca and me and so many others, it was a period of quiet. We were both fortunate enough to be able to work from our apartment, and in between the moments of disbelief and disorientation that we shared with the rest of the planet, we found ways to enjoy small moments of domestic bliss. After being apart for so long, it was a time during which we grew closer and got to know each other in a totally new way. We appreciated so many small things we might not have otherwise. But as it did for so many, the pandemic encouraged us to think more critically about our future. We had conversations about what we wanted in the long term, what was most important to us. We took that time to consider our next steps, envisioning as much as we could what life would look like "after."

We'd always talked a lot about the importance of family. I had spent most of my adult life living far from my parents and have always been very sensitive to their aging. Between losing Bianca's father and the forced perspective of the pandemic, and as we came to recognize and appreciate the unpredictability of life, we decided to start discussing our options. We loved our apartment, but we always knew we wanted a home that reflected us individually and as a couple, one we could create together and that would have space for our family and friends to visit.

Our Manhattan place was a great start, but moving out of the city just about guaranteed that we'd have much more space to stretch out. Before we knew it, we found ourselves again looking at another major life change, and in March of 2021, we spent our first night in our new home in a New England suburb.

I had always promised myself that I would make decisions that would take into account the people I love most in life; now, we were certain we could provide space and support for those people if the need was there. And once we were settled in our new home, we knew it was time to make good on another promise.

During a conversation, early in our dating days, I told Bianca I had no intention of getting married. I had seen firsthand the way the institution had failed so many people in my world. And I was also angry at the exclusiveness of it, because for much of my life, gay people weren't able to get married.

I think if I'm being honest, though, there was also an element of fear. For reasons of insecurity that plagued me for so many years, deep down I worried I'd never meet someone who wanted to be with me forever. But with Bianca, that fear—along with so many other fears—was erased, and my position on marriage evolved as time went on and as we talked about it more.

People often talk about proposals being special because of the surprise element of it all. It's not that Bianca and I don't know how to have fun or be spontaneous. We follow our hearts, and we love an adventure. But when it comes to the *really* important stuff, our relationship is characterized more by intention and stability, and on the night that I proposed to Bianca in 2019, she already knew it was coming. In fact, we even had the rings. We picked them out and bought them together on a trip to Australia while her father was still with us. She was able to show them to her father before he passed, which was really important to her, and I got to ask his permission, which was important to me, but we decided then to wait to get officially engaged.

I really wanted to be the one to propose, and Bianca knew that. I tried to hold out as long as I could, but with the rings sitting in a safe in our apartment back in New York, I was like a kid on Christmas morning. I was trying to wait, to come up with the perfect way to do the thing, and I could have gone a million ways with the proposal. At the end of the day, though, I decided what made it special wasn't some contrived circumstance—it was *us*. I knew this was something we'd remember forever, so I wanted the whole thing to reflect that and be uniquely ours.

We already had a special ritual every night to wind down together. We lit candles, used a cleansing spray for the air, and set an intention out loud. I figured there wasn't any intention greater than the one to dedicate myself to our future together, so I decided to lean in to it. One night with the candles lit, I told Bianca to close her eyes before we did the spray, and when she opened them, I was on one knee. When she saw me and realized what was happening, we both immediately started crying. She crouched and came down to my level, and then we were both on the floor crying together. I was so totally overwhelmed, and in retrospect, it reminds me of that first kiss in the car that day—that sense of total, complete, and utter joy that just takes over. The feeling that, for me, can only be associated with Bianca.

We always like to write little notes to each other, and we had each written one for this occasion, knowing it was coming. Eventually, when I was keeping it together enough to speak, I read her my note, then I asked the most important question of my life. Bianca responded with the only word I ever needed to hear. Then she read her letter, and all those moments, all the lead-up, all the questions and the conversations and the honesty, and the work and the care, and the intentionality—it all came together in that moment. And while I didn't technically surprise her by jumping out of a bush or baking the ring into a cake for her to stumble upon, our love still managed to surprise me, to exceed expectations, to leave me in total awe that a human so perfect could choose me. That, more than anything in my life, was totally stunning.

After being adopted and raised in a loving family, then finding my own along the way and ultimately being a part of creating a family at Arlo Grey, I was about to start my own—this one, just the two of us. We were committing to a totally surprising new adventure, and I couldn't wait to start the ride.

Originally, we envisioned a big bash where we could celebrate and share our love with all our friends and family, but later, as COVID carried on, we realized that wasn't going to be possible anytime soon. We considered waiting, but nothing was certain except the fact that we wanted to be committed to each other. So at the end of the day, we decided that we would do it, for us, in a way that was possible in those days.

Shortly after we moved, we started planning to have a wedding right in our own backyard. Just because we couldn't have the traditional elements of a wedding didn't mean we weren't going to make it special or reflective of us. We relied on our new community and met with a justice of the peace recommended to us by our real estate agent. The justice then spent hours talking to us and really getting to know us—who we are individually and as a couple. She wanted to create an experience for us that would be customized and authentic. We felt so seen and could not have been more appreciative.

As hospitality professionals, we are people who have spent large parts of our lives creating memorable experiences. We're resourceful and know how to work with what we've got. And what we had was Marshalls, so on the morning of our wedding, we took a ride to the store and scoured the aisles for decor. We found bookcases that we could set up with photo frames and flowers, which my parents sent from the local florist. Since our yard isn't exactly secluded and we wanted some privacy for the ceremony, we got an old bedsheet and cut slits into it to account for the windy day. We set up tables and our laptops so our families could join us via Zoom.

We've both been to a lot of weddings, but this one was entirely without distraction. It felt like the only things that really mattered were the things that were there, and it felt like the things that were there were the only things that mattered. We didn't have a giant audience. There was no buildup to a massive wedding with friends and food and fanfare. And while weddings like that are exciting and beautiful, this was quiet and peaceful. It was everything we could have possibly wanted or needed, and it was the most present I've ever been with anyone, at any time of my life.

We stood in our fancy outfits in our little outdoor space, with our people watching from thousands of miles away, in the presence of our officiant and nature, beneath a blue spring sky, and we exchanged the vows we'd written for each other, and I knew I would never be the same.

Afterward, we cried and drank champagne, and I made tacos. We had a little wedding cake from a local bakery. I think we were in bed by 10:00 p.m. It was nothing like what we would have expected for our wedding day, but it was absolutely perfect and perfectly us.

Bianca calms me—oh, my God, she calms me. I knew it so early on. She brings me to a place where I can be present in my own body. It's because I trust her, and she trusts me, and we both trust in our relationship. Sometimes I hear couples say, "My partner makes me a better person." But I believe that's not the responsibility of your partner. Bianca brings me up. She brings me to a place where I am present with myself, which then makes me a better person for me and, in turn, for her. I don't feel like I need to be any particular version of myself. I'm allowed to be *all* of them. I can be vulnerable and weak. I can be the one who has it together, and I can be the one crumbling apart, and she will not look at me any differently, and she doesn't make me feel bad for being all those things at different times or all at the same time. And if I'm a better person with Bianca, it's because I *want* to be—for her, for us, for our future.

I look back sometimes at my favorite picture from that day. My parents bought us two dozen long-stem white roses from the local florist. I went and picked them up and brought them home, and when I came into the kitchen, there was Bianca, sitting on the floor in our brand-new home, in her sweatpants with no makeup on and her hair tied back. It was just the way she always is when she wakes up in the morning, except that morning, at that moment, she was arranging flowers for our wedding. It's one of my favorite images because it's just so naturally *her*. Such an ordinary moment on an extraordinary day. It's so Bianca, doing this thing that means so much to her, putting in that work, and when I saw her like that, it totally caught me off guard. I was in awe, and I remember thinking, *Wow, you're doing this for us.*

I believe that every story is a love story. For Bianca and me, that story didn't start with some lightning strike or in a chaotic, high-intensity whirlwind romance. With Bianca, I recognized that love is not magic, or fate, or coincidence, or luck. It's dedication and authenticity, perseverance and work, understanding and acceptance, and emotional availability and awareness. It requires softness and an openness to all the ways two people can be, individually and together, and it requires appreciation of each other in all those ways. Love *isn't* actually magic; it's a daily practice.

In our backyard with our homemade wedding and ripped-bedsheet backdrop wasn't some far-off, exotic destination—but I knew that with Bianca, I would always find that love, safety, and awe. They would be present in moments big and small, extravagant and simple, and sometimes messy, everywhere, for the rest of my life. Our love has astonished me and surprised me at every turn. It has defied my expectations and redefined the way I look at the world. It never ceases to amaze me.

Now, with my feet firmly on the ground, fully rooted in love and trust and with a sturdy foundation, I felt ready for takeoff, for whatever might come next.

15

When I was growing up, my generation used cell phones to make actual phone calls. Watching TV was a planned activity; we were more often encouraged to go outside and play.

That said, when I did get to sit in front of a screen, I understood that my relationship to TV *was* actually founded on learning. Right from the jump, with *Great Chefs of the World*, I looked to that little screen for information, whether for practical culinary tips and skills to apply to my "pudding" experiments or just to see places that sparked something in me. (Although that's not to say I didn't zone out purely for entertainment over the years.) But even though I found inspiration and ways to explore my curiosity through television, I never had any grand visions of being on-screen. As I sat still, watching those programs in my childhood days, I never could have dreamed the ways in which it would affect my life and take me so far from my parents' kitchen back in Michigan. Aside from my career as a chef, the medium has allowed me to embody roles and try on hats I never would have imagined for myself at any point in my life. I've gotten to be a competitor and an explorer, a performer and an anthropologist—and then briefly, in 2015, a sort of journalist.

The *New York Times* has long produced a column called 36 Hours, a guide for readers on ways to spend a brief trip in a given city, which changes from week to week. The feature tells travelers how to prioritize that city's most important sites and get to know it on the level of a local. During the column's run, the nation's paper of record has covered countless locations—occasionally revisiting them with updates—and it's a useful resource for travelers who are tight on time and just need to be directed to the highlights. At some point, the Travel Channel saw potential for the column to be turned into a hosted TV show, taking viewers by the hand and walking them through those recommendations with on-screen guides. It translated well and was timely, particularly as there were record-breaking numbers of international travelers in 2015, the year it launched.

Just after I had left Menton and was working independently, I was standing outside on a sunny Boston day in front of Barbara's restaurant, the Butcher Shop, when my manager, Tory, called and informed me that I was being invited to screen-test for the job of cohost on *36 Hours*. I'm not entirely sure how my name wound up in the hat, but I was in such an open, exploratory place in my life that it felt like there was nothing to lose. And before I knew it, I was in New York City running through tests with three other possible cohosts.

I hadn't had my sights set on hosting television, but there were a lot of reasons the opportunity was exciting. For one thing, there was an appealing level of prestige to both the *New York Times* and the Travel Channel, and I was honored to be considered for the series. The lineup of places they had planned for the first six episodes was pretty great, too. On the list were Barcelona, Berlin, and Istanbul as well as domestic stops: Nashville, Portland, and—most meaningful to me—Boston.

Beyond that, it was a way to keep me on the road and fulfill some of my earliest dreams about travel. When I was a kid watching *Great Chefs of the World* and fantasizing about seeing new places, it never occurred to me that it could be possible at all, let alone that I'd be paid to do it. And in addition to the idea that I was going to make money from going on these trips, I saw great value in the fact that they would be arranged for me. I had already learned how freeing it could be to have someone hand me an itinerary, as the producers did back in my *Top Chef* days, knowing that they'd checked all the boxes and managed all the minutiae and all I had to do was go out there and experience the thing. That trustworthy, controlled element to making TV is totally freeing for me, and now I was going to have that same reliability applied to my longtime travel aspirations.

That said, once I signed on and we got underway, there were parts of the *36 Hours* experience that felt controlled in a much less liberating way. It became quickly clear that there was a certain aesthetic and vibe to the show with which I was going to have to comply. There were expectations—let's call them guidelines—regarding how I presented myself on-screen. It's not totally unusual for that to be the case, particularly with such big names behind the series, but in retrospect, part of the problem was that I didn't quite know myself yet. I was newly out of the closet, still finding my sense of style, my voice, my way of moving in the world. I was cohosting the show with Kyle Martino, a pro soccer player and a super-charismatic, good-looking guy who had great TV presence, but by contrast I sometimes felt like I didn't know how to carry myself.

The people on the other side of the camera were trying to make "good" TV, but it sometimes felt at odds with what came naturally to me, especially evidenced during one episode when we visited the legendary Prince's Hot Chicken in Nashville. Anyone who has ever experienced this rite of passage in Music City or the many places to which it has migrated over the years knows that there's not really an elegant way to eat hot chicken. This stuff is spicy in the extreme, saucy and intense, and honestly, that's part of the fun. But I was expected to look professional and, maybe for lack of a better word, *ladylike*. Which meant trying not to take a bite so big that it would prevent me from carrying on my conversational hosting duties or cause me to wind up with spicy oil all over my clothes.

That was almost impossible for this kind of food, and because I was overthinking *how* I was eating—and trying to keep clean and be what the sponsors wanted me to be—the effort also sucked the joy out of eating something I would otherwise have been so stoked to try.

I also think it would be nearly impossible for *anyone* to keep neat and tidy in the clothes they had me wearing—a wardrobe that included khaki shorts. Okay, so there's nothing wrong with khaki shorts, just as there's nothing wrong with taking small bites of food, but if you know me now, you understand that this is just not *me*. (To be fair, it also wasn't me back in middle school, when my friends were coming up with my makeover wardrobe. Some things just never change.)

Although the powers that be had ideas of what they wanted for their program, the problem wasn't so much that they were polishing me but that I wasn't sure yet of who I was or how I wanted to be seen. I remember meeting with wardrobe early on and being presented with racks of silk blouses and striped shirts in various colors and patterns. I was wearing my black skinny jeans and black boots along with a white Hanes V-neck shirt and wondering, *Why can't I just wear this?* Maybe if I had spoken up, they'd have been accommodating, but

I hadn't yet learned how to ask for what I wanted—in part because I hadn't figured that out. I'm not sure if viewers would have picked up on it, but if I look back at those episodes now, it's clear to me that at times I was so busy trying to be exactly what I thought they wanted me to be that I lost my ability to live in the moment, to request what I needed in order to feel comfortable and present. These days, I would ask to wear the black jeans if I wanted to. I would take the big bite and laugh if I made a mess.

But there were destabilizing factors for me happening off camera, too. I discovered that the person I'd been dating was cheating on me. It forced me to question so much about myself and my self-worth. I was still very much learning how to be in a relationship, feeling behind after so many years in the closet, and I found myself internalizing the betrayal. Had I done something wrong? Was I not enough in some way? Of course, I would later understand that infidelity—and the dynamic between a couple in general—is so much more nuanced and complicated than I could have imagined then and that blame can't be placed on a single person or factor. But it all compounded the discomfort and insecurity I was feeling professionally.

That said, I was grateful to have this totally unique and unexpected adventure as a very effective distraction from my broken heart. There were so many unforgettable moments while we were filming the show—running around Barcelona and Istanbul, standing in the presence of art and monuments and architecture, having my mind expanded by every new sight and smell, and experiencing the world in a totally new way. Shooting *36 Hours* affirmed for me how much I love to travel and how much more of it I want to do in my life. I got to expand my culinary horizons and enjoy some truly life-altering food that would go on to inform some of my own philosophies about cooking.

I also had a very sweet Boston homecoming. During one episode, we featured a segment at Stir with Barbara, and I had a chance to shine a spotlight on my mentor the way she had on me so many times in the past. And while I was uncomfortable at times, I also recognized the shift when we got into kitchens or filmed segments focused on food. I relied on those beats to help buoy my sense of confidence, and in those moments, I knew exactly who I was—a person who had authority and expertise, who belonged in those rooms and conversations.

This was also the first TV experience for me in which I wasn't the one answering the questions but asking them. I learned how to interview people—how to read them, listen, and learn from them.

And while I didn't love those moments of control when it came to how I was expected to be and behave, I look back now and realize how necessary that was for context and contrast. If I hadn't had those experiences, I might not have later recognized and really appreciated when I *was* able to freely and authentically be myself.

Another lesson from that first hosting experience with *36 Hours?* Television is extremely unreliable. It may seem to viewers that there's an abundance of options on TV today, and it may even appear that these shows crop up quickly. But the truth is that the number of pitches and ideas that seem promising is an ocean compared to the thimble of content that ultimately gets greenlit, funded, produced, and picked up. And even then, it may be for only a single season, a few episodes, or just a pilot in some cases. The rationale can range from audience reception to budgets to logistics to analytics beyond viewership that I still don't fully understand. There are never any guarantees that a show will stick around forever, and *36 Hours* ended after those six episodes.

Naturally, I was disappointed. At the time, I think part of me did believe it had the potential to be a peak career moment. Of course, in retrospect, it's funny to imagine how many times in my life I had that feeling, never knowing what was just around the bend. But as unsure of myself as I felt, I didn't internalize the news. I recognized that there were a lot of reasons the show wasn't picked up for a second season and that none of them had anything to do with me.

Part of the beauty of the unexpected is that you're less likely to be crushed when it doesn't work out. I didn't set out to be the host of a TV show. I didn't have it on a vision board and didn't pursue it single-mindedly. It was a surprise from day one, even though it was a welcome one. It was also never part of my plan to hedge my bets professionally, but it had happened naturally. And because I had a lot going on, it wasn't the blow that it might have been had I put all my eggs in that basket.

Afterward, I went about my life. For years, I occupied other spaces and had other adventures. I traveled on my own, doing pop-ups, writing my cookbook, and really living. Then I opened a restaurant and fell in love. I did the things I was meant to do at that time. Once again, I thought perhaps the TV life had reached its conclusion for me. But then, a few years later, when the restaurant had reached a steady point and I was once more without any expectations, I was approached again.

The people who know me best know that I love fast food. I always have. Whether it was visiting my brother at his Pizza Hut job and snacking on stuffed-crust pepperoni pizza while I helped him fold boxes, devouring the McDonald's number 2 combo on my shift breaks at Twist & Shout, crushing curly fries at Arby's back in my Midwest days, or basically making a mental map of the best chicken fingers in just about every state to which I've ever traveled, I consider fast food part of my soul. So when I was approached with the concept for *Fast Foodies*, I was immediately interested.

It was late September and early October of 2019 when the emails started arriving. A few years had passed since the cameras stopped rolling on *36 Hours*, and my life had changed dramatically. I was no longer living a no-strings nomadic life. I was operating a restaurant that had my name on it—with partners and a team to whom I was responsible—and I was in an authentic, stable relationship to which I was entirely devoted. I had learned so much in the intervening years—about business, about love, about life. I had also learned about myself and had come into my own during that time in so many ways that made me a very different person from the one in those khaki shorts.

I believe the universe is selective about the moments in which it introduces life-changing prospects. Had it been a year earlier, I'd have been up to my neck preparing the restaurant and tending to an avalanche of other responsibilities. But as it happened, the restaurant was up and running, and I had a team I trusted. I had moved to New York to be with Bianca and was traveling back and forth to Austin to check in, but I did have bandwidth and was once again in a headspace that allowed me to be a little experimental.

And while the universe may be deliberate about the timing for something new, sometimes what you've already put out into the world is still working on your behalf, even when you don't know it. There was an executive producer on *Fast Foodies* who had once been part of *Top Chef*, and although we never overlapped, he thought of me and reached out when it came time to cast the show.

The concept for *Fast Foodies* appealed to me for several reasons. The fast-food hook was fun and totally unlike so many of the serious shows that had cropped up over the years. It was also an actual cooking show, and I liked the idea of being able to apply my culinary skills again. There's a strange thing that happens when you own a restaurant: One of the marks of strong leadership is, in some ways, to make yourself obsolete. And although it did feel like a sign of success that the team didn't need me as much, I wasn't making food with my own hands as often anymore, and I missed it. I longed for the creativity and practice of it—and honestly, I even felt in some ways that I had to prove I still *could* do it.

This show was an opportunity to cook again, but in a playful way. I loved that it was a competition, but one without the super-high-stakes intensity of *Top Chef*. It was all friendly, meant to be fun and funny, and that was new for me. Despite how serious I have had to be at times in my life, I really do consider myself to be a fun-loving person and was ready and freed up to embrace that frivolity.

After some negotiations and dealmaking, I signed on to film a pilot, which we did in Los Angeles in November of 2019. It was, as promised, a ton of fun, but once again I carried on with my life afterward. As I said, making TV is subject to a *lot* of variables, and can take a very long time. I wasn't interested in or able to sit around wondering about what would happen next. I had other things going on—there was the restaurant and partnerships and other side gigs as well as early conversations about another TV show project (more on that soon).

I remained hopeful about the show while I went about other things, but then there was a period during which it really fell off my radar altogether. In the time between the filming of that pilot episode and what would be the next steps, the world was turned on its head by the pandemic. TV production, like everything else in the world, came to a screeching halt, and I became focused on surviving the situation and making sure my restaurant did, too. It wasn't an era in which I was placing much weight on anything, because everything felt completely uncertain, in the way TV does even under the best of circumstances.

And yet the world did so desperately want to carry on eventually, so in the summer of 2020, when it felt like there might be a bit of a reprieve from the virus—or at least a way to continue living with it—the show resurfaced. Although we still didn't have a vaccine, the production company and network decided to move forward with filming in the safest way possible, which meant being in compliance with a cascade of restrictions and guidelines.

That time was scary in so many ways, and honestly there were moments when it almost seemed too trivial to make television—let alone the kind that was just for fun. And yet that notion was powerful in its own way. There was something I loved about the idea—that during a time when the world felt so intense, so bleak in so many ways, this was a chance to offer a simple service people really needed: pure entertainment. A chance to escape through the TV screens that had become a main point of contact and comfort for so many who were isolated. Part of the value of TV is that—like a restaurant—it can serve as a connection point. And although the show wouldn't technically reach homes until early 2021, and although we had no way of knowing what life would be like when it did or how long we would be in this limbo, it was heartening to think we were putting something purely positive into the world. Plus, on a personal level, after months of quarantine, the thought of being around other humans did have an appeal.

And so I followed protocol and prepared to fly to LA, collecting proof of negative test results, loading up on hand sanitizer and airline-approved masks, doing my best to be extra vigilant in my precautions so I could protect myself and not compromise the production. I was also grateful that Bianca was able to come with me, because neither of us loved the idea of being separated during such an uncertain time. Her job had gone remote during the pandemic, and we were fortunate that we could set aside a budget for her travel. It helped put my mind at ease that we'd be together, and I always took comfort and inspiration knowing she was close.

Just before we got down to business with shooting, I met with Jeremy Ford and Justin Sutherland, the latter of whom was new to the show, having replaced one of the chefs who filmed the pilot with us. Both men were also *Top Chef* alums. It's hard to look at contemporary food television and not take note of the fact that so many of the shows, regardless of network, feature *Top Chef* talent. I believe it's a testament to the quality of *Top Chef*'s casting and production that these other projects can draw from its pool of strong candidates who have been solidly vetted and, in a way, are almost "trained" for television. It's like a preparatory school for food personalities—not to mention culinary stars.

But that wasn't the only reason that Justin, Jeremy, and I bonded. When we met that first day, I can't explain the way we just clicked. Even though they were both new to me for the most part, it had the vibe of finding out you were assigned a group project with your two best friends. It was a perfect fit, and instantly I knew this was going to be a great show, if only because I would get to hang out with these guys.

The format of the show was also lighthearted and amusing. The concept was to have a celebrity guest join us and tell us their favorite fast food. From there, the three of us would try to first re-create and then riff on the dish—this was the "remix" round. The guest ultimately tasted each of our interpretations and chose a winner, who was awarded the Chompionship Trophy. As you can probably tell, even if you've never seen a single frame of the show, absolutely nothing about it was super serious, and it was a huge departure from so much of my own life and career in that way—not to mention the mood of the world at that moment.

I believe our dynamic worked so well in part because we all knew who we were at that point in our lives, and it was a very live-and-let-live situation. On camera, the three of us bantered and trash-talked, and when we were off duty, we did our own things. After we wrapped, the guys might go out for drinks or to hang out, and I would go back to the hotel and crash. And as silly as the project may seem on-screen, we each showed up ready to go when the time came. We all respected the work and one another, a fact that became extra important to me as the show progressed.

Although I never felt out of place or as if I were being polished on *Fast Foodies,* I was very much aware that I was outnumbered. The crew did boast some incredible women working in capacities from camera to audio to production, but I was the only one on-screen. I'd had early lessons in the importance of representation through *Top Chef,* thanks to those who rallied around and supported me, whether Asian American or adoptee or, after I came out, the queer community. Each one reminded me that when I was in front of an audience, I was there not just for myself and my own purposes—I was being given a platform.

Although Justin and Jeremy were great guys and we all got along so well, there was no question that the show had a very male-centric vibe. It didn't help that the guests were also mostly men. At first, it wasn't such a big deal, but after a while, I began to get tired of that energy—the relentless sexual innuendo, to which food language and culture lends itself so well; the seemingly endless supply of dick jokes that comedians would come up with when they got into our kitchen. Naturally, Jeremy and Justin laughed at this stuff, and I did, too, for a while. But it got to the point where I felt like I really could not handle more of the same. Plus, that kind of repetition is also just not interesting television, to be honest.

It was a challenging situation, because I could have simply refused to engage with it on-screen or made it known that I thought it was tiresome, but then I'd be the "angry" woman rolling her eyes episode after episode. And yet I knew that remaining silent could be a problem. It's not that there was ever abuse or harassment on the set to my knowledge (which was very much top of mind in a post-#MeToo era), but I also believe that it shouldn't have to get to such extremes in order for people to demand some kind of culture change. I knew I had to put some of the lessons I'd learned about representation to work in order to learn new ones, to grow as a person and a professional, and to live up to my responsibility. I realized that I might have been outnumbered on-screen, but I *did* have something to say, and even a single voice matters.

Particularly when you're a woman, it's very easy to second-guess yourself or decide to keep quiet for fear of how you might be painted if you speak up—especially because women often have to be blunt and direct in order to be taken seriously. Of course, when a woman *does* speak up, she can be read as being a bitch, not soft and nurturing and maternal. I have at times been referred to as intimidating, which always feels so incongruous with the person I believe I am. I aim to be both kind and nice, depending on the circumstance, and I always strive to lead with respect, intention, empathy, and care for others. But I am also honest and clear, and I do believe that in women, seriousness and honesty are sometimes taken as harshness. I'm sure just about any woman in any professional space can sympathize with that conundrum.

There are a lot of things that go into mustering up the courage to use one's voice. I believe that personal satisfaction and life experience work together in so many ways, and when we filmed *Fast Foodies*, I was happily partnered. There was a level of confidence and stability for me that made the professional stakes feel much less intense. I knew that at the end of the day, the most important thing was that I could go home to my person, and no amount of pressure at work could take that from me—even if the powers that be didn't like what was on my mind. My partner also supported me: Bianca has always encouraged me not only to say what I want to say but also to *think* before saying it. Admittedly, I'm still sometimes working on that latter part, but having that encouragement has been so important at many times in my life.

Motivation is also part of the equation. I have always been better about doing things for others rather than myself. If I had reservations about speaking up before, now I knew that it wasn't just about me or my comfort level. I was representing a lot of people up there. I learned that I had a voice—and with it a certain level of power. And so, during the course of the show, I came to understand how to use both. I felt that as a woman—as a *human*—I was allowed to have an opinion, and that opinion mattered and had value. And whether or not it made a huge difference, I wasn't going to stay silent and maybe regret it later.

I tried to apply Bianca's advice—to thoroughly think through what I wanted to say and how. I started by sharing my frustration with the guest lineup. I tried to be clear about wanting more women on the show and explaining why it was important. And because I believe in presenting a potential solution when raising an issue, I did my own research to come up with ideas for more women and people of color. That said, I did know that the casting team wasn't being deliberately exclusionary. I recognized the challenges they were up against—particularly in the midst of a global pandemic, when guests weren't highly compensated—and kept all that in mind during our conversations.

But then when I saw one particular name on the schedule, I really had to put my foot down. I always did my research beforehand to learn more about our guests, and this guy had some troubling discourse around him at the time. Although it was all speculation, I didn't want to be associated with him, and I couldn't understand the benefit of bringing him on. If we passed him over and it turned out he'd done nothing wrong, then maybe we'd have missed out on having a cool guest—which, okay, bummer. But if the opposite proved true, did we all really want to have this episode out there in the world? I knew my answer: I did not want to be the woman on-screen buddying up to him, making him feel welcome on the show. There were plenty of other people out there we could invite who wouldn't put us—all of us—in a potentially compromising situation, and I made my thoughts clear on the matter.

In the end, he was replaced, and I was relieved. But just as rewarding as that peace of mind was the fact that I was 100 percent supported. I felt seen and heard by the entire production team and the network, as well as Justin and Jeremy.

There were times in my life, at restaurants like Menton, when I used my voice and the response was utterly demoralizing. This experience helped me revise my feelings about doing so. Having that support—from Bianca first, and then from the people involved in the show—made me see that there is a world where my opinion matters, where I'm not risking my livelihood, my reputation, my relationships, or my spirit by saying what I believe to be true and important. There is no trophy that could have matched that reward from this show.

I also learned another practical lesson about making TV. While *36 Hours* had already proved that there are no guarantees that a show will keep running even with major names and players involved, *Fast Foodies* was a crash course in mergers and acquisitions and what those behind-the-scenes machinations might do to a project.

We'd filmed two seasons and were deep into strategizing about more. Typically, I'm pretty measured when it comes to getting excited about "potential" projects. Until the ink is dry, it feels dangerous to get too attached to an idea, no matter the industry or issue. But in this case, it felt like we were already there, so I let myself get into it a little more. Which is why, when truTV was purchased by Discovery, thus halting our momentum and placing the fate of the show in purgatory indefinitely, it *was* a disappointment.

The politics and details of it all could take up several pages here, and certainly removed a few from my own story, but I still look back on this experience as one of my favorites in television. Despite the challenges, making *Fast Foodies* was almost always just a purely good time. I got to cook with two people I genuinely enjoyed. I made friends on both sides of the camera and, frankly, some of my best food. There's something about joy that is really freeing, and I believe that sense of fun and playfulness and frivolity does come through in cooking. I was sad to say goodbye to the guys, the crew, and this gig, and when we parted ways, I genuinely hoped we'd find a way to come back together eventually for more. But in the meantime, there were things percolating on other channels in my world that helped soften the blow.

When you're making TV, sometimes you're so in it that you don't even recognize that someday, someone out there will watch what you're working on. And while I was busy having a blast on the set of *Fast Foodies,* there were indeed people at home enjoying the show—and some were in the television industry, too.

I didn't have the same fears about how that show had come off as I had had about other shows in the past. I wasn't so preoccupied with the expectations placed upon me, the way I was with *36 Hours,* and I definitely was not experiencing the stress and pressure of *Top Chef.* Which was why, when Jenn Levy—who was the VP of non-fiction at Netflix and formerly worked on *Top Chef* when she was at Bravo—later told my manager that she had seen me on *Fast Foodies* and thought, *Kristen has found her voice,* it was especially validating, because the person Jenn saw wasn't a pretense. That person was entirely, authentically me.

But that discussion with Jenn didn't happen right away. The conversation that came first was with my manager about the show *Iron Chef.* This was one of the original cooking competitions. It was iconic. It started in Japan in the early 1990s and then transformed into *Iron Chef America* in the hands of the Food Network, where it ran from 2005 to 2018 before going on an indefinite hiatus. There weren't a lot of details about why production stopped, but my manager informed me that Netflix had bought the rights and intended to revive the franchise—and that they were interested in me.

At the time, I didn't know what that interest meant. There are several capacities in which someone can be cast for *Iron Chef,* and during that initial conversation it was unclear where they saw me fitting in. And while I didn't know exactly what they were hoping for from me, I knew for certain what I did not want for myself: I had zero interest in being an Iron Chef (one of the show's regular roles) or a competing chef (a visitor who "challenges" the Iron Chef in an episode). I was no longer at a place in my career where that kind of intensity and pressure felt like an attractive challenge—especially not after *Fast Foodies*, which really was just all for fun. I loved the idea of being part of this legendary series, but I also knew I didn't have to say yes to everything, that just because an offer came in didn't mean it was the right one for me.

Since we didn't have a clear ask from the production company, I agreed to a meeting to discuss what they had in mind. Bianca and I had just moved into our newly built home in the suburbs, and I remember trying to find a good place to take the call amid the boxes and general moving chaos. I wound up sitting on a stool in the wet-bar area of our new house. We were very much in transition, experiencing a period of growth together, creating a place of comfort and safety. In retrospect, I can see the ways in which I was cultivating the same for my professional life.

Part of what made me comfortable speaking up during *Fast Foodies* was this more measured sense of what was at stake in my life and career, and that applied to this conversation, too. We evolve so much as we grow and age, with experience and time. Something like this meeting might have caused me so much anxiety in other eras—it might have caused me to lose sleep and feel fearful about the possibility of losing a thing that really didn't belong to me and, frankly, that I wasn't even sure was *for* me. And it's not as if anxiety is eliminated as you mature, but life reveals itself to be complex and nuanced the longer you live it, and a yes or no doesn't feel as if it'll make or break you. You can feel a sense of peace and acceptance about the outcome—whatever it may be.

All that is to say that I was feeling fairly calm when we started that call, despite the fact that I was speaking with some industry heavy hitters. On the other end was Eytan Keller, a longtime producer of *Iron Chef* on the Food Network, among other notable food TV projects, and Daniel Calin, who had also worked on *Top Chef,* although our paths never crossed there. We had a casual conversation in which I reiterated what I told my manager—that I wasn't interested in cooking. When they asked what I *was* interested in doing, I said I'd be open to floor reporting, commenting on what challengers were up to during the cook, much like a sportscaster. Prior to the call, another member of my management team and I spoke about possibilities, and he'd suggested hosting. I hadn't given it much thought at the time—we were just talking it through at a high level. But then on the call, I realized I really had nothing to lose, so I added, "I'd also be open to hosting."

They hadn't asked me about it, and I'm not even sure I had given that idea real thought before we started talking. I didn't say it because I had been scheming about it. I said it because, well, why not? Why not throw it all out there? I was lobbying for myself, and I decided to aim for the highest rung and see which one I landed on. The worst they could say was no.

If you showed a recorded version of this call to me at age twenty or twenty-five, or maybe even thirty, I might've reacted with a dropped jaw and bated breath. But my wife was in the next room. My restaurant was up and running (albeit in a limited capacity because of COVID). My family loved me and my communities embraced me and honestly no one in my life would have cared if I didn't get this job—most of them didn't even know it was a possibility.

It's not that I didn't care, but I cared exactly the way I care about everything else in my life. If I got the gig—whatever version of it felt right to all parties involved—I would dedicate myself entirely to it. I had never done and would never do anything halfway if I committed to it. But I had learned my value. I had a sense of self, and I was proud that I asked for what I really wanted regardless of the outcome.

If it surprised them half as much as it might've surprised the younger me, the team didn't react strongly one way or another. We carried on our conversation, and when we finished, I thanked them for their time, turned off the computer, and returned to my wife.

It only took a couple of weeks to get the news—lightning speed in TV land. And it was an official offer to be the brand-new cohost of the next era of *Iron Chef.*

Once the offer was made, there was another decision to be sorted out—my cohost. At the time, there were a handful of options, but the powers that be weren't sure yet who would be up there with me. I speculated about some possible names, but when they came back and confirmed that it would be Alton Brown, I was floored. First of all, he was a Food Network fixture. It shocked me that he would be stepping outside of that stable and into the Netflix world. And then of course there was his reputation, which was formidable, to say the least. I had watched Alton for many years, and the idea of sharing a job with him—on equal footing—was exciting, and intimidating.

Alton Brown is best known for his show *Good Eats,* during which he gets into the nerdiest details of culinary science and history. I imagined that this man's brain must've been loaded with facts and information that I couldn't begin to assimilate in the time before we started filming together—particularly given that this wasn't the only thing I had going on and that I had only so much time to dedicate to preparing. But I was about to learn more from our partnership than I could ever have picked up from Alton's show—and it didn't have anything to do with food or television, for that matter.

I had my very first call with Alton from a hotel room in Santa Barbara, where I was doing work for another project. This was just weeks before we would commence filming. He was cordial and enthusiastic and very professional, and it was a lovely conversation that gave me a glimpse of what was ahead. But although I felt good about it, there was nowhere near enough time to put me at ease about getting started.

A few weeks later, we convened in person in LA to do a rehearsal. We had a single day and ran through the show with local culinary students. I had already learned so many times in my life that feeling prepared is critical to my sense of confidence and peace of mind. I did my due diligence as best I could by studying up on the competing chefs and our hero ingredients in the time that I had. But the fact that I had not more than one day of practice with a man who had twenty years of experience in this role terrified me.

Still, it never occurred to me initially that Alton would be feeling out of his element, too. Early on, I told him my concerns—that I had never hosted a show like this before and had nowhere near his level of experience. His response surprised me. He reminded me that while I'd never done the job before at all, he'd never done it with someone else, and it was then that I realized we were both in totally new territory, together.

But even though we shared some sense of apprehension beneath the surface, there were differences between us, some of which were apparent in more visible ways. For example, we each had a desk where we could spend time preparing and researching and comparing notes. And whereas Alton's was covered in Post-its and books and a computer, mine contained nothing but a pen and a notebook, which gave me a sense of calm. I needed to have the mental and physical space, but it was interesting to see someone else's process.

When we officially got underway with shooting, though, I realized I needed to negotiate a different relationship with space—this time, I needed to take up more of it. Alton had held this role for so long by himself and he was very good at it. That's not to say that I wasn't, but I couldn't quite figure out how to find my way into some of the conversations and commentary when we were filming, and I did worry that by comparison, I appeared more like a prop than an on-camera personality.

This wasn't about ego or airtime, though; it was about doing my job. And unless I asked for some space for myself, I wouldn't be able to execute that responsibility, which I took very seriously. This was my opportunity, too, and I couldn't let it slip away by allowing myself to be small. There was a time when I'm sure I would have let it go on that way, when I wouldn't have felt as if I could, should, or deserved to try to find a place for myself on that stage. But by that point, I had learned the power of using my voice.

Alton is accomplished and knowledgeable, but he is also warm and open to anything I had to say, and from day one I felt like I could talk with him—just as I had about our differences in experience. When I did approach him and let him know how I was feeling about our on-camera interactions, Alton really listened and heard me. And because I took the steps to advocate for myself, and he was receptive and supportive, we adjusted our dynamic and were able to have natural exchanges on the show that felt really good.

It can be so easy to get mad when you feel sidelined in the world.

It's a much lower lift in some ways to just be angry and put off by a situation. It's harder to say what's on your mind and ask for what you need. Although communication isn't always easy, the experience with Alton and *Iron Chef* was another lesson that the effort is worth it, and that it is critical to a relationship of any kind. That level up in professional communication also had an added benefit—it allowed us to develop a lovely friendship beyond the *Iron Chef* set.

That said, while we got our bearings as a cohosting team and were feeling good on camera and having a blast on set, I almost always felt under water while filming that show. Shoot days were long, sometimes with a call time before the sun came up, and filming stretched into double-digit hours well after dark. But that part was expected, and, honestly, I was well-conditioned for it after so many years in restaurants.

It wasn't the filming that exhausted me, exactly. It wasn't even the fact that I always stayed up way too late, studying ingredients and our chefs for the following day. It was my nerves that kept me wound up and spinning, staring at the ceiling and worrying that I wasn't ready, no matter how many facts I memorized. I knew by then how important preparation is for me to manage my anxiety, but I never felt like there was enough time. For that reason, I never slept more than maybe five hours a night and rarely soundly or straight through.

It was a brief period—about three weeks in total—and I did my best every day. I showed up and participated, fulfilled my responsibilities, and I really did have so much fun. I loved the job and the people with whom I got to spend time. And I was able to sneak in thirty-minute lunchtime naps in my trailer, which honestly saved me.

As with any situation, you often walk away taking note of not only what you *do* want for the future but also what you don't want. *Iron Chef* was so much of both. I loved the experience, the team, and the ability to participate in a project that held such significance for two industries that were really meaningful to me—food and television. But I also recognized that I did not want to feel that underprepared or exhausted again. That's not to say you can always arrange perfect circumstances, but I knew that going forward, I would at least try to get closer to them.

Still, it didn't change the fact that by the time we wrapped and I returned home, I was so grateful and proud of what I'd accomplished—what we'd all created together—and eager to share it with the world.

The filming of *Iron Chef* was a whirlwind, but while I would have loved a little time to pause and recuperate, or even just reflect, I can't say I was exactly sitting around waiting to watch the episodes from the comfort of home. In fact, before the show officially dropped on Netflix, in June of 2022, I had already begun my next television adventure—and this one was truly worthy of the word.

In 2021, more than half a decade after my debut with *36 Hours* and before *Iron Chef* began filming, I got the news that I was getting another crack at a travel show. I'd been approached about the idea back in 2018, during its early stages. In the TV world, those first steps include building a "deck" that details the idea and refining a pitch to take to networks in hopes that someone will bite. But as I mentioned, making TV is a long game, and this one took a bit more time to get off the ground, in part because of the COVID interruption.

Once the world started opening up again, though, the idea was resurrected, refined, and finally pitched, after an immense amount of hard work, patience, and planning. It was shopped to several networks, and ultimately it was purchased by National Geographic. Subsequently, a production company called World of Wonder, the same team behind *RuPaul's Drag Race,* was brought on board. And thus *Restaurants at the End of the World*—a show in which I would travel to restaurants in remote parts of the world—was born.

There was a cachet to the show and a particular association for me. I could recall seeing copies of the iconic yellow-bordered covers of *National Geographic* magazine back when I was a kid, knowing that the pages within were windows into other worlds, filled with stories about far-off locations that were beyond my wildest dreams. Working with this legendary brand in a medium in which I was becoming more comfortable was exciting. The concept itself was super cool, too, and combined so many of my interests and skills. Over the course of four episodes, I would travel to some almost literally off-the-map locations in Panama, Norway, Brazil, and even an island off the coast of Maine and meet with chefs who ran restaurants there to talk through the challenges of operating in such places. It would be my job to be curious, to learn from other humans, and to transmit those findings and stories to the folks at home. It felt meaningful and would also give us a chance to celebrate those cultures and the hardworking people who might be in the margins and not otherwise have a way to reach a broader audience.

Personally, I would also have the chance to see the world in a much deeper way than I ever could as a tourist. And as an adoptee, this was especially significant to me. When I began really traveling in my early thirties for work and experiencing the world, a thought continued to run through my head whenever I went somewhere new. I would look around and think, *This could have been my life.* Because I really could have ended up anywhere. That idea shaped the way I enter a new place, always wanting to experience it all—through the lens of a parallel universe, in a way. I knew this show would give me that depth and opportunity and that it would be dense with unforgettable experiences.

I was also aware that once again, it would all be coordinated for me, with the protection of insurance and safety teams and under the supervision of companies who wouldn't spare any expense to protect themselves and everyone involved from liability. So many opportunities had been presented to me in the previous decade or so, and I was grateful for every one of them, even if I didn't always say yes. But this one did feel like a once-in-a-lifetime kind of thing. Every adventure sounded thrilling and included so many excursions and explorations I knew I'd never plan for myself, not only because of my well-documented aversion to logistics but also because I was no longer worried about just myself. I had to learn to take care of myself for Bianca, too. My life had become a two-player game, and what happened to me also happened to my wife.

Which is also why, when it came time to negotiate the contract for *Restaurants at the End of the World,* Bianca was worked into the deal. It was an unusual stipulation, but we were able to arrange it so the show would cover travel expenses for her when she wanted to come with me. We knew I would have to travel a ton with the show, not to mention for other projects, and as exciting as it all was, my priorities had changed—my family had to come first.

Fortunately, there were people on the other side of the contract who understood that philosophy. Courteney Monroe, president of National Geographic Global Television Networks, is also a working mother and wife, and I very quickly came to respect her immensely. I knew it was her stamp of approval that made that provision possible, and later I had a chance to thank her and express how much that meant to me. When I did, she reacted as if it was a totally natural decision. The way she saw it, it was her job to create a great TV show, and how could she expect the host of that show to bring the best version of herself to work every day if she didn't have what was necessary to be exactly that? I've heard people claim that entertainment executives are cold and unfeeling, obsessed only with ratings and the bottom line. But Courteney understood the value of family and love. She treated me like a human being rather than a commodity, and it was an example of being cared for that I will never forget.

With the contract in hand, it was time to film the pilot. For that first episode, which was set in Panama, I did go alone (in the end, Bianca would join me for two and a half episodes out of four). And that is how I wound up watching my very first episode of *Iron Chef* from a hotel restaurant at the end of the world (if the title of the show is to be believed). And by "watching" I mean scrutinizing video clips of our TV screen that my wife was texting me from back home, where *she* was watching it. I had very little Wi-Fi service and no access to Netflix, so this was our improvised solution.

To say it was a surreal experience could never do it justice. There are times when it's just impossible to reconcile your own reality. Once again, it's easy to imagine blowing the mind of a younger Kristen, who was so unsure of herself, who wanted to travel simply so she could go someplace where she might be accepted because she wasn't sure she'd ever find love or a place where she belonged. And now there I was, in the rainforest on the isthmus between Central and South America, trying to get a sense of my performance as the cohost of a legendary TV show alongside a culinary icon, thanks to my *wife* giving me the blow-by-blow from the home we built together with the foundation of a love I once believed would never be available to me.

Whether or not the show that was airing on a whole other continent was a "success," this scene alone was surreal and unforgettable.

I would eventually get to watch that season of *Iron Chef* back home (as well as on the road, once I figured out the magic of a VPN), and although I had some apprehension about my performance initially, I felt proud of the way it turned out. Which was a good thing, because during the height of production on *Restaurants at the End of the World,* I had to begin promoting *Iron Chef.* For four months that summer, I was simultaneously doing press for that show and filming for Nat Geo. I was flying all over—to California, to Norway, to Austin to check in on the restaurant, then stopping home before the next leg. It was absolutely insane at times. Everything was happening all at once.

You could look at this overlap in different ways. On the one hand, it was unbelievable to think that the stars aligned in such a way that I was allowed to do both (the alignment had some help from contract carve-outs that prevented any conflicts of interest). On the other hand, it was also the closest I've ever come to actually falling apart. One of the biggest lessons from this period was recognizing that I had a limit and knowing when I was approaching it. I had a job to do—two of them, in fact—for major networks. These were amazing opportunities, and I was so elated and appreciative. But I also realized that both things could be true: that sometimes it's okay to vent and even ask for a break, all while being truly, genuinely grateful.

No matter what was happening in the "real world," though, when I was out on shoots for *Restaurants,* it was hard to think about anything except what was right in front of me. The idea of social media posts and promotional meetings, press opportunities and television ratings, simply couldn't compete with the moments when I got to swim in the Arctic Ocean or float on a boat among walruses or step onto an actual glacier. Somewhere in the back of my mind I knew I was doing a job. But for the first time in any professional capacity, I was also just *living*, because there are some wondrous, all-consuming experiences that simply take precedence over productivity.

When Bianca came along on one of the trips, I always made sure to offer her an out, so she could stay in our hotel or explore a place on her own. Those shoot days could be long and grueling and a little boring for a spectator, even in the most awe-inspiring circumstances. But she was such a trooper, always happy to come along. Bianca frequently tells me that my joy is her joy, and I felt that so much in those days when I would look up from whatever it was that I was filming and see her watching me with a smile. For the most part, just knowing that she was there with me took the experience to another level—it was something we were both living together in a way, and I could feel her support just by proximity.

There were other times, however, when it was impossible to let a moment pass just because I was "working." One such instance was during our trip to Norway. We were set to film a scuba scene with a chef, but a polar bear had been spotted too close to the original dive location. And as cute as those things are in stuffed-animal form, they're not exactly what you want as a spectator for your film shoot. The team went into logistics mode and found us a new location within an hour. We had to hustle, and after being slipped into a seven-millimeter wet suit with the help of two grown men and a bottle of wet-suit lubricant (that's a sentence I never thought I'd write), we were off. It was a gray, foggy day, and for all the times people use the word *arctic* as a synonym for "freezing," the water was cold but not actually unbearable.

Viewers would eventually see me paddling around in the

Arctic off the coast of Norway's Svalbard archipelago, near the seventy-fourth parallel north—a landmass that is among the closest to the North Pole. What viewers wouldn't see was that I was also surrounded by a crew—there was a camera boat and a safety boat and, in the distance, another boat carrying producers and gear. Bianca was on the boat with the cameras. I looked up at one point and saw her there, watching me with that familiar smile. I knew I'd never forget it either way, but to really and truly *live* it, I wanted to share it with her in a more intimate way. I can't explain what came over me: I was well aware that I wasn't supposed to break the fourth wall, but I didn't care. I swam over, lifted myself up on the boat like a seal on a rock, and kissed my wife in the middle of that ocean. Afterward, I slid back into the water and proceeded to finish my job.

Maybe I felt compelled and liberated to act upon impulses like that one because I was already in the midst of a sea change in my life, understanding that there are some things that are so much more important than work—than a dish, a scene, an "outcome." That to live life and recognize those moments when they are happening is the true goal, and to share them whenever and however possible is the way to make them transcendent.

I also believe that the Nat Geo experience freed me in a profound way. I was never nervous on that show. There were no expectations other than to just be myself—all the versions of me, natural and unimpeded—and communicate what I was witnessing to the world beyond. In that sense, it was unprecedented for me in ways that had nothing to do with the totally novel surroundings. I may have been traveling to the end of the world, adventuring through the unknown, but I had never felt more at home in my own skin.

Restaurants at the End of the World aired in 2023, and while once again the complications of network mergers and politics left us in limbo, I had made friends and memories and walked away with more major lessons—those learned on both sides of the camera.

I cannot overstate the value of working in television and other media in my life—for myself, for my team at the restaurant, and for the communities I have come to represent. Growing up, I never imagined I had a story to tell or a message to spread, but I've since learned that every life has value, a narrative, and to share it is to connect, humanize, and create empathy. These projects are more than just television programs; they're a powerful opportunity to transmit those narratives. In doing so, I can demonstrate that a gay Korean adopted woman, born in Seoul and raised in Michigan, can be a chef, a character, a host, and a cultural communicator—as well as a human being with a beating heart, with all the aches and pains and challenges and triumphs and rewards that come along with it.

Being a TV "star" was never part of the plan. In fact, most of the time, when I was growing up, I didn't want to be seen at all. But had I seen someone like me on TV when I was a kid, I might not have spent so much of my life trying to be someone different. In the future, I hope to help more people in the world feel as if they can be the heroes of their own stories, no matter who they are or where they're coming from.

I've never been a big reader, which was sometimes a challenge when I was in a traditional academic setting. But as the world has come to understand the many ways in which human beings can grasp new concepts and ideas, I have recognized that I am a visual learner. I might read one particular instructional paragraph ten times, but once you show me how something is done, I can replicate it and retain the information. I can even share it. Maybe in that way, it's no surprise that I wound up finding a place in the world of television. And after absorbing so much—yet knowing there is so much more to learn—these projects helped me open the door for whatever might come next and approach it with clear eyes—wide open.

16

Spend enough time in airports, and they all start to blur together. Hudson News. McDonald's. The same bags of chips and trail mix and granola bars at impulse-purchase stands (with slight variations for international trips). The same souvenirs, just stamped with different city names.

Airports occupy a strange, liminal space. You're in an in-between, and it's almost like what happens there doesn't actually apply to the real world—kind of like Vegas, but less scandalous. It's easy to forget what happens in an airport sometimes, and given that I've traveled so much in my life, I occasionally have a hard time even remembering which one I'm in at all.

That dreamlike quality is part of why what I experienced in the security line in early June of 2023, on a layover in Dubai between Thailand and New York City, felt especially surreal.

Bianca and I had been in Thailand the previous week, enjoying the hell out of a trip that was planned around a few work events for me. I was there for a brand collaboration, doing some around-town filming for a hotel's content platforms.

I was also scheduled to participate in a panel for queer people to celebrate Bangkok Pride Week. This was one of those things that I never even knew to dream about when I got into the culinary world. That I could represent and learn from others in my community and celebrate queer culture on the other side of the world—that was a kind of gratification I couldn't have imagined when I picked up my first knife roll decades earlier.

In addition, I was promoting my soju line with a fun and educational mixology class. The brand and product had been another one of those random surprises in my career, one I'm super proud of—as is my dad, who tells anyone who will listen about it. It was a busy schedule, but in the downtime, Bianca and I got to enjoy some gorgeous beach life together. We had breakfast in bed, kissed on the shore at sunset (and posted selfies for proof and posterity), and enjoyed remarkable hospitality on Koh Samui, an island in the Gulf of Thailand. These were incredible perks of the job, and I couldn't have been more thrilled to share them with the love of my life.

Overall, the trip was fantastic, and we were so happy for the getaway. And while I was continually stunned to be able to call these experiences part of my job, it was still work somehow, so we weren't totally off the grid. Both Bianca and I were staying connected to the so-called real world, even if it was occasionally with the privilege of using a hammock as an office chair. And of course, I was staying connected to the rest of the world by way of social media, and it was during one of these Instagram check-ins from our hotel room on June 2, that one specific post got my full attention.

⸻

There have been certain elements in my life that have always been the same. Little reliabilities that don't rock the boat and are just a dependable part of my world, no matter how much time passes or things evolve. There are universal ones, like the sky being blue, and the personal ones, like the fact that my parents will always be Michigan State football fans. Sometimes I'm aware of that immutability. Other times, I simply don't notice it because I never question it—it just is.

For me, *Top Chef*—the show that shaped so much about my life, from my relationships to the way I cook—was one of those things I expected to always stay the same, exactly as I left it.

In part, that's because the series was cemented not only in the food world but also in the cultural zeitgeist. And it was hard to imagine anyone, even outside the industry, who didn't hear those two words together and immediately think of three very specific people: Tom Colicchio, Gail Simmons, and Padma Lakshmi. Which is why the Instagram post I read at our sun-drenched Bangkok resort stopped me cold.

"After much soul-searching, I have made the difficult decision to leave *Top Chef*," Padma's Instagram post told followers.

It was a message tailor-made for social media. It was honest, brief, and to the point, designed to connect with a specific audience and deliver major news to the masses in a personal way.

I knew Padma from our interactions over the years, including the times during my more nomadic period when she opened up her home to me, and she was always a consummate professional—committed, thoughtful, deliberate about her career and her relationships. I also knew what likely went into making that decision, because I knew firsthand how much she'd put into the show. That was why the message struck me in such a big way.

The announcement wasn't just a surprise for me as a casual bystander, though. This was one of those moments that reminds you that nothing—even what you consider to be a reliable, unwavering reality—is entirely resistant to change.

I had been involved with *Top Chef* during the COVID pandemic, when I was brought on as a guest alumni judge for seasons 18 and 19. At the time, it was a fun way to return to that stage, despite the unusual circumstances. Because of the restrictions around travel and the logistics of testing and quarantine, they created a COVID bubble for filming, so I did four consecutive episodes for one season in one shot, then returned later to do two more—the first and semifinal episodes—for the following season.

My experience with *Top Chef* had started way back in 2012, and it changed my life and the trajectory of my career. It altered not only what I *did* dream; it also entirely altered what I *could* dream. It put me in another category altogether. Coming back as an alum was an honor, but I also took it as a responsibility to the show that had given me so much.

I was able to come back not only with fresh eyes and perspective but also with a lot more experience—in life, in the kitchen, and in media. And yet none of it was enough to keep my nerves at bay. The first day brought back all kinds of emotions. Even though I wouldn't be cooking or evaluated in any kind of concrete way, I don't think that association with judgment—the nerves that come with taking on those challenges and not succeeding—has ever really left my subconscious. Each of the three judges was supportive, but that didn't stop me from feeling intimidated because of my own internalized fears.

As an Asian woman in this business, and in this world, for that matter, I'm very familiar with the additional lengths we sometimes must go to in order to be taken seriously. Padma has been supportive and generous when someone is in need of help. But she also exudes authority.

Many times in my career (and my life), I have been subject to evaluation, assessment, and appraisal, whether as a student, as part of a demonstration for a job in a restaurant, or in front of cameras on the *Top Chef* stage. But the idea of judgment has never really sat well with me. Particularly when it comes to food, who's to say that my opinion of what tastes good should carry more weight simply because I'm trained in technique? I had learned this lesson time and again working in restaurants: Not everyone's palate is created equal, and preference can vary wildly. But especially at Arlo Grey, we learned early on that many factors, including regional culture and expectations, could affect the lens through which food is received and reviewed.

But *Top Chef* has never been about arbitrary judgment. It's not Yelp. The systematic evaluation is done by skilled culinarians with decades of experience and, in my opinion, good intentions.

Having been a contestant, I had some idea of how the discussion went down, and it may seem strange to think I was just as fearful on the other side. But there's a power to judging, and I wanted to wield that power delicately and constructively. I didn't want to tear anyone down. My own time in the competitors' circle stayed with me. Even though I was the winner, there were plenty of moments when I wished I could have done better, and I never wanted anyone to walk away feeling like a failure or defeated, even if they didn't win.

Those guest-judging episodes helped me get a better, behind-the-scenes understanding of the system, a comprehension that not only gave context to my own memories as a contestant in a deeper way but also added a dimension to my style of leadership. Arlo Grey had been running since 2018, and coaching my team is a hugely important part of the job, especially since these days I'm not on-site for every service. I've had to learn to walk a line between being instructive on the one hand, offering guidance, support, and encouragement, while also being gently authoritative on the other, correcting missteps and directing people toward improvement and growth. I also had to learn when to step back, be more hands-off, and let them steer the ship.

In addition to making entertaining television, I do believe the goal of *Top Chef* has always been similar to mine—to help contestants recognize hitches in their performance so they can address them and improve. Because the show's structure was so well established, so dialed in, I learned a lot that translated practically to my working life as a manager. The framework of the challenges, with a particular and clearly communicated objective, is an ideal sort of training device in a way. The evaluation system excludes any kind of arbitrary "judgment." While the process isn't a set of hard-and-fast rules, and the strategy varies a bit from person to person at the judge's table, there's an understanding that across the board we're all looking to track quantifiable metrics, like technical ability and creative interpretation, and that we'll be able to back up our critique.

Having those parameters allowed us to provide insight as to why we made our decisions, which helped eliminate ambiguity for the contestants. They could walk away not with a sour taste in their mouths and a set of questions about their performance and likability (or popularity, for that matter) but instead with a clear idea of something concrete they could work on and strengthen for the future. For me, it helped clarify my role and provide my own parameters for how to deliver valuable feedback.

That said, for as much fun as it was, and for all that I learned, I never got 100 percent comfortable as a judge in a guest role. I'd spent so much of my life losing sleep over expectations and terrified to let people down in my life, and Tom, Gail, and Padma remained major figures in my world. I couldn't shake the stress of disappointing them.

Afterward, I didn't see Padma regularly. After my appearances as guest judge, time just passed, and before I knew it, years had gone by. I had no reason to believe the world of *Top Chef* wasn't preserved in amber, exactly as it lived in my memory. Until that June afternoon.

In Thailand, I showed the post to Bianca, who was equally floored, before sitting down to compose a message to Padma. I took my time. I wanted to convey my support, my hope that whatever it was she was on to next would be something that filled her soul.

Still, although I felt so deeply in my heart for Padma—and the rest of the *Top Chef* family—I was also still on my own work trip, with my own professional life to conduct. After I sent Padma my support, I mostly put the news out of my mind for the remainder of my time in Thailand (aside from the inescapable, omnipresent industry and social media chatter). Eventually, I finished my obligations, and although the trip was lovely, I was ready to get back home with my wife and back to our version of normal. Then I got a call that would change my life once again.

I often think about the chains of events that lead us to particular moments in life. *Top Chef*'s first season aired in 2006. Padma joined in season 2. At that time, fourteen years earlier, when a production company called Magical Elves pursued an Asian American woman to host their show, it was practically unheard of at the time. The definition of trailblazing.

Simultaneously, I was living my own life, taking opportunities and stepping through open doors, making decisions (and, arguably, some mistakes). But all of it—the confluence of factors and decisions made by so many people—came together that summer when my phone rang in that otherworldly realm of the international airport.

Bianca and I were waiting in line for security, exhausted by travel and going through the motions, when I spoke with my manager, Tory, formerly a director of communications for Bravo. I called her in response to a slew of text messages I'd received in-flight, which came through once we were on the ground and out of airplane mode. We were getting close to the front of the line, so I knew it would have to be a brief conversation, which I let her know when I picked up. But we didn't need much time, because the message came through loud and clear when Tory delivered a single line:

"Kristen," she said, "Bravo wants to meet with you."

Since Padma's news broke, I'd had plenty of feelings: surprise, some sadness on behalf of the *Top Chef* team, happiness for Padma, and curiosity about her next moves. But not once did it cross my mind that in their quest to find a successor, the team's searchlight would land on me.

Later, I was astonished and so honored by how many people would comment that they saw this coming or that there was no question in their minds that it could be anyone but me. But I wasn't thinking about the show as much in those days, and the thought never once went through my head. I was operating my restaurant and running brand partnerships, and my own TV reality had expanded, too. I'd just wrapped up *Iron Chef* on Netflix and hosted *Restaurants at the End of the World* for Nat Geo. I was preoccupied with keeping my eye on the many balls that sometimes seemed to be coming at me from all directions, grateful for the continued interest in me and trying to both enjoy the experience and live up to the expectations of each.

But even though the job hadn't been on my radar, something about the tone of Tory's voice that day while I pushed my suitcase through the metal detector snapped it into stark focus. I had to hang up quickly, and I told her I'd call her back on the other side of security, once the powers that be decided I was approved to fly. But somehow, I already knew what she was going to say when we reconnected.

I looked at Bianca, who was in front of me, taking our belongings out of the bins. I leaned down and relayed the news:

"Bravo wants to meet with me," I told her.

I'm a daydreamer and always have been, and Bianca has always been supportive and beyond encouraging, but neither of us is the type to count our chickens. In fact, I tend to err on such a conservative side when it comes to possibilities that it borders on skepticism, because a major part of my life has been about managing expectations and approaching opportunities logically. Neither of us assumed it was a done deal based on a single sentence. So when Bianca responded with a beaming smile, then stood up on her tiptoes to wrap her arms around my neck, I knew it wasn't because she believed it was a foregone conclusion or that her love for me would be somehow enhanced by or contingent on my getting this gig. Even if it went nowhere beyond that call, she was already expressing her immense pride. She was just happy for me to be considered and recognized. That alone would have been enough for both of us.

But that wasn't all it was. We were back in New York twelve

hours later, and it took barely another twenty-four hours before I was wheels-up once again—this time, headed due west, to LA.

———

By that point, I'd taken a lot of meetings in my career that could be classified as scary. But although the guest-judge gig did make me nervous, one of the great things about returning to *Top Chef* in any capacity was a sense of comforting familiarity, something I found in friendly faces. Whenever I'm in LA, one of the first people I always see is Derek, who has been cutting my hair forever. This trip was no different, and I was thrilled to see him when he arrived at my hotel, shears in hand. Then my ride to the meeting was with Ron Mare, the vice president of casting for Magical Elves—someone with whom I'd had many conversations and interactions over the years. He picked me up, and we drove to the Bravo offices on the Universal Studios lot. It gave me a sense of calm to be surrounded by people I knew.

And although I was tired from the whirlwind of travel, and a little keyed up by the uncertainty of it all, I can't say I was super nervous, exactly. That's because I wasn't under the impression that I needed to be. Before I left town, I tried to clarify with Tory that this was *not* an audition. I'd been through plenty of those before. I understood it was a necessity in some situations, but I was not interested in that process or in being a name on a long list of candidates who would be clawing for the crown. I told her if they wanted me, they'd get me, but if I was going to be fighting for the job, it was not for me. Tory assured me that to her knowledge, that was not the case.

When I finally found myself at the table in Los Angeles that morning, though, it was hard to tell. I was acquainted with some of the people in the room, including Ron, Casey Kriley, also from

Magical Elves (the company's co-CEO), and Ryan Flynn, a senior vice president of current production at Bravo. These were people who knew and had seen me far more than I'd seen them, being as they were always behind the scenes, but they were familiar faces, and the vibe was cordial.

Still, the questions that followed the pleasantries had a distinctly interviewish flavor to them. Queries like, "How would you host *Top Chef*?" and "What would this role mean for you?" and "How do you see yourself growing?" made me uneasy. I answered thoughtfully and honestly, but I also felt confused. It's not that I was defensive, exactly, but I was concerned with being clear about the dynamic. In my experience to that point, not being direct with your intentions, hopes, and deal-breakers rarely leads to a positive outcome. So while the conversation toggled between interview-style questions and very casual, complimentary language, a number of lines began with an unsettling qualifier:

"So, Kristen, if you get this job..."

There are moments in life when you surprise yourself and realize how far you've come. You understand that you actually know yourself, your capabilities, and your boundaries better than you even realized. There is great power in coming to that point in a career or relationship or life in general—when you recognize that you don't *need* something. I was interested in the job. I was curious about it. Hell, I can even honestly say that I *wanted* it, truly. But I absolutely did not *need* it. And that information can lower the stakes of any conversation. It can give you an unbelievable amount of comfort. It gives you leverage. I'd played the "act as if" part many times in my life, and I didn't have to do it anymore. After another of the questions began with this opener, without even thinking I looked Ryan directly in the eye and started my response with "*When* I get this role…" And I realized that this was one of those life moments. That alone might've been worth the trip.

The meeting lasted about an hour, at the end of which I hugged Ryan and thanked him. He informed me that they had a few other people to talk to (although Ryan later admitted that this wasn't the case—it was a 'play it cool' comment), and this was definitely not the news I wanted to hear. I had expected to walk out of that building with a hint that I'd be getting the job. Instead, I had an invitation to lunch.

In television, there are several entities involved in making a show, including the network and production company. In this case, that was Bravo (network) and Magical Elves (production). That first meeting on the Universal lot was with the network, and now I'd be sitting down with just Ron and Casey from production. Either way, I still didn't really have a good sense of what I was working with, and despite the much more relaxed setup—a Mexican spot surrounded by chips and guac and queso, picking at shrimp tacos and Sprites on a sunny LA summer day—I didn't let myself relax. I didn't know if I was having a meal with friendly industry acquaintances or potential employers.

The conversation meandered, but the show was definitely the focus. It was a different set of questions, more about logistics like wardrobe. For example, they asked, "So would you wear a dress?" To which I replied, resoundingly, "No," in yet another sign of personal growth and self-assuredness. But I also got the sense there was some hyping happening. It's evident to me now when I'm being sold a little. I've come to understand that there's a strategy in these situations, to get someone to feel like they need to be a part of a thing they didn't know they wanted. Even with good intentions and good people at that table, this was the vibe I was getting from the way they described this changeover as a moment to "shake things up" for *Top Chef*, promising that this as-yet-unnamed new host would have the chance to be part of this progress.

Later that night, after I had a conversation with Tory in my hotel, during which I conveyed some of my confusion and frustration, I fell into bed. I didn't have the luxury of losing sleep over this. I had to wake up early to catch a flight, to begin another day tending to other obligations, responding to other people who relied on me. Still, as I lay in my hotel bed that night, digesting the events of the day, I was certain this one would be nagging at the back of my mind.

———

Every season, the winner of *Top Chef* gets a coveted multipart prize. It has changed slightly over the years, and starting with season 17, the cash part ballooned to $250,000 from $125,000, which is what it was in my day. But one element has always been part of the package: an appearance at the Food & Wine Classic in Aspen, Colorado. That may not sound like much compared to the dollar amount, because the money is huge, obviously. Some winners use that cash to open restaurants, grow the businesses they already have, pay off debt, or go on a vacation. But the latter part of the prize is a big deal, too.

Within the industry, it's an honor to receive an invitation to the Food & Wine Classic. It's attended by so many influential figures in the food world, all doing demos and panels and shaking hands and making connections. It's one of those events that can open doors and help you forge a larger network.

In 2023, I was slated to be part of the *Top Chef* panel, moderated by *Food & Wine* editor Khushbu Shah. Other participants included seasons 19 and 20 winner, Buddha Lo; season 7 alum Tiffany Derry; and Gail. Under normal circumstances, this would have been a fun and casual reunion. But this happened to be taking place less than a week after my ambiguous LA trip and less than two weeks after Padma's news.

Now, I've lived with secrets often in my life. First and most significantly as a closeted gay woman. I've also been with women for whom I was literally a walking secret. And then, when I won *Top Chef*, there were months when I couldn't reveal that information to anyone. Sure, it can be argued that secrets can be fun and exciting in some kind of way. But at a certain point, and under certain circumstances, it is at best exhausting and at worst isolating and destructive.

I'd gone about my business after LA, and by the time I went to Aspen, I had no further information, just a swelling secret. Despite a brief follow-up call with Casey and Ron after I'd left town, I had no clarity on the gig or where I stood in the process. With the panel on the schedule and Padma's departure news fresh in everyone's minds, there was no doubt I was going to be faced with questions, and I had no way of knowing how to answer. I'd already had to dodge inquiries from people like Derek, my hairstylist, who had innocently just wanted to know why I was in town that day. I needed to get my story straight and my poker face down pat—fast.

Of course, when the day of the panel arrived, to absolutely no one's surprise, the first question from the crowd was, "Who will be the next host of *Top Chef*?"

Khushbu was a skilled moderator and knew to shut that question down in a kind and professional way. With the Bravo PR and comms teams on-site, we did our best to skirt the issue. And while I could stomach the idea of talking to the press or strangers and avoiding the truth, it was something else entirely to do the same with someone I considered a trusted friend. To me, that was Gail.

Gail was no stranger. I'd been to her home as well as Padma's. I knew her family. And yet before I flew to Aspen, I was strongly encouraged not to speak to Gail until I signed the contract. And look, I understand why some rules are in place. I get the need to protect certain elements and control the narrative—and the need to get ahead of rumors. I even know that some of this is to protect me, too, from internet trolls and even the possibility that something might kill the deal before a decision could be made.

But in some cases, rules just can't apply, especially when it comes to human relationships—particularly those that were built over the course of years with investment and care. It's not that Gail and I regularly had super-deep discussions whenever we were together, especially not in the context of an event like this, but the awareness that I was keeping a secret made me uneasy.

I'd seen Gail at the opening party, during which there was just too much going on to have this subject top of mind. But one afternoon later in the week, we walked back to our hotel together and were able to have a lovely moment of quiet conversation, and there came a point where I felt like I was watching a sitcom scene—the point where you as the viewer know both parties are aware that something is up but no one discusses it. It felt unnatural to dance around something so significant to both of us, so after a sufficient amount of small talk and surface-level chat, I turned to her.

"Gail," I said. "Do you know…"

I didn't finish the sentence. Some people might have forced the issue, insisting that I be clear and say the damn thing out loud, in full. But not Gail. She didn't press me for anything more or put me in a position where I might be further compromised. But she said she did know. And that was that.

Knowing that she knew that I knew, and that I knew that she knew, was a massive relief. It was also a strong indicator of where I stood. Given her history with the show, Gail's opinion and influence would matter to the powers that be.

But more than anything, it meant so much to me to hear this person, who had been such an influential figure in my life for more than a decade by that point, offering me affirmation—this validation and her support. Whether or not I actually got the role, it felt damn good to know that Gail thought I could do it. And if nothing else was a sure thing, I knew our friendship was secure, and that was what was most important to me.

I left Aspen with no further information, so again I returned to life as usual. Or at least as close to usual as possible. This is a motif when you're making television: hurry up and wait. In the meantime, I went along with daily life, as I would have had I never received that call in the security line and had Padma never decided to leave the show. I had a personal life full of loved ones who didn't judge me or question whether they wanted me. They were people who loved me back. People who didn't ambush-interview me or make me question my self-worth. At the end of the day, I really did like the people who made the show, both at Bravo and Magical Elves. If I hadn't, I wouldn't have wanted the position as badly as I did. And while I didn't love waiting—when something is so exciting, it can feel interminable—I was conditioned to that part of the process. It's just part of the game.

I remained in professional purgatory, so it was good timing for a personal interlude, and my family had a very good reason to refocus and get together. My father was turning seventy-five, so Bianca and I were traveling to Michigan to celebrate him. It had been a very long time since we'd last gathered, and frankly, after so much chaos and the emotional roller coaster of the previous month, I was really looking forward to the homecoming.

An added bonus was that my big brother had just gotten a new boat and was taking us all out on it—which would be the first time for Bianca and me. He was so excited to share it, and we were super enthusiastic to play crew to his captain. As we prepared to board that day, I looked around at the lake and my family, and I knew that despite our being out there on the water, it would be the first time in a while that I would feel entirely on sturdy ground. I could put it all aside for a while and just enjoy my family's company. At least that's what I thought.

But whether it was the universe's sense of humor or the team's sense of decency, I got a call a few days before we left for the trip. Casey and Ron informed me that the role was going to be offered to me—they didn't want to leave me hanging over the long Fourth of July holiday weekend. And while that conversation alone might have seemed like enough to let us pop the champagne, I couldn't let myself really feel the relief—the elation, the joy—until I had a signed contract. That part came at a less opportune time, after we'd made the trip to Michigan and just before we were about to board the boat. On our way, Tory explained that I was going to receive an email with the agreement, which I wanted to sign ASAP. Which was going to be interesting, considering I was about to be in the middle of a giant lake. For a moment, I worried that I wouldn't have cell service, and that was enough to send me into a small panic again. I just wanted the damn thing done.

Fortunately, I didn't have to worry, thanks to the reach of modern technology, and so despite the fact that the process had been so stressful, so grueling, so destabilizing, in the end it was while I was beneath a beautiful summer sky, in the middle of Lake Michigan, surrounded by the most important people in my world, and reclining in Bianca's lap that the deal of a lifetime was closed. I e-signed the contract and exhaled. My parents, my brother, my wife—everyone I loved most in the world was within arm's reach. Even though I'd wanted answers so many different times in the preceding weeks, I couldn't have asked for a more perfect scenario. The ink, at least in digital form, was officially dry.

When Tory alerted me that I could expect the offer, I had two questions. The first was "When can I tell my family?"

I hadn't looped them in yet, because again—logical daydreamer. I didn't see the point in getting everyone all whipped up if I didn't have something real and solid to say. Now I had a black-and-white contract and a green light.

"You guys know that Padma is leaving *Top Chef,* right?" I asked as my brother piloted along and we enjoyed a gentle summer breeze. My parents nodded.

"You know who's going to take over?" I asked.

No one said anything for a beat, until my mom let a little smile creep up.

"You?" she asked.

I nodded. I let my own smile—the one I hadn't truly allowed myself until that moment—explode across my face. I didn't need to say anything more. There were hugs and congratulations, and everyone was so proud. But the beautiful thing about my family, and that moment in my life, is that they probably had the same reaction the day I told them I'd lost my first tooth. Throughout my entire life, they were evenly, reliably, *always* proud of me. No matter the scope of the achievement.

That weekend, we celebrated my dad's birthday as planned. We let all the noise and intensity of the last weeks fall away and focused on the family time that was so rare, the time I always missed so deeply when I was far from home and that was more valuable than any contract could ever be.

My second question to Tory had been a no-brainer, too. "When can I tell Padma?"

I did not want her to hear it from anyone but me. So later, after disembarking from Jon's boat, in the basement in my aunt and uncle's house in Michigan, I made the call. I'd rehearsed it in my head, thinking so carefully about how to phrase the news. I wanted to make sure I accurately conveyed my respect and a sense of appreciation, knowing that she carved this path, created this role, and paved the way for a woman like me to succeed her—and succeed in general.

I wanted it to be authentic and professional but express the emotional side of how I was feeling, too. I knew Padma would appreciate these qualities, because I'd learned them in part from her, observing how she carried herself and conducted her own career and her life.

In the end, I simply said, "Bravo has extended me your role."

I didn't say "*the* job" or "*the* role," because truly, it belonged to Padma. She created it, and in a way the baton was hers to bestow. I knew much would be made in the press about Padma being the one to blaze the trail, to pass the torch to another Asian American and another woman. But the significance of it all for both of us, and for so many people *like* us, was not lost on me in that quiet, private moment.

We had a brief conversation after that. Padma was congratulatory and cordial. She offered support and reminded me of that open door, the one she'd made sure I knew was there since the very beginning. I was appreciative. I knew it was a phone call and a moment I'd never forget.

The whole process had taken less than a month, but it *felt* like an eternity at times. Now, with so many conversations and questions finally behind me, I was able to get to the exciting part. Sure, there were still details to sort out, and I had major nerves about diving into the role, but the first step was to tell the world. Bravo informed me of their schedule for making the announcement on social media, and I couldn't wait to share the excitement that had been practically bursting out of me since that first call in the Dubai security line, long before I really even let myself experience it.

But there was also a moment during which I was really worried. The internet can be a brutal, ruthless place—I'd witnessed it before, personally and with colleagues—and people tend to really dislike change. They can also be extremely vocal about it from behind their phones and computer screens, so I braced myself for a potential backlash. I reminded myself, and Bianca especially emphasized, that the opinions of real consequence to my life had already been voiced by the closest people in my world. The ones who truly mattered. I knew she was right.

It turned out I didn't have to worry. What I did have to do was turn off my phone, because the unbelievable outpouring of support and enthusiasm was absolutely overwhelming. Sometimes you can plan for the worst and not even allow yourself to imagine that things might go *well,* but it's surprising how positive the world can be. I've been lucky that life has been like that so often for me, thanks to fans and communities that have been kind, enthusiastic, and boundlessly supportive, and I'm so grateful for that experience. I wouldn't consider myself a negative person, exactly, but I cling to that logical streak, and the inclination to manage my own expectations is always a tactic of self-defense. And yet the number of times that life has surprised me, given me an affirmation of goodness when I might have expected otherwise, has been a reminder to leave room to be awed by the unexpected. Because those moments and those reactions—the ones for which you could never have planned or dreamed—are true magic.

Another surprising part of this whole thing has been how frequently people have echoed sentiments similar to the ones Gail shared with me on our walk on that Aspen afternoon: "I knew it'd be you" and "Of course it was you, Kristen." I never once had that expectation in my own mind, nor did I realize how many people thought of me as being that capable. It has been humbling, affirming, and, frankly, so moving. Now, when I feel scared, or like I'm slipping into a nervous or anxious place, I try to see myself through the eyes of the people who love and believe in me. I always do my best to live up to their expectations. I also remind myself now that these are the people who will love me no matter what. I don't have to punish or push myself. I just have to *be* myself, trust myself, set and live by my own standards, because this person—the one I've always been—is the one in which they already believe.

After so much buildup, starting the show was a total trip. Tom and Gail are such pros by now that they only need to show up and roll. I, on the other hand, opted to fly in four days early to try to get comfortable with my surroundings. Even though there was a welcome familiarity to the franchise, and even though I'd hosted TV before, this was a completely different animal. I wanted the time to go through the motions of setting up my hotel room, mapping out my routines, removing some of the guesswork and variables that might make me anxious when it was go time.

That first morning, as we prepared for filming, everyone was so supportive. Gail set my mind at ease, emphasizing that I could do as many clean reads as I needed, assuring me that everyone would be patient and accommodating. I replayed her words from that day in Aspen in my head, reminding myself that I belonged there. The crew—some of whom I knew well and others whom I was meeting for the first time—were all welcoming and enthusiastic. Whatever opinion they might have had of the torch-passing, I was fresh blood, and this was a new season. It was such good vibes all around as we prepared.

And then, just before we got rolling, Tom pulled me aside. I was already in full hair and makeup, shaking out my hands, trying to move energy and adrenaline around and expel some nervousness. Tom had always been kind to me, but this was a different side of him—I could tell from the way he approached me. There was an air of ceremony, a weight to the scene that reminded me that I was living through a pivotal moment in my life.

"Listen," he said once we had a little peace. And whether sensing my nerves or reading my mind, he gave me the brief pep talk I needed. "All you have to do is just talk to these chefs like you would talk to your cooks at your restaurant. It's preshift. That's all this is. Just talk to them."

It was such simple advice, to strip away the flash, to zero in on what matters, what's real. This is the objective not only of the show but also of life itself. To make a meaningful connection to other humans. I was once so accustomed to forging those connections at a dining table, in a restaurant, where I could see how people were doing, whether they were enjoying themselves, whether my work was landing. Where I could tell for sure if I was reaching them. And here I was, in this entirely new capacity, yet the goal was the same. Tom was helping me pull back, take a breath amid the chaos, and recognize that.

I thought about the experiences that had come from my time on *Top Chef.* The opportunities. The adventures. But above all, the connections. I thought about the way the Asian American and queer and adopted communities came out for me, how they reframed my sense of self, how supporters shifted my priorities and my intentions for the work I do. I thought about the small moments with humans like Gail, Tom, and Padma that had happened behind the scenes— on studio lots, on walks, on phone calls from family homes.

The show wasn't all cameras and dramatic challenges and flash-bulbs and fanfare. It was a conduit for connection. That was something I held sacred, on-screen and off-screen.

When we finally got out in front of the camera, I was positioned in the middle, with Gail and Tom on either side. I looked around at the crew—the AD, the camera operators, the set photographer, the audio team. I knew a lot of these people and had built a rapport with them over time. I could feel their pride in me, which made me so emotional and proud of myself, in a way, for participating in the creation of this network. And when we finally started rolling tape, I took a deep breath from a well of confidence, secure in the knowledge that I was surrounded by so much support, mutual respect, and love.

Later, after we'd filmed all the episodes for the season and arrived at the finale, I geared up for a major moment, one in which I'd be the one to deliver the iconic closing line: *You are Top Chef.* This was to be the first time since Padma had assumed her role in season 2 that this message would not come from her.

I felt the exuberance of the whole cast and crew waiting for that moment around the set. It was an immense responsibility. This single sentence was a brand-new starting point for the winner, a first impression in a way, a launchpad for possibilities they might have never imagined for themselves. It was a place I remembered very well.

After the cameras had been switched off, after the celebrations and congratulations and hugs and laughter and toasts, when I went back to my room and was able to sit and reflect and hear my thoughts clearly, a phrase passed through my head—one that had found its way into so many conversations about my returning to the show.

Full circle.

The thing is, that phrase indicates closure, completion. But for me, returning to *Top Chef* wasn't about closing a loop or arriving at a conclusion. As I sat there thinking about all I'd learned, how I would apply it all in my new role and in my life going forward, I was reminded of how many surprising, unimaginable new beginnings I'd had in my life. I could recognize the feeling now, like taxiing on a runway, preparing for takeoff. This was in no way an ending. It was just the beginning.

EPILOGUE

ACCIDENTALLY ON PURPOSE

Sometimes I think back to the "start" of my adult life, when I was trying to pick a path post–high school, looking at all those road maps and attempting to see into the future, to anticipate exactly where my choices would take me so I could plan accordingly.

But in the course of my life, I've repeatedly found myself at intersections where I've been offered chances to reroute, reconsider my path, reevaluate what I thought and said I wanted. And instead of doubling down on my own direction, I've accepted many of those suggested course changes. I followed sound advice from trusted sources, turned down open roads, and listened to my own instincts, which sharpened with time and reflection. Because opportunity alone doesn't move you forward—choice does that.

But then sometimes a path can come full circle, back to where you started, too. And that doesn't always mean you're not getting anywhere.

I'm often asked about my relationship to Korea and Korean culture. There seems to be a general expectation that adoptees must at some point feel compelled to go diving deeper into their place and biological family of birth. There are so many reasons one might want to explore that option, and I can absolutely understand why so many adoptees want to travel that road—even in situations like mine, where they are loved and happy with the families into which they've been adopted.

But for much of my life I have subverted that expectation, too. For me it just wasn't something I felt compelled to pursue. Truthfully, I only ever really considered it once. It was way back during that time when I moved home after the tumultuous period in Chicago. I was feeling severely lost. I hadn't yet considered moving to Boston, but I knew I couldn't stay in Michigan. I was in search of a direction, something to guide my next move, a fixed point on the horizon that could be a destination. It seemed like going to Korea could be that thing.

I did some cursory research and quickly realized that it wasn't something I could really afford, but beyond that, it would require a lot more time, energy, and other resources than I was willing and able to dedicate to it just then. In retrospect, I can see that for most of my life, when I wanted something, I found a way to make it happen. I think at the time, my heart just wasn't really in it for a variety of reasons.

After that, years passed, and the idea didn't preoccupy me. I was never averse to going to Korea, but as I've explained throughout this book, logistics really aren't my thing—and that was a journey that would require a lot of them.

I think I believed that someday I would be struck by the motivation and have the means to make it happen. But if I had some ideas about how that would play out, they were about a million miles off from the way I'd actually, finally find myself with a ticket to Korea.

In 2022, during the period when I was actively shooting *Restaurants at the End of the World* and simultaneously doing press for *Iron Chef*, the universe intervened, and an opportunity showed up in my path. Well, actually, on my schedule. The calendar was packed wall-to-wall with events and stops that season, and I was traveling all over the place. I was trying to take it in stride even though I was exhausted, but when I reviewed the rundown, there was one stop that gave me pause. There, in a five-day block, smack in between two other confirmed obligations, was a trip to Korea.

The plan was to send three Korean Americans—me, Esther Choi, and Kevin Kreider—as a cross-promotion with *Money Heist: Korea*. I had two initial reactions: One was *Fuck, how am I going to do this?* And that was purely from a practical standpoint. I was already teetering on the edge, trying to somehow manage it all. The other was more of a gut reaction: *This isn't how I want to go to Korea for the first time.*

I tried to convince myself that it wasn't going to work, but I couldn't argue that the trip fit perfectly in schedule. Still, there was so much going on that it was hard to even process the idea. I remember thinking it was just too much. That felt like a logical reason to say no, so before I could spin about it, I told my manager that I couldn't make it happen. It was rare for me to turn down anything that felt like part of the job. But if it seemed out of character, my team didn't argue with me. And neither did Bianca, who listened and accepted my initial decision.

But although no one was pushing me, I couldn't stop thinking about it and revisiting the internal debate. I'd been to so many new places in my life, but when it came to Korea, I always felt that when I went for the first time, I needed to go and go all in—really *do the thing.* Spend weeks traveling around, doing a cultural and personal deep dive, allowing myself time to explore and process in a carefully planned fashion. That's how I expected it to go down.

But then somewhere in my brain, I couldn't help asking myself the follow-up question: *Why haven't you done it yet?*

I had realized by that point in my life that when something nagged at me this way, when I felt I couldn't fully turn away from a possible path, it might be for a reason. It might be a sign. And so, ultimately, that was the sign I followed.

A few days later, when I said to Bianca, "I think I need to go," she gave me her enthusiastic support. ("Thank God, yes!" is how I believe she responded.) It was clear that her mind had been on a parallel track.

With her support and that change of heart, my perspective changed. I thought, *Maybe this* is *how I need to go to Korea*—in a way that is without so much pressure, without the insistence that I have to *find* something specific. Rather, I could just go and experience and *discover.*

That revelation shifted my mindset from "I *need* to go" to "I *want* to go." And that one word changed everything.

I called my manager back and told her, "Okay, let's do it."

The trip was an unexpected development, and now that I planned to go without any expectations of Korea, I intended to fulfill *my* expectations, professionally speaking. I went and did my job, but I was also very fortunately able to rely on someone else to plot the course again.

Whereas Kevin and I were Korean adoptees, Esther had experience living in Korea, and she knew the language, which was huge. I'd known her for a while by then (the food world is a small one, and we'd met a few years earlier), and long before any of us knew to anticipate this trip, she'd told me she wanted to be the one to take me to Korea and show me around. I'd always loved the idea: Knowing Esther, I was sure she'd put together a thoughtful itinerary, and she did. It was so wonderful. She asked what I wanted to do but made informed suggestions and mapped out a schedule based on what was feasible, trying to maximize our limited time there. She showed us around and gave us a full food tour of Seoul squeezed in between our responsibilities.

During those five days, I planned nothing. I went along for the ride. I didn't go searching for any ancestral threads or distant family. For one thing, there wasn't time. But more important, that wasn't the purpose of the trip. And because I approached it without those expectations, the same way I would any other adventure in my life, I was able to really enjoy myself.

The thing is, building up some profound scene in your mind prior to any experience imbues it with immense pressure. The best moments of my life have been the ones free of that expectation, when the stakes felt so low because they were a total surprise, because I didn't know what to want or hope from them. Like *Top Chef.* Like that first meeting in Austin about Arlo Grey. Like the morning I was scheduled to pick out plates for my restaurant and was introduced to my future wife. Without pressure, I was able to have clarity in those moments—the ability to see what was wonderful right in front of me without being preoccupied by my own plans or preconceptions.

I've also learned that the most significant impressions often come from the smallest moments, and the most lasting memories come from the most fleeting moments—a conversation with my parents, a morning coffee with Bianca, a humble meal when I hadn't anticipated the menu.

One morning during that trip to Korea, Esther introduced me to a breakfast place. It was maybe 7:00 a.m. We'd been unable to sleep, thanks to the time change, so as soon as the world was awake and open and we were able to go out into it, this was the first spot we headed to. It was a part of the culture she was really excited to share.

I've never been a sweet-breakfast person, so I was happy to see that we weren't sitting down for anything that resembled pancakes or pastries. Instead, what we were served was a braised pork neck stew with kimchi. Once we were finished, the pot was taken away, and the kitchen used the same vessel to prepare fried rice in the leftover broth, which concentrates all those layers of flavor from the pork and kimchi. Then they pack it with fish roe and bring it back to you as a sort of follow-up course.

It may sound unusual to people from the West, where this seems like something you'd eat at lunch or dinner, but I could see how this could be a strong start to the day. It felt at once restorative and fortifying. It was so satisfying on a soul level and made me wonder whether this is why I've always preferred a savory breakfast. Even though I'd never encountered that dish before, maybe that sensibility is somewhere in my blood.

It was also a strange sensation in that although it was different from anything I'd ever eaten, it wasn't unfamiliar. I grew up eating cabbage rolls with sauerkraut, and this wasn't actually far off—the comforting braised meat, the funkiness of the cabbage. What made it different was its form and seasoning—the product of culture and adaptation, environment and evolution.

This is what it is to be human, too—to be the result of these same influences. I was elementally the same person inhabiting the same body as I had as a kid back in Michigan (and then in Chicago, Boston, Austin, and all the other places I'd been in my life). But I sat at that breakfast table in Korea as a product of my own culture and adaptation, environment and evolution. All those versions of me, seasoned by experience and concentrated over time.

When they say timing is everything, it's usually applied to some major event or a hairpin turn that alters the course of your life. But it's also about what leads you to these small moments that become unforgettable memories. It's about arriving at one of those intersections and having your eyes open to what is being presented to you, evaluating what serves you at that particular juncture, and making a judgment call.

That trip to Korea came up at a time when I'd sufficiently learned the benefits of being open. I might not have been ready before then. And although I didn't go with expectations, I did go with purpose—even if it wasn't the one people might have expected of me.

As an adoptee, I know I was no accident—I am evidence of my parents' deliberate decisions, their dreams and their deep love. I have wondered at times whether that instilled in me a sense of purpose and intentionality. To this day, those are values that are integral to who I am and strive to be.

My understanding of those qualities has evolved, though. Back when I was eighteen, I thought I was starting my adult life with purpose when in fact I was often trying to be in control. Accidents—or anything that would indicate a lack of control—would have been terrifying to me. I had too much to lose. But I've since learned the difference between control and agency. You can be open to "accidental" developments, to rerouting your course—sometimes even in the absence of a map—without relinquishing your agency. If you accept and embark upon that new course and do so with commitment, devotion, and intention, it becomes your own decision—one made in collaboration with the universe, the world, and the communities around you.

I don't have any plans to go back to Korea in the immediate

future, but I do intend to go back one day when the time is right. I loved Seoul the way I have loved many great cities—as a tourist, a curious explorer with an appreciation of culture and humanity. But perhaps as was to be expected, visiting also sparked a lot of deep questions and emotions. I wasn't there long enough to unpack it all, but I boarded the plane back home with a clear "to be continued" in my mind—a future step on a circular path that began at my birth.

When I was a kid, there was no road map that could have directed me to all these key points and places—the mall food courts of Michigan, the classrooms of Chicago, the kitchens of Boston and Austin, the television sets, the streets of Seoul, or the homemade altar where I professed my vows to Bianca. Call it fate. Call it a grand design. Call it a series of happy accidents—whatever you want to call this trajectory, it was always in harmony with awareness, intention, and a decision to increasingly open myself up to the unexpected as I travel my path. Your life can change in an instant, in ways you never imagined. There's a general perception that, like accidents, the "unexpected" isn't a good thing. But I'm here to say that my life has proved otherwise. The truth is that staying open to discovery, surprise, awe, wonder—*that's* what makes living so magical.

I've always had a complicated relationship with the concept of expectations. When I was younger, I worried that because I am an adoptee, my parents might have certain expectations of me and that I wouldn't live up to them. Then I saw back in middle and high school what I thought the world would expect from me as a woman, while all the while I grappled with what I could reasonably expect from my life as a gay person. Later I wanted to live up to professional expectations, first as an employee and then as a leader, when I honed ways in which to convey my expectations of others in a kind and encouraging way.

My life has defied expectations from the moment I was born. I know now that my family expects nothing of me—they only want my happiness. And if I feel expectations now, they're the ones I place on myself for reasons that are enriching to my world and the world of the people around me. I'm not worried about what society expects me to look like or how it wants me to behave. I want only to live up to my own standards, to be the best version of myself for my team, my family, and my wife, and so I can proudly represent my communities. Staying open helps me meet those expectations by providing me with resources and opportunities I might never have known to seek out.

I often think back to that first real date with Bianca, the way we just set out on an open road in Texas after our first kiss. No plans. No expectations. And how it was in that open space that we discovered and realized our love. Years later, we make sure to always give our love that kind of space to grow and evolve, to have the chance to surprise us.

Going on little adventures like that first one is something we still do today. When we have a day off together, we pull up a map and find an open space—something that looks like pure possibility—and we go there. We go with the intention of seeing what we run into or stumble upon. We make the active decision to take a detour. We opt for the unexpected. We intend for the unintended, and we lean in to letting go. These adventures may not be in the plans, and they may even fall into the category of accidents. But one thing my life has taught me time and time again is that even accidents can have purpose.

ACKNOWLEDGMENTS

To Vivian Lee: Thank you for believing in me, for finding meaning in this story, and for seeing value in sharing it. You championed this book from day one and put immense heart and care into shaping it, and your efforts will never be lost on me. Thank you to the team at Little, Brown, who provided a platform for this book and dedicated considerable talent and resources to bringing it to life.

To Stef: Thank you for being so easy to talk to, for capturing my voice and putting words to my story, and for making this process a true collaboration.

To Kim Witherspoon, for your persistence in finding the right home for this story. To Tory, Andrew, Danielle, and Jacob: Thank you for maintaining order while always keeping the plates spinning. Above all, thank you for being good, thoughtful people whom I'm proud to call my friends.

To the *Top Chef* family: Everyone has stories and lessons, but without this show, I may never have had the chance to share mine.

To Barbara: When others said I couldn't do it, you never doubted me. You changed my life in so many ways, and I will never take your unwavering encouragement for granted.

To Steph, Scott, and Auntie Kim: Thank you for being steadfast and integral to my adulthood, for helping me see my own worth, and for being my family.

Thank you to the people I have known in my life, supporters and detractors alike, who have taught me countless lessons, including the one that every experience—big and small, happy and hard—has value.

And to everyone who has supported me, embraced me, welcomed me into a community or a room with open arms, and given me space to become myself: Thank you.

ABOUT THE AUTHOR

KRISTEN KISH was born in South Korea and adopted into a family in Kentwood, Michigan. At a young age, she showed an affinity for cooking and, prompted by her mother, attended Le Cordon Bleu in Chicago. After culinary school, Kristen spent the next ten years in Boston honing her skills in several high-profile restaurants, ultimately becoming the chef de cuisine at a Relais & Châteaux property. From 2012 to 2013, Kristen competed on Bravo's *Top Chef* season 10 and ultimately won the coveted title. From there she went on to cohost *36 Hours*, a Travel Channel show that partnered with the *New York Times* to bring the hit newspaper column of the same name to television. In October of 2017, Kristen released her first cookbook, *Kristen Kish Cooking: Recipes and Techniques*, and in 2018 she partnered with LINE hotels to launch her first restaurant, Arlo Grey, in Austin, Texas. The restaurant reflects Kristen's playful yet refined cuisine, pulling inspiration from her classical training as well as nostalgic dishes that highlight her upbringing and love of travel. In 2023, Kristen became the new host of Bravo's *Top Chef* for its twenty-first season, a true full-circle moment, rejoining the *Top Chef* family on air a full ten years later. Kristen is the costar of *Fast Foodies* (truTV/Food Network), a cohost of *Iron Chef: Quest for an Iron Legend* (Netflix), and the host and producer of *Restaurants at the End of the World* (National Geographic/Disney+).